Foundations of Parallel Programming

A Machine-Independent Approach

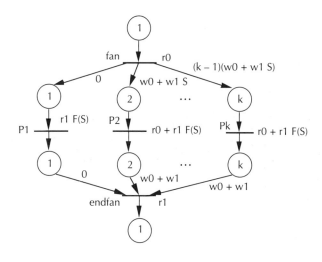

Ted G. Lewis

IEEE Computer Society Press

Los Alamitos, California

Washington • Brussels • Tokyo

Library of Congress Cataloging-in-Publication Data
Lewis, T.G. (Theodore Gayle), 1941–
    Foundations of parallel programming: a machine-independent approach / Ted G. Lewis
        p.   cm.
    Includes bibliographical references and index.
    ISBN 0-8186-5692-1 (case). — ISBN 0-8186-5691-3 (fiche)
    1. Parallel programming (Computer science) I. Title.
QA76.642.L48 1994
005.2 — dc20   94-4873
                                                    CIP

Published by the IEEE Computer Society Press
10662 Los Vaqueros Circle, P.O. Box 3014, Los Alamitos, CA 90720-1264

Technical Editor: Jon Butler
Production Editor: Lisa O'Conner
Cover Artist: Alex Torres

IEEE Computer Society Press Order Number 5692-04
IEEE Catalog Number EH0393-9
Library of Congress Number 94-4873
ISBN 0-8186-5691-3 (microfiche)
ISBN 0-8186-5692-1 (case)

Additional copies can be ordered from

IEEE Computer Society Press
Customer Service Center
10662 Los Vaqueros Circle
P.O. Box 3014
Los Alamitos, CA 90720-1264
Tel: (714) 821-8380
Fax: (714) 821-4641
Email: cs.books@computer.org

IEEE Service Center
445 Hoes Lane
P.O. Box 1331
Piscataway, NJ 08855-1331
Tel: (908) 981-1393
Fax: (908) 981-9667

IEEE Computer Society
13, avenue de l'Aquilon
B-1200 Brussels
BELGIUM
Tel: +32-2-770-2198
Fax: +32-2-770-8505

IEEE Computer Society
Ooshima Building
2-19-1 Minami-Aoyama
Minato-ku, Tokyo 107
JAPAN
Tel: +81-3-3408-3118
Fax: +81-3-3408-3553

This book was acquired, developed, and produced by Manning Publications Co. 3 Lewis Street, Greenwich, CT 06830.

Design: Frank Cunningham
Copyediting: Margaret Marynowski
Typesetting: Aaron Lyon

Printed in the United States of America
10   9   8   7   6   5   4   3   2

Contents

Preface

In parallel computing applications, one faces the difficult challenge of building software which can take advantage of highly parallel systems. Parallel software is so poorly understood that a new branch of software engineering will be required to achieve the transition from sequential to parallel applications. At the heart of this transition is parallel programming.

The "genius compiler" advocates believe it is possible to construct compilers that translate sequential programs written in our favorite sequential languages into parallel programs. In this scenario, FORTRAN, Pascal, and C source programs are converted into highly efficient parallel equivalents. Thus, a sequential program can be moved onto a parallel processor, compiled, and run many times faster than on a sequential processor.

The problem with this approach is the underlying assumption that sequential algorithms *can* be converted into parallel algorithms. In many cases this is true, but in other cases it is impossible to convert a good sequential algorithm into a good parallel algorithm because the two approaches are radically different. For example, a binary search is known to be a good sequential search algorithm, but a linear search done on N processors is better, given enough processors. Yet, it is unlikely that a genius compiler will ever be able to convert a program which implements binary search into a parallel program which implements a much faster linear search algorithm.

The second option is to discard all sequential programs and start over again! This extreme view has the advantage that one can redesign programs to use algorithms which are efficient on parallel processors. Clearly, it will be a long time before the world converts all of its existing sequential software into parallel programs which implement efficient parallel algorithms.

An intermediate prescription borrows from both extremes. Some sequential programs can be converted automatically into parallel equivalents, and others will need to be thrown away and rewritten. In this approach, new applications would be coded directly in new explicitly parallel languages so that after a period of perhaps decades, the transition to parallelism would be 100% complete. Sequential programming would become a subset of parallel programming, and there would no longer be a division between the sequential and parallel paradigms.

The problem with this approach is that it is still too early to decide on the features of a good parallel programming language. Each parallel computer seems to offer its own dialect of parallel FORTRAN, parallel C, or some new language altogether. If we are going to begin now, what language should we use? Selecting a new parallel programming language at this early stage might be just as wasteful as continuing to program in sequential languages.

This book is not about parallel algorithms; nor is it about how to write parallel programs for a specific machine. Instead, it is about the *design* of parallel programs using a small number of fundamental constructs which are powerful enough to express any parallel algorithm. Its emphasis is on foundations and concepts rather than syntax and machine dependencies.

This book's approach might also be called *performance-based design*, because it develops analytical measures of performance for each of the fundamental constructs of parallel programming. These analytical results can be used by a human programmer or a machine compiler to optimize the performance of any parallel program. This is especially important in parallel programming, because the object of parallelism is performance.

This approach is also machine independent. The only assumption made is that the parallel processor has N processors, linked by some interconnection network. Different machines may exhibit different performance characteristics, but they all possess multiple processors and some form of interconnection. One can use the performance-based design formulas to optimize a given program for a given architecture.

How can a programming book be both language and machine independent? This book proposes a simple *pseudo-code* notation for describing parallel programs. This notation is rigorous enough to be incorporated into a language some day, but for the purposes of this book it is strictly a pedagogical device. Even so, one can express any parallel algorithm succinctly and correctly in this notation, and derive performance formulas accordingly.

In a sense, this notation is a specification language for parallel programs. These blueprints are given in a very structured manner, so that students of parallel computing can understand the ideas without getting lost in details. Thus, the concepts of data distribution, synchronization, tasking, allocation of tasks to processors, and the trade-off between communication and computation are all made explicit without obfuscating details.

What are the fundamentals of parallel programming? Each chapter of this book, commencing after the introductory chapters, deals with a major building block used in parallel programming. Each of these building blocks is rooted in a fundamental concept which can be expressed as a programming construct. Thus, Chapter 4 introduces the data-parallel **fan**; Chapter 5 introduces the reduction **tree**, and so forth. These building blocks are sufficient to express any parallel algorithm. Furthermore, each construct corresponds to a fundamental concept of *flow-correct* programs.

The text covers concepts of both *fine-grained* and *large-grained* parallelism, beginning with low-level fine-grained parallelism at the statement level, and working up to procedural parallelism. This also corresponds to increasingly more difficult control problems, e.g., synchronization and race conditions.

This book is designed for an upper division undergraduate course for students in the physical sciences and engineering. Many of the examples are taken from science and engineering. Most students will have had calculus, programming languages, and operating systems prerequisites.

The author would like to thank the students of Oregon State University who have suffered through early drafts of this book. Their comments and questions have vastly improved the material. In addition, the manuscript has benefitted from a number of unknown reviewers.

TED LEWIS
lewis@cs.nps.navy.mil

CHAPTER 1

Models and Measures of Parallelism

There are many varieties of parallelism; each variety is called a *paradigm*. A paradigm is a way of viewing the world, and in computing, a world view becomes a program design and coding style. Therefore, a *programming paradigm* dictates the abstractions used by programmers. One abstraction might be represented by message-passing, while another abstraction might be represented by synchronization mechanisms called *locks*.

We classify parallelism according to two broad paradigms: control-flow and data-parallel. We claim that the control-flow paradigm is the most general, but does not yield a high degree of parallelism. Data-parallelism is more restricted, but generally yields very high levels of parallelism. We will show that control-flow parallelism can be implemented efficiently on multiple-instructions–multiple-data (MIMD) machines using either message-passing or locking. Message-passing is preferred on distributed-memory machines, while locking is preferred on shared-memory machines. Further, we will show that data-parallel parallelism can be implemented efficiently on message-passing machines in either the single-procedure–multiple-data (SPMD) or single-instruction–multiple-data (SIMD) form. Thus, MIMD, SPMD, and SIMD are architectures for supporting either the control-flow or data-parallel paradigms.

We claim that the *Amdahl Law* of speedup governs control-flow parallelism, while the *Gustafson–Baris Law* governs data-parallel parallelism. We will briefly derive these laws to gain an understanding of their bases; one in the world of control-flow parallelism and the other in the world of data-flow parallelism. These are idealized laws, so one must turn to a more detailed analysis of each parallel algorithm to determine practical bounds on performance. We will define scalability as the ability to obtain N-fold speedup in the face of communications overhead; parallel-computable algorithms as scalable algorithms; and quasi-scalability as speedups in excess of unity, but short of parallel-computable speedups.

We will present Petri nets and Gantt charts as means of visualizing the execution semantics and performance of arbitrary parallel programs. In addition to providing a crisp definition of the semantics of each construct, these diagrams allow performance analysis, and lead to greater insights into parallelism.

The models presented here assume a linear relationship between processor speed and process execution; and message-passing and communication delays. Furthermore, we will assume very simple interconnection networks, ignoring contention, for example, as well as routing overhead. These assumptions may not hold in general.

1.1 PROCESSORS, MEMORIES, AND NETWORKS

A *process* is any single flow of control through a set of instructions stored in a computer, and a *processor* is a hardware device for executing a process. A *parallel computer* is a collection of two or more processors connected to one another through an *interconnection network* or memory. A *parallel program* contains more than one process. The purpose of a parallel computer is to run parallel programs. Note that it is possible for a parallel program to run on a single processor, sequentially, such that each of its processes runs one after the other. Clearly, the advantage of parallel computers is that they deliver greater performance than single-processor computers.

The most general form of a parallel computer is shown in Figure 1.1. If the processors operate independently of one another but with occasional pauses to synchronize their processes, we call the parallel computer a multiple-instruction–multiple-data (MIMD) system. Alternately, if the processors operate in lock-step unison, synchronizing with one another after every instruction, we say the parallel computer is a single-instruction-multiple-data (SIMD) system. SIMD processors simultaneously execute exactly the same instructions, but on different data.

Examples of MIMD machines are the Intel iPSC series, nCUBE series, and other commercial products that link a number of commodity microprocessors together to form a single system. MIMD systems contain multiple sequencing units, which means that they can operate asynchronously and independently. Each processor runs under the control of its own sequencing unit, which means that many different instructions can be simultaneously executed, one in each processor.

Examples of SIMD machines are the Thinking Machines, Inc., Connection Machine (CM) series and the Maspar Computer Corp. MP series, products that link together a number of processing elements under the control of a single

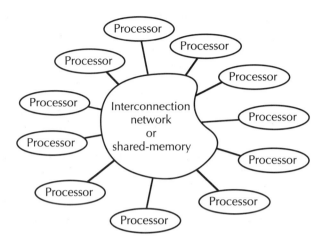

Figure 1.1   General model of a parallel computer

sequencing unit. In a SIMD system, all processing elements do the same thing at the same time, or else they are idle. The processing elements may be incomplete computers that perform simple arithmetic operations on distributed data, or as in Thinking Machines' CM-5 series, they may be entire computers. The most important distinction between MIMD and SIMD architectures is the degree of synchronization among processors: SIMD architectures are much more tightly synchronized.

Processors in SIMD computers are almost always connected by some form of interconnection network that permits them to pass messages among each other. In such systems, memory is associated with individual processors rather than the group of processors; hence, there is no *central memory*. An application's data must be copied and sent to where they will be processed. Thus, SIMD machines are also *distributed-memory machines*.

For example, in the Maspar series, processors and memory are arranged as a mesh-structured array. Each processor/memory subsystem is connected to its nearest neighbors on the north, east, west, and south (NEWS) borders. Other distributed-memory SIMD machines are linked together by *hypercube* interconnection networks, or even more exotic networks. In a hypercube interconnection network, processors are given a binary number designation such as 011 (3 in decimal), and only neighbors that differ in one bit are connected. Thus, processor 011 is connected to processors 111, 001, 010.

The trend has been toward more and more sophisticated interconnections of memories and processors. If the interconnection creates one path through all processors, it is called a *1-D network*; paths that can be drawn on a single sheet of paper without crossing each other are called *2-D networks*; *3-D networks* must be drawn in 3 dimensions, and so forth. Interconnection networks are called *static* if their connections are hardwired into the machine at the factory, and *dynamic* if it is possible for processor–processor connections to be switched while the machine runs.

Some networks collect data into *packets* before transmitting them from one processor to the other, while other networks establish a route between two processors, and transmit data for as long as the route exists. *Packet-switched networks* break messages into packets; *circuit-switched networks* operate like a telephone system and send messages over closed-circuit routes. In a packet-switched network, delays may be introduced by intermediate processors, because the message hops from one processor to the next, along the network. *Worm-hole routing* bypasses intermediate hops, thus achieving greater performance than that of purely packet-switched networks.

MIMD machines are usually either distributed-memory or shared-memory systems. If the architecture is a shared-memory design such as the Sequent Symmetry, Silicon Graphics Onyx, or Sun Microsystems multiple-processing system, processes must synchronize their access to shared data, or else *indeterminate* results may occur. Thus, shared-memory MIMD programmers must be concerned with locking and protection mechanisms.

A distributed-memory MIMD machine like the Intel Paragon uses message-passing to synchronize the parallel parts of an application program. When the message-passing style of parallel programming is adopted, an application's data are distributed among the processors' local memories, where they are processed in parallel. In this paradigm, the MIMD programmer must be concerned with copying and distributing the data.

Thus, even the MIMD paradigm calls for two radically different styles of programming. This necessity is a major hindrance to the progress of parallel computing, because details of the machine architecture creep into the design of software. Portability, and reuseability of software are greatly hampered by such machine dependencies.

For example, shared-memory programming is similar to operating systems programming, where processes are forked and joined to achieve a level of concurrency. No message-passing or copying of data is needed, and data are shared merely by declaring them as shared. But, in distributed-memory systems such as the nCUBE and Intel iPSC series machines, message-passing is used to distribute the data. These machines use Send and Receive primitives as illustrated by the following example. A Send primitive places data in a buffer, which is then emptied by the operating system. A Receive primitive forces a processor to wait for some message, then to copy it into the address space of a waiting destination process. Once distributed, additional effort is needed to update the copies and collect the results.

Example 1.1

Suppose two processors want to access the same value, stored in variable Y, as follows. Processor 1 runs a part of a parallel program that sets the value of Y, and processor 2 runs a part of the parallel program that increments Y. The following code is shown graphically in Figure 1.2.

Processor 1	*Processor 2*
Y = 100;	
Send(Y) to B;	Receive(X) FROM A;
Receive(Y) FROM B;	X = X + 1;
Output(Y);	Send(X) TO A;

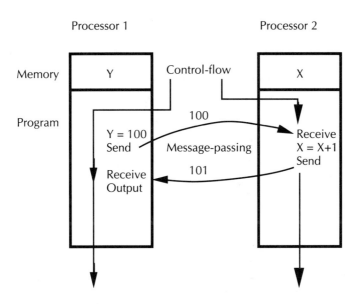

Figure 1.2   Synchronization in distributed-memory machines is achieved by message-passing.

The progress of each parallel part of the program is shown as a time-line in Figure 1.2. Both processors begin at the same time, but 2 immediately blocks on the Receive, waiting for a value to be received from 1. In the meantime, processor 1 sets Y to 100, and then places its value in a buffer so the operating system can send it across the interconnection network to processor 2's buffer. Processor 1 continues on to the next statement which is a Receive primitive. The Receive forces processor 1 to block, waiting for a returned value to fill its buffer. In the meantime, processor 2 receives 100, stores this value in its local variable X, increments X, and then sends 101 to processor 1.

When 101 is received by processor 1 and stored in variable Y, the processor unblocks and resumes. The Output function writes 101 from variable Y. Thus, the synchronization between these two processors is achieved by message-passing between the two local memories of the parallel computer.

A *shared-memory system* is one in which parallel parts of an application program are synchronized by setting and clearing *locks* on data stored in a centralized, shared memory space, or by synchronizing processes through programmer-created *barriers*. A lock prevents access to data unless certain conditions have been met, such as "only one process has access." A barrier forces any process to wait until all processes have arrived at the same point in the parallel program. Shared-memory MIMD machines share access instead of duplicating data.

A shared-memory MIMD machine like the Sequent Symmetry series, uses locks to coordinate access to shared data as illustrated by the following example.

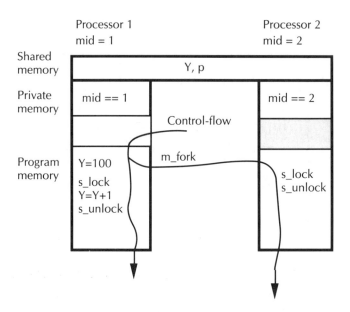

Figure 1.3   Shared-memory locks synchronize access to shared data.

Example 1.2

Suppose the previous distributed-memory example is repeated for a shared-memory machine. Once again, the problem is to simply increment the value stored in Y. But, this time, Y is a shared variable stored in shared memory. We use a simplified version of the Sequent DYNIX model to illustrate how this is done on most shared-memory MIMD machines.

shared int Y;	/* Declare Y to be shared
shared lock p;	/* Create a lock variable
.	
.	
.	
Y = 100;	/* Set Y
m_fork(2);	/* Fork program into two programs
s_lock(p);	/* Set lock so only one process can access
	critical section of code
if (mid == 1) {Y = Y + 1};	/* Processor 1 increments shared Y
s_unlock(p);	/* Clear lock so all can access
output(Y);	/* Output the result
.	
.	
.	

In this version, the two processors (identified as mid = 1 and mid = 2) are activated by two copies of the same program. In addition, the data that are shared must be placed in a special shared partition of memory, see Figure 1.3. This is done by declaring Y to be a shared integer.

When the original program executes the m_fork(2) primitive, the operating system makes a copy of the program and starts running identical code on two processors. That is, the program is halted, and two copies instantiated. Both copies run in parallel, from that point on, as illustrated by the lines in Figure 1.3 that show the flow of control.

When each copy executes the s_lock primitive, the operating system forces one copy to wait while the other copy continues through the critical section of code. It is nondeterministic which processor reaches the s_lock primitive first, but assuming 1 is faster than 2, the lock is set by processor 1. Later, when processor 2 executes its copy of s_lock, it is blocked until shared lock p is cleared by processor 1.

Continuing, processor 1 is allowed to increment Y, because mid is equal to 1. The s_unlock primitive is executed next, causing processor 2 to become reactivated. But, mid is equal to 2 in processor 2, so the increment is skipped. The s_unlock clears p, leaving p unlocked.

The observant reader will also notice that both processes output Y, but the value of Y is different in each one!

Example 1.2 shows how a single copy of an application program can become a model for a parallel program consisting of many parallel parts. These parts must be coordinated by careful placement of locks. This is in stark contrast to message-passing. However, the reader should note that this is a software paradigm; it is possible to implement message-passing on a shared-memory computer. If we were to do so, the paradigm would shift from locks and barriers to sends and receives, regardless of the underlying hardware.

1.2 PARALLEL PROGRAMMING PARADIGMS

Regardless of the architecture of the target parallel computer, parallel programs must harmoniously coordinate two or more program segments to assure correctness as well as high speed. This is the challenge of parallel programming. Exactly how parallelism is controlled is largely determined by the particular *paradigm* used by the programmer and programming language designer. Thus, parallel programming reduces to the study of programming paradigms.

A *parallel program* is a collection of *processes* connected to one another through either message-passing or access to shared data. If the processes operate independently of one another, we call the parallel program *trivially parallel*. If they operate independently but with occasional pauses to coordinate among themselves, then the program must adopt one of two general styles to properly synchronize its parallel parts: *control-flow* programming or *data-parallel* programming (see Figure 1.4).

A control-flow program is one in which more than one thread of control is supported by the underlying hardware, and thus by the parallel program. This means that a single program can perform different operations in the same time interval. Control-flow parallelism is also used to indicate that the order in which (parallel) parts of a program execute is governed by program control rather than by the availability of data.

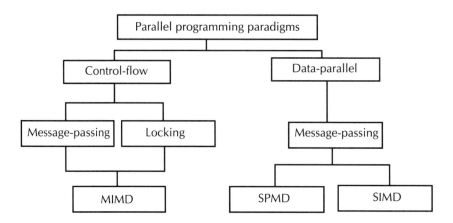

Figure 1.4   The paradigms of parallel programming

When using the control-flow style of parallel programming and a distributed-memory paradigm, the programmer is forced to use message-passing. We say the program is written in the *message-passing paradigm*. However, when a control-flow program is run on a shared-memory machine, it most likely uses locking to coordinate access to shared data. In this case, the program is also an example of the *locking paradigm*. In both cases, the parallel programming paradigm belongs to the class of *MIMD programs*.

At the other extreme, a parallel program might use a data-parallel paradigm, whereby the application's data are partitioned into separate sets, and then identical operations are performed on all sets at the same time. Because this requires distribution of the data across the parallel computer, message-passing is always employed. Hence this is also an example of the *message-passing paradigm*.

Data-parallel programs execute processes in lock-step unison, each process executing exactly the same instruction at the same time, but on different data. If synchronization is tightly controlled as is the case in a SIMD machine, we say the program uses the *SIMD paradigm*. If the synchronization of the SIMD paradigm is relaxed slightly to permit entire procedures to complete in between synchronizations, we say the program is written in the *SPMD paradigm*. Therefore, SPMD and SIMD programming styles are forms of data-parallel programming, because parallelism is derived from distributing the application's data across many processor or memory units.

The control-flow paradigm for the message-passing and locking styles of parallel programming were demonstrated by Examples 1.1 and 1.2. Both styles are control-flow oriented because the two parallel processes perform different operations on the data. In addition, there is no centralized synchronization mechanism; thus both processes run asynchronously. Whenever synchronization is required, the programmer must insert locks or message-passing to force synchronization through the exercise of control-flow. This is the "traffic cop" approach to parallelism.

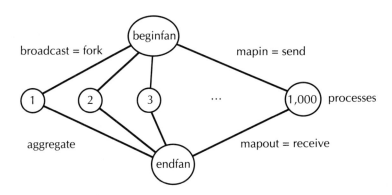

Figure 1.5   The broadcast-aggregate form of data-parallel programming

The data-parallel paradigm is not meaningful until we attempt to process large arrays of data. That is, data-parallelism works best on vectors and matrices. Thus, in the next example, we show how to increment all elements of a vector, $Y[n]$, instead of a single value, as in the previous examples.

Example 1.3

Suppose we want to quickly increment all elements of vector $Y[N]$, where each element of Y has been previously entered as input, and N is 1,000. In a serial program this might be done by an iterative loop, such as:

for(i := 1; i <= 1000; i++) Y[i] = Y[i] + 1;

Ignoring time lost due to overhead, this would take 1,000 additions in sequence on a single processor. Also ignoring overhead due to communication, we can execute this loop in the time that it takes a single processor to do one increment, if we use 1,000 processors. The idea is to replace repetition with replication of the code for $Y[i] = Y[i] + 1$.

The code to do this must distribute one element of Y to each of the 1,000 processors, perform all increments in lock-step fashion, and return the incremented value to the original processor. This is the well-known broadcast-aggregate algorithm of the data-parallel paradigm, see Figure 1.5. The code for this would perhaps look like the following (using a notation similar to that introduced in Chapter 4):

```
begin fan
broadcast i := 1 to 1000;          /* Start 1,000 processes on 1,000
                                      processors
mapin  Y[i] to LocalY;             /* Make 1,000 copies of LocalY variables
{ LocalY = LocalY + 1    }         /* Do 1,000 increments at the same time
mapout LocalY to Y[i]              /* Collect 1,000 results
endfan
```

Because of the fan-like appearance of the broadcast-aggregate form shown in Figure 1.5, we call this a data-parallel **fan**. Conceptually, the **fan** runs identical copies of a segment of code on different processors, but with each (identical) instruction in lock-step harmony with the corresponding instructions in other processors.

In this code, we see the three phases which always accompany the data-parallel paradigm: broadcast via the **mapin** statement, SPMD calculation, and aggregation of the result via the **mapout** statement.

The simplicity of data-parallel programming is startling, but that is not the end of the story. We need to consider what happens when many broadcast-aggregate computations are combined with other forms of parallelism to achieve a complete parallel program. This problem will be discussed throughout much of this book, as it is a major issue of parallel programming.

In summary, we have identified three distinct paradigms of parallel programming: control-flow with message-passing, control-flow with locking, and data-parallel with message-passing. The message-passing of data-parallelism is hidden within the broadcast-aggregate operations. We have used **mapin** and **mapout** to implement message-passing. This high-level construct will be developed further in later chapters.

Note that programs written in all three of these fundamental paradigms can be implemented on one or more of the machines described above. But clearly, the MIMD architectures are the most general parallel machines, because they can implement all three paradigms with little concession to inefficiency due to overhead. Thus, the architectures of parallel machines are merging toward a MIMD style, with SIMD features to make data-parallel programming highly efficient. For example, the Connection Machine CM-5 is a MIMD machine with SIMD properties. The iPSC series of Intel machines are MIMD machines with fast enough interconnection topologies to achieve reasonably rapid SPMD computation. While shared-memory machines do not need to pass data from one processor to another, they can be programmed in all three of these fundamental paradigms.

One can argue that the basic constructs of control-flow and data-flow parallelism are necessary and sufficient to represent all parallel computations. The argument goes as follows. First, we know from the theory of serial computation that all algorithms can be written in serial languages containing only sequences (assignment, function calls, etc), loops, and if–then branching. We can mimic these constructs within our paradigms of parallelism. Thus, the necessary condition is met by any set of constructs that simulate sequencing, looping, and branching.

Example 1.4

The following sequential program is written using only sequence, loop, and branch constructs. Can it be written as a parallel program? The answer is "yes," because we can substitute a parallel construct for each sequential construct that permits parallelization (a topic we discuss in greater detail later). We substitute the data-parallel **fan** in place of the sequential **for**:

Sequential program	Equivalent data-parallel program

```
input(x[1..N]);                    input(x[1..N]);
for i := 1..N do                   fan i := 1..N
begin                                mapin x[i] to LocalX
  if x[i] = 0 then x[i] := 1         { bit LocalX;
          else x[i] := 0               if LocalX = 0 then LocalX := 1
end;                                             else LocalX := 0}
                                     mapout LocalX to x[i]
                                     endfan;
```

The sequential program flips the bits in array $x[1..N]$ such that 1 is changed to 0 and 0 is changed to 1. It does this in time proportional to N, because it must run through each element of $x[1..N]$, one at a time. The parallel program does exactly the same thing, except it first distributes one element of x to each of N processors, and then simultaneously flips the bits from 0 to 1 and 1 to 0. The result is returned to the bit array, again simultaneously, by message-passing. The parallel version might run as much as N times faster, depending on overhead.

The data-parallel program runs identical instructions at the same time on each processor. Also, each processor receives a copy of its data as LocalX, and returns the data as $x[i]$. That is, there are N copies of LocalX throughout the collection of processes.

This shows that it is possible, in our limited example, to represent a sequential program as an equivalent parallel program. That is, we have illustrated the equivalence of sequential and parallel constructs for the sole purpose of showing that an algorithm can be expressed in both. We claim that this is possible for all uses of sequencing, looping, and branching necessary to write any sequential program. Thus, it is possible to write any parallel program in the parallel equivalents of sequencing, looping, and branching. We will show which parallel constructs are necessary to do all of parallel programming in the remainder of this book.

The question of sufficiency of constructs is left unanswered by this example. Even if we have all constructs necessary to express any algorithm as a parallel program, is the set of parallel programming constructs sufficient?

Our argument is that all *parallel algorithms* can be written in terms of control-flow or data-parallel constructs. But, what is a parallel algorithm? Let a parallel algorithm be any algorithm that executes N times faster on an N-processor computer. If such an algorithm can be written in terms of sequences, loops, and branches, then all we need to do is show that these constructs can be implemented N times faster on an N-processor parallel computer. We will do this in the remainder of this book. However, even so, we have not proven that these are the fewest number of constructs needed. Might there be fewer, more powerful constructs that also speed up a program N-fold?

As a preview of the constructs we will propose throughout the remainder of this book, consider this: sequences can be replaced by **par**, which executes all statements in the sequence at the same time. Loops can be replaced by **fans**, **trees**, or *pipelined stages*, which distribute the iterations of a loop over many processors. When no data dependencies exist we use a **fan**, as in Example 1.3; when dependencies are present we use either a **tree** or a **pipe**. We leave branches alone, and merely rewrite sequential if-then-else constructs as sequential if-then-else statements within the parallel program. In other words, if-then-else statements cannot be parallelized.

We seek techniques and representations of control-flow and data-parallel constructs that approach the ideal of a truly parallel program. But, we are pragmatic computer scientists, so we assume that it is not always possible to achieve the ideal of N-fold speedup. Instead, we focus attention on the problem of representation. Can we represent all parallel algorithms in terms of control-flow or data-parallel constructs? We claim an affirmative answer. In the remainder of this book we will attempt to convince you that the combination of control-flow and data-parallel paradigms is necessary and sufficient to represent all parallel algorithms, even if speedup is not always N times that of the original sequential program.

1.3 PERFORMANCE MODELS

Parallel programming strives to achieve two fundamental goals: to represent parallel algorithms as correct parallel programs, and to achieve N-fold speedups when using N processors. The first goal is one of representation, as discussed in the previous section. The second goal is one of performance, a topic which we can now address in more detail.

The idea of *speedup* is somewhat confusing to many practitioners of parallel programming. Originally, speedup was defined as the ratio of the execution time of the *best* known serial program to the execution time of the corresponding implementation on an N-processor parallel computer. This definition is often too difficult to use because the best serial program execution time is not known, or else the parallel algorithm differs so greatly from the serial algorithm that a comparison is meaningless.

As a consequence, a practical definition of speedup has evolved which can be measured by running the parallel program using 1, 2, ..., N processors. We let the execution time of the single-processor version be divided by the time taken to run the program on N processors. This ratio gives the same result for a lengthy program as a speedy program, if the two programs actually run N times faster on N processors. That is, the speedup is defined as the ratio of the execution time of the parallel program running on one processor to the execution time of the same program running on N processors:

$$\text{Speedup} = \frac{T_1}{T_N}$$

where T_1 is the execution time of the program running on 1 processor, and T_N is the execution time of the same program running on N processors.

In addition, the *efficiency* E is a measure of how well we utilize parallel processors:

$$E = \frac{\text{Speedup}}{N}$$

We are most interested in *linear speedup*, Speedup = $O(N)$, which is equivalent to *isoefficiency*, $E = O(1)$. But is this a practical expectation? In the following example we derive the famous Amdahl Law of speedup, and show that only scalable algorithms are isoefficient, meaning they show linear speedup when run on N processors.

Example 1.5

Amdahl's equation assumes that the time to run a parallel program on N processors depends on the fraction of program β that is inherently serial, and the remaining fraction $(1 - \beta)$ that is inherently parallel. That is, $T_N = \beta T_1 + (T_1 (1 - \beta))/N$. Substituting into the formula for speedup, we get

$$S_A = \frac{N}{\beta N + (1 - \beta)}$$

Suppose one-half of the program can be run in parallel, and that the other half must run serially due to the nature of the program. This means $\beta = 0.5$, so that $S_A = 2N/(N + 1)$. As N increases, the speedup goes asymptotically to 2, which means that the best speed improvement using any number of processors is only twice that of a single processor.

The Amdahl equation is very pessimistic. It assumes that speedup is governed by the fraction of the program that can be executed in sequence, as dictated by a control-flow paradigm.

Now, suppose we define any algorithm that can be run N-fold times faster when run on N processors as a *scalable algorithm*. Then, Speedup $= O(N)$. Is Amdahl's Law a model for scalability? $S_A = O(1)$, so it is not scalable.

While Amdahl's Law may accurately model many control-flow programs, it does not properly model data-parallel programs because it ignores the parallelism that might be exploited in the data to be processed. That is, it overlooks the possibility of SIMD or SPMD computation, where the amount of potential parallelism increases with the size of vectors and matrices in the application. The following example derives an alternative formula for speedup based on the claim of John Gustafson and Ed Barsis.

Example 1.6

The Gustafson–Barsis equation starts with the same ratio for the speedup, but makes an entirely different assumption for T_1 and T_N. Suppose the time to compute a solution to a data-parallel problem using N processors is normalized to unity, e.g., $T_N = 1$. Now, what happens to T_1?

When the program is run on one processor, it must compute the serial part, in time $\beta T_N = \beta$, plus the parallel part, in time $N (1 - \beta) T_N = (1 - \beta) N$. Thus, the formula for T_N is simply the sum: $T_N = \beta + (1 - \beta) N$. Substituting into the expression for speedup, we get

$$S_{GB} = N - (N - 1) \beta$$

When $\beta = 0.5$ as in the example above, we get $S_{GB} = N - (N - 1)/2 = (N + 1)/2$.

The result in Example 1.6 is quite different from the pessimistic prediction of Amdahl (see Figure 1.6). Speedup is proportional to N. Why? And, $E = O(1)$, so data-parallel algorithms are isoefficient; i.e., they maximally utilize all processors. Data-parallelism can achieve speedup proportional to the size of the data. The number of parallel parts does not matter so much as the number of data parts, hence the designation *data-parallel*.

But, both the Amdahl and Gustafson–Barsis Laws ignore overhead. And, as we now know, overhead is very detrimental to parallel algorithm performance. What is needed is a performance measure that considers overhead in the form of time to communicate data to the parallel parts of the program. In the next example we derive a general expression for speedup that considers communication time delays, and that leads to the important concepts of *parallel-computability* and *quasi-scalability*.

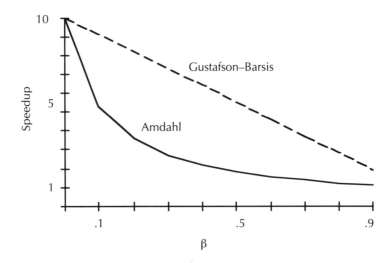

Figure 1.6   **Amdahl versus Gustafson-Barsis speedup Laws as a function of fraction of serial program code, β**

Example 1.7

Suppose we add communication overhead to the Amdahl and Gustafson-Barsis Laws, and then obtain speedup formulas, following the same arguments used above. Let the communication overhead be given by some function $W(N)$. Then:

Amdahl Law

$$S_A = \frac{T_1}{\beta T_1 + \dfrac{T_1 (1 - \beta)}{N} + W(N)}$$

$$= O\left(\frac{1}{W(N)}\right)$$

Gustafson–Barsis Law

$$S_{GB} = \frac{\beta T_N + N(1 - \beta) T_N}{T_N + W(N)}$$

$$= O\left(\frac{N}{W(N)}\right)$$

We can now classify each of these according to their scalability, parallel-computability, and quasi-scalability. If overhead permits, an algorithm is scalable if Speedup $\geq O(N)$; parallel-computable if $S = O(N)$; and it is quasi-scalable if Speedup ≥ 1. Thus, we find:

	Amdahl Law	*Gustafson-Barsis Law*
Scalable	$W(N) \leq O(1/N)$	$W(N) \leq O(1)$
Parallel-computable	$W(N) = O(1/N)$	$W(N) = O(1)$
Quasi-scalable	$W(N) \leq O(1)$	$W(N) \leq O(N)$

Clearly, parallel-computability is implied by scalability. A scalable algorithm is *superlinear* if Speedup $> O(N)$. However, some algorithms are not parallel-computable even though their performance is improved by parallelism, because $1 \leq$ Speedup $< O(N)$. These algorithms fall into the class of quasi-scalable algorithms.

We are most interested in algorithms that are at least parallel-computable. As a practical matter, most algorithms will only be quasi-scalable, because they fail to run N times faster on N processors.

It would seem that data-parallelism achieves the performance goal of perfect parallelization, but it does not guarantee that all parallel algorithms can be expressed in the data-parallel paradigm. On the other hand, control-flow parallelism seems capable of modeling both data-parallelism and control parallelism, but it cannot guarantee the N-fold performance improvement we seek.

These general results cannot tell us the performance of a specific parallel program. In addition, these formulas ignore important details such as the speed of the machine, the bandwidth of the interconnection network, the overhead in sending a message or starting a process, and so forth. To properly model the performance of a parallel program, we need to model machines and programs more accurately.

1.3.1 Estimating Execution Times

A performance model for the underlying parallel computer is needed so that we can estimate the performance of specific programs. For this reason, we will develop formulas for processor speed, network speed, the activation and execution of a parallel process, and a similar expression for message-passing delays. These models are approximations to reality. For example, they ignore network routing and contention delays common in many interconnection networks. However, they provide a basis for comparing parallel algorithms and will help us to understand the underlying semantics of parallel program constructs that we will introduce later.

We use linear approximations in the following definitions, even though the phenomenon we are modeling is rarely linear. The following symbols will be used throughout:

p The parallel processing hardware contains p identical processors and their memory.

N The parallel program can be partitioned into N tasks.

t_i Task i takes t_i time units to execute. Times t_j and t_i may differ for $j \neq i$.

r_1 *Processor time* (the inverse of processor speed), measured in units of time to perform some operation. The definition of an operation may change from instance-to-instance, but in general it is some basic arithmetic operation, such as addition, multiplication, move, copy, etc.

r_0 *Processor setup time*, measured in time units. This is the time it takes to initiate a process on some processor. This estimate includes overhead due to the operating system.

In addition, we assume that the execution time of a task is a function of the length of its input data S. Therefore, the estimated *execution time* of a task is $F(S)$. The *execution time delay* of a task includes its setup time, and depends on processor speed.

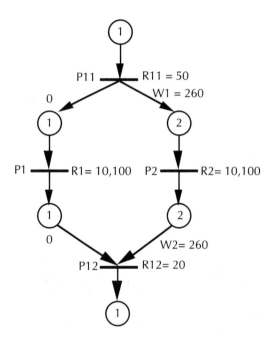

Figure 1.7   Petri network graph showing two parallel processes

R Execution time delay of a process. $R = r_0 + r_1 F(S)$

We use the following to estimate communication times:

w_1 *Transmission communication time* (the inverse of bandwidth) of the interconnection network, measured in time units to move a character. This time delay is caused by transmission speed, routing delays, and other overhead.

w_0 *Communication setup time*, measured in time units. This is the time it takes to initiate a message, including buffer creation, packaging the characters, and so on.

W_{ij} Communication time between tasks t_j and t_i depends on locality and processors: if t_j and t_i are placed on the same processor, $W_{ij} = 0$; otherwise W_{ij} = startup time + message size × transmission time per character, e.g., $W_{ij} = w_0 + S_{ij} w_1$

I Processors are connected by some interconnection network, which we ignore. We also ignore network contention. Both of these factors can alter our estimates in dramatic ways, but we will not address them here.

Contention   One network link needed at the same time by two or more messages.

PN   The parallel program is represented as a *Petri network* graph, where each place is marked as follows (see Figure 1.7): place label = task number i, transition label = name, execution time t_i.

In a Petri network (PN), we designate states as round "bubbles," and transitions as straight horizontal "bars." Arcs and arrows show the flow of control from state to transition, and transition to state. Arcs are never allowed to connect two states or two transitions.

The meaning of a PN is as follows:

1   States (bubbles) represent zero-time delay pauses in the execution of a program.

2   Transitions (bars) represent time-consuming actions made up of one or more sequential instructions, executed by one parallel task.

3   Arcs represent time-consuming flow of control and passage of data through the parallel program, inclusive of parallel tasks.

4   Labels are used to designate which processor is in the state, designate how much time is absorbed by a transition or flow, and indicate which task executes each transition.

Figure 1.7 models a simple fork-join parallel program. The fork, P11, and join, P12, are represented as transitions which consume times R11 and R12, respectively. The numerical labels on the places in Figure 1.7 indicate the location, processor 1 or 2. The communication delay is zero between tasks on processor 1 and nonzero between processors 1 and 2.

The PN models parallelism because it is possible for more than one transition to be executed at the same time. Indeed, execution order and timing are a function of time delays, and not a function of the placement of instructions in a program. The two parallel tasks in Figure 1.7 are modeled as two paths running from top-to-bottom on the PN. P11 splits the program's control into two tasks, P1 and P2, and then joins the control together again at P12.

Such a graphical model is useful for estimating the performance of a parallel program, because we can simply add the delays along a path to obtain the total. The *critical path* is the longest path through the graph, and represents the *elapsed time* of execution of the program. A similar elapsed time can be obtained for the same program running on a single processor, and this value used to compute a speedup ratio.

Example 1.8

Suppose we are given processor parameters as follows: $w_0 = 250$, $w_1 = 0.01$, $r_0 = 100$, and $r_1 = 10$. Furthermore, assume that all messages are of constant length, $S = 1000$ characters, a fork takes 50 time units, a join takes 20 time units, and P1 and P2 take time proportional to their inputs. What is the execution time of the parallel program represented by Figure 1.7?

Given the general formula $W = w_0 + w_1 S$ and the values above, we can compute the message delays by simple substitution:

$W1 = 250 + 0.01 \times 1000 = 260$
$W2 = W1 = 260$

Given the general formula $R = r_0 + r_1 F(S)$, and assuming $F(S) = S$, in P1 and P2, we get the following estimated parameters:

$R1 = 100 + 10 \times 1000 = 10{,}100$
$R11 = 50$
$R12 = 20$
$R2 = R1 = 10{,}100$

Now, we can compute the execution time along each of the two paths. The first path represents work by processor 1, and the second represents the work of processors 1 and 2:

Processor 1: $R11 + 0 + R1 + 0 + R12 = 50 + 0 + 10,100 + 0 + 20 = 10,170$
Processors 1&2: $R11 + W1 + R2 + W2 + R12 = 50 + 260 + 10,100 + 260 + 20 = 10,690$

Therefore, because the two paths are executed partially in parallel, we take the longest path as the elapsed execution time. Hence, this program runs on two processors in $T_N = 10,690$ time units.

What is the speedup? If this program had run on a single processor, there would have been no communication time delays, nor any fork/join overhead, but the two processes would have run on one processor. Hence, the single processor performance is the sum of the two process execution times.

$T_1 = R1 + R2 = 20,200.$

Therefore,

$$\text{Speedup} = \frac{T_1}{T_N} = \frac{20200}{10690} = 1.89$$

Petri net graphs are simple to construct. Each bar represents a computation at some level. It might be a single instruction in one application, or an entire procedure in another. The level of detail is determined by the application and the programmer. Each bubble is a zero-time delay state that roughly corresponds to the program counter of the processor whose number is in the bubble. That is, a bubble numbered 2 represents the place in the code where processor 2's program counter is pointing. Bubbles are simple program counter states.

Bubbles always connect to bars and bars always connect to bubbles. If an arc connects two bubbles or two bars, the graph is not drawn properly. The only exception to this rule is that the start bar has no input arc, and the stop bar has no output arc.

Bars represent parallel processes; hence the graph visualizes parallel execution. Sometimes this is shown by placing tokens in the bubbles. A *token* signifies that the bubble is enabled. A bar is executed only when all input bubbles contain at least one token. For example, in Figure 1.7, bar P12 cannot execute until a token appears in both of the bubbles before it. Tokens are created and passed along all output arcs of a bar, signifying a fork. In Figure 1.7 the bar labeled P11 creates two tokens, one of which ends up in each of the output bubbles.

1.3.2 The Gantt Chart Model

The placement of processes on processors, and the time history of their execution may not be clear from the graphical model illustrated in Figure 1.7. For this reason, we often use a *Gantt chart* to show how the parallel program executes (see Figure 1.8). A Gantt chart lists the physical processors vertically, and time horizontally, left to right. The blocks inside the chart represent the start time, duration, and ending time of each process in the program.

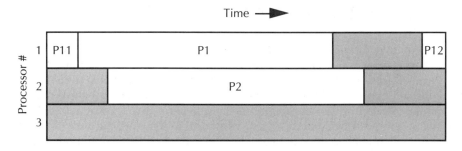

Figure 1.8   Gantt chart model of parallel program execution shows which processor runs what process, and in what order.

Gantt charts show execution schedules. A *schedule* is an allocation and time ordering of all processes in the parallel program. The length of a chart is equal to the critical path length, and shows the elapsed execution time of the program. The chart also reveals inefficiencies in the program. For example, empty space in a chart indicates idle processors.

Sometimes communication time delays are also shown in a chart. This reveals bottlenecks due to communication delays, and possibly communication-intensive parallelism. Communication can be reduced by moving send–receive process pairs to the same processor. This eliminates the communication bottleneck, but also reduces parallelism. This phenomenon is sometimes called the *max–min problem* of parallelism because of the seemingly paradoxical trade-off obtained by maximized parallelism versus minimized communication.

An *optimal schedule* is a shortest-length Gantt chart. That is, the best placement of processes onto processors leads to the shortest critical path, and hence the least elapsed execution time. The *scheduling problem* of parallel programming is to find the optimal schedule. This is a well-known computationally complex problem, and is almost always solved by heuristics rather than by exact methods.

It may not be possible to find a parallel-computable function that solves a certain problem because there may be no known parallel algorithm that gives an N-fold speedup. But, if the scheduling problem can be solved, and the result is a Gantt chart schedule that gives N-fold improvement, then we know we have found a parallel-computable function. But we know that finding optimal schedules is NP-complete, thus, finding parallel algorithms is, too.

On a pragmatic level, we are driven to find the best solution possible using heuristics to solve the max–min problem and yield practical parallel algorithms. This will be the approach taken here, but the reader should be cautioned that such heuristics cannot guarantee near-optimal schedules every time. In fact, the resulting Gantt chart may be far from optimal.

1.4 KEYWORDS AND CONCEPTS

We have discussed three important concepts: programming paradigms for parallelism, measures of performance, and the Petri network computational model. Parallel processing systems can be broadly classified according to the paradigms described here, e.g., control-flow versus data-parallel. The measures of performance also depend on the paradigm used. In general, the traditional control-flow model is governed by Amdahl's Law, while the newer data-parallel model is governed by the Gustafson–Barsis Law. These are idealized laws, and may not be very useful for estimating the performance of a specific parallel program. Therefore, we have described a control-flow Petri network model which is the basis for a more detailed performance analysis technique.

This tour of paradigms, measures, and models introduces the following concepts and keywords, given here in alphabetical order for convenience.

1-D network, 2-D network, 3-D network   A parallel processing system combines hardware and software into a computer system containing many processors linked together by either shared-memory, or distributed-memory. In the distributed-memory case, an N-dimensional interconnection network is used to link processors with other processors or memory. A 1-D network is a linear link, such as a bus-structure or a local area network. A 2-D network is planar, such as a ring or tree. A 3-D network uses three dimensions to connect processors, such as a hypercube or fully connected network.

Barrier   A barrier is a synchronization mechanism which forces all processes to wait for the latest process, before allowing all processors to continue. Barriers are control-flow synchronization mechanisms, used to force processes to meet at some point in the program, such as occurs in a join.

Broadcast-aggregate   The broadcast-aggregate model of parallel computation uses a barrier to coordinate parallel processes as follows: a single process is forked into N parallel processes, and data is broadcast to all siblings. The siblings complete their tasks in parallel, and possibly at different speeds. They meet at a barrier, collect results, and then are joined back into a single process.

Circuit-switched networks   An interconnection network such as a hypercube or mesh can be implemented electronically as a packet-switched or circuit-switched routing system. If circuit-switched, the network operates much like a telephone system whereby a connection from one processor to another is held constant as long as the communication takes place. Data are sent or received as one continuous stream. Compare this to packet-switching in which the data stream is broken up into packets, and each packet is sent separately, possibly over different links.

Communication setup time   Whenever a message is sent from one processor to another, the message must be created, buffered, and packaged before it can be sent. The time taken to do this is called the communication setup time. It will vary depending on the operating system, the size of message, the size of buffers, and the speed of the processor.

Communication time   The time to set up and send a message is the total communication time. The setup time may be the largest component of communication time, but transmission time is also included in this total.

Control-flow   There are two fundamental models of programming: control-flow and data-parallel. In the control-flow model, the sequencing of program statements are dictated by a control path or thread. This is in contrast to data flow or data-parallel, in which the next statement to be executed is determined only by the availability of (input) data, and not by the flow of control.

Critical path   A parallel program has many threads of control through it, and each thread touches on one or more processes. The longest execution path is called the critical path. We are concerned with critical paths because they determine the time it takes to complete the program. If we can shorten the critical path by properly scheduling the parallel parts, we can improve performance by a mere rearrangement of parts.

Data-parallel   This is a major parallel programming paradigm in which the program is divided into separate but identical processes; each process operates on different data. In a data-parallel program, performance is improved through partitioning the data and processing each partition in parallel. This is usually a three-phase process: data partitioning and distribution, parallel processing, and aggregation of the results into a single partition. Data-parallel contrasts sharply with control-flow parallelism.

Distributed-memory machines   The hardware design of parallel machines can be generally divided into shared-memory and distributed-memory architectures. In the latter, processors own their local memories, and so data must be sent across a network whenever one processor requests access to another processor's memory.

Dynamic   The difference between a dynamic interconnection network and a static network is in the length of time a connection remains in force between nodes on the network. A static connection remains fixed forever. A dynamic connection changes as messages are passed through the network. This is typically done to route the message along various links to avoid contention, failures, or simply to make or break point-to-point connections.

Efficiency   An algorithm is said to be efficient when it is run on a parallel processor system and it keeps all processors busy. Efficiency is a relative concept, however, so we quantify it in a variety of ways. Each way is usually measured on a scale from 0 to 1.0. In this book, we measure efficiency as $E = \text{Speedup}/N$.

Elapsed time   A parallel program's elapsed time is its execution time. It is also the time to execute the critical path through the program. Unlike a serial program, a parallel program may have a variable elapsed time, because it may be run faster by using more processors.

Execution time   The time to perform a process is its execution time. The elapsed time of a program is also its execution time. Execution time is a function of the number of processors, the number of parallel processes, the cost of communication and message passing, and the size of each process. Predicting the minimum execution time of an arbitrary parallel program is an NP-complete problem.

Fan   Fan is another name for SIMD broadcast-aggregate data-parallelism. We use a fan to partition and distribute data, carry out the SIMD or SPMD processes, and aggregate the results. This is perhaps the most common form of parallelism in practice.

Gantt chart   A Gantt chart is a pictorial representation of the schedule of a parallel program. It shows the number of processors used, the order of activation of each process, and the critical path through the program. The execution time of the program is equal to the length of the Gantt chart.

Hops   In some networks, a message is stored and forwarded each time it passes through a processor node. This takes time. The process of receiving and then passing on a message in such networks is called hopping, and the number of hops is equal to the number of times a message is passed through a processor node. This is in contrast to worm-hole routing.

Indeterminate   A value of a variable is indeterminate if it depends on the execution order of the tasks in the program. Nondeterminism can lead to indeterminism if a parallel program is not properly synchronized. This is a form of flow-error in parallel programs.

Isoefficiency   The idea of isoefficiency comes from the idea of scalability. That is, if we can run a parallel program twice as fast on twice as many processors, it must be scalable, because each processor is just as efficient when used in either case. If we continue to increase the speed by increasing the number of processors, the algorithm is said to be isoefficient, because the processors retain their efficiency throughout the scaling. This is rarely the case, except in data-parallel algorithms which ignore communication overhead.

Linear speedup   Linear speedup is an ideal situation in which a parallel program can run N times faster on N processors than on 1 processor. It can rarely be achieved because of communication and process overheads.

Locks   A lock is a synchronization mechanism. Spin locks, semaphores, barriers, and atomic queues are examples of shared-memory locks.

Message-passing paradigm   Message-passing is more than a mechanism, because it changes the model of computation. In place of shared global variables, a message-passing program copies values from one local space to another. Therefore, there are no global variables, and the program may contain many copies of the same data throughout the program. When one variable changes, its new value must be propagated throughout the program.

Min–max problem   The min–max and grain size problems are different facets of the same problem. If we attempt to minimize overhead due to communication and process creation, we risk lowering overall performance due to loss of parallelism. If we attempt to maximize performance by maximizing parallelism, we risk lowered performance due to high overhead. The min–max problem is solved by optimization which balances overhead and parallelism.

MIMD programs   Multiple-instruction–multiple-data programs are the most general form of parallel programs. They may be implemented as either shared-memory or distributed-memory programs.

Optimal schedule   A schedule is both an ordering in time and an allocation of tasks to processors. A schedule determines the critical path of a parallel program and thus its performance. An optimal schedule is one that results in the shortest possible elapsed time for the entire parallel program. In general, finding optimal schedules is NP-complete, and so heuristics are often used.

Packet-switched networks   A packet is a collection of data plus a source and destination header. A message is divided into packets and sent through a packet-switched network, one packet at a time. The packets may arrive in different order and at different times. Therefore, they must be reorganized into their original form at their destination. Contrast this with circuit-switched networks.

Par   A par is a programming construct that forks N different processes, executes each parallel process independently of the others, and waits at a barrier for all N processes to finish. This is the equivalent of a fork–join operation in a multitasking operating system.

Process setup time   A process is a locus or thread of control through code. It takes a finite amount of time to create a process. This is called the setup time.

Quasi-scalable   An algorithm is scalable if it can be run N times faster if we add N processors. However, this is an ideal which is rarely achieved. It is more likely the case that an algorithm will run faster and faster as we add processors, but fail to achieve an N-fold increase in speed as we add N processors. If the algorithm speed can be improved, but not by a factor of N, we say it is quasi-scalable.

Scheduling problem   The scheduling problem is NP-complete. It is the problem of placing the tasks of a parallel program in time and processor space such that the program runs as fast as possible. Thus, the scheduling problem is the problem of finding the optimal schedule for a parallel program.

Shared-memory machines   A machine which stores its data and instructions in a shared address space is called a shared-memory machine. However, some shared address machines are actually implemented as physically distributed memory machines, even though their address space is shared. Therefore, we will define a shared-memory machine to be a physically shared-memory machine. Contrast this with a distributed-memory machine.

SIMD paradigm   The single-instruction–multiple-data paradigm assumes there is only one thread of control in a parallel program. Therefore, the processes in the program operate in lock-step. Only the data varies from process to process. Hence SIMD is a restricted form of parallelism. The data is partitioned and distributed to all processors, all processors do the same thing at the same time, and the results are collected from each processor.

SPMD   The single-procedure–multiple-data paradigm is a modification of the SIMD paradigm whereby the granularity is larger. Instead of one instruction at a time, the SPMD paradigm executes an entire procedure at a time, in lock-step.

Static   A network is static, if its links do not change while messages are being passed. The network topology remains unchanged.

Worm-hole routing   A worm-hole route is established much like a circuit in a circuit-switched network, but the worm-hole routing network has many characteristics of a packet-switched network. This approach avoids the multiple hopping that occurs in a purely packet-switched network. Large messages are transmitted much faster.

PROBLEMS

1   What is the speedup of a program that executes 75% of its code in parallel and 25% in serial?

2   When is it impossible to write a data-parallel program?

3   Is the control-flow programming paradigm more general than the data-parallel programming paradigm? Why?

4   Draw the Petri net graphs of these examples:

a   Shared-memory

```
shared int Y;              /* Declare Y to be shared
shared lock p;             /* Create a lock variable
   .
   .
   .
Y = 100;                   /* Set Y
m_fork(2);                 /* Fork program into two programs
s_lock(p);                 /* Set lock so only one process can access
                                critical section of code
if (mid == 1) {Y = Y + 1};  /* Processor A increments shared Y
s_unlock(p);               /* Clear lock so all can access
output(Y);                 /* Output the result
```

b   Distributed-memory

begin fan
broadcast i := 1 **to** 1000;   /* Start 1,000 processes on 1,000
                                          processors
   mapin Y[i] **to** LocalY;   /* Make 1,000 copies of LocalY variables
   { LocalY = LocalY + 1   }   /* Do 1,000 increments at the same time
   mapout LocalY **to** Y[i]   /* Collect 1,000 results
endfan

5   Draw Gantt charts for **4a** and **4b**.

6   List the differences between SIMD and MIMD.

7   List the differences between the control-flow and data-parallel paradigms.

8   Is communication delay considered part of the Amdahl and Gustafson–Barsis Laws?

9   What is the "traffic cop" approach to parallelism?

10 Derive the Amdahl and Gustafson–Barsis Laws when communication overhead $W(N)$ is included.

REFERENCES

T. G. Lewis and Hesham El-Rewini, *Introduction To Parallel Computing*, Prentice-Hall, 1992.

CHAPTER 2

Principles of Concurrency

In this chapter we will introduce concepts needed to analyze concurrent systems, whether they be distributed or highly parallel. We are most concerned with processes and their synchronization. Synchronization is typically supported through a variety of mechanisms such as *locks* and *messages*. But because of the high degree of complexity associated with locks and messages, we will propose a much higher level of abstraction called a *path expression*. Path expressions permit separation of *policy* from implementation, and elevate programming to the level of design.

Determining if a distributed or parallel program is flow-correct is made even more difficult by asynchronous processes. We will develop two techniques to check for flow-correctness: the *timing diagram*, and the *interleave matrix*. These are visualization techniques which, when applied carefully, can reveal flow errors of the most subtle kind.

The concepts of *safe*, *live*, and *fair* synchronization will be introduced and claimed to be the most significant synchronization challenges facing parallel programming. Timing diagrams and interleave matrices are the tools we use to analyze parallel systems for unsafe, unfair, and deadlock-prone programs. These tools can reveal errors, but they cannot guarantee the absence of all errors.

We will give novel solutions to two important concurrency problems in the literature: the *bounded buffer problem*, and the *multiple readers/writer problem*. The solutions are unique in that they separate synchronization from coding, and they are easily shown to be flow-correct.

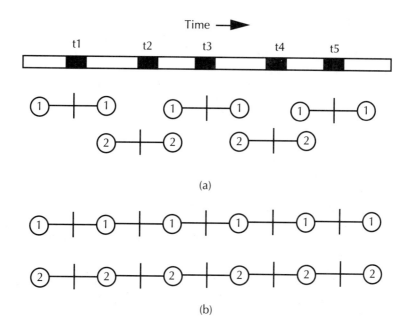

Figure 2.1   Petri network representations of (a) concurrent processes and (b) parallel processes

2.1 PROCESSES

A *process* is a locus of control. That is, a process is the single threaded trace of a program counter as it moves through code. We can use a Petri network to model a process as a series of transitions (operations) and places (states of the process), see Figure 2.1. A process is defined as the path of a token through the Petri network.

We can think of an interval of time as divided into *quanta*, or finite length subintervals. When a process executes for one or more of these quanta, we say it is *active*. When two or more active processes alternate between successive subintervals, as in Figure 2.1a, we call them *concurrent processes*. Each transition takes one or more quanta of time to execute. Places take zero time.

Note: We will elaborate on the ideas of *messages* and *locks* later on. For the time being, it is useful to know that the progress of a process as suggested in Figure 2.1a, is affected by message-passing or locking. In a message-passing system, a process may be delayed while it waits for a message from another process. In a locking system, a process may be similarly delayed by a lock. Thus, a message send or receive or a lock can cause a process to pause. (In the following, we use locks to synchronize access to shared data.)

Informally, a lock is any mechanism for pausing a process. Its purpose is to implement some kind of *synchronization policy*, such as "only one process can access these data at a time," or "these data can only be looked at, they cannot be changed."

A concurrent process may be paused by a lock, or by the need to wait for a message to arrive. But, it is also possible for a concurrent process to be paused so that another concurrent process can use the processor to execute its code. The idea of alternating concurrent processes is the basis of all *preemptive multiprogramming* systems where the operating system divides time among several programs. Each program is allowed to run for a quantum, or until it interrupts itself to do input/output. This use of concurrency is not the same as the use of concurrency in parallel programming.

We distinguish between concurrent processes and truly parallel processes. The key difference is that concurrent processes are active during *different*, nonoverlapping time quanta, while a *parallel process* runs in the same time interval as other processes. The time quanta of a parallel process overlap or coincide with the time quanta of other parallel processes (see Figure 2.1b).

We define a *parallel program* as a program consisting of two or more parallel processes. Thus, parallel processes of interest in this book are those that are members of the same program.

The distinction between parallel and concurrent processes is sometimes not recognized, because multiprocessor systems can also be used to run multiprogramming operating systems that support concurrency. However, it is important to know the subtle difference, because solutions that might work for concurrent processes often fail for parallel processes.

To implement a process, we need a segment of code, a segment of data to be manipulated, and a machine to run the process. When a process is created, we allocate these three things (code, data, and machine). Figure 2.2 illustrates three process models. In Figure 2.2a, two concurrent processes maintain two separate loci of control, and two separate data spaces, but run on one target machine. Because only one process can be active at a time in a single processor system, these two processes merely *time multiplex* their single target machine. This is a model of the classical *time-sharing system*.

One of the immediate consequences of the process model in Figure 2.2a is that only one lock can be set or cleared at a time, because there is only one processor to do the setting and clearing. This greatly simplifies things. If two concurrent processes vie for the same data at the "same time," in reality only one of them is allowed to set the lock. The other one must wait until its time quantum before it can run the corresponding lock code.

Figure 2.2b illustrates a true parallel processing situation. The two processes maintain two separate loci of control, two separate data spaces, and run on two separate processors. They run on different target machines so they can run simultaneously.

The immediate consequence of Figure 2.2b is that two processes can simultaneously set or clear a lock, with neither knowing the true state of the lock. Now, if two parallel processes vie for the same data at the "same time," in reality both of them are allowed to set their local versions of the lock. Unless the lock designer is careful, both processes may think they have sole access to shared data, while in reality they do not. This is one of the subtleties of parallelism versus concurrency.

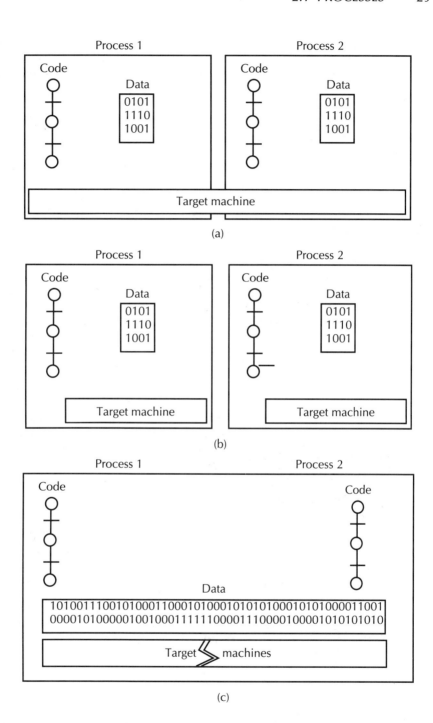

Figure 2.2 Process models: (a) concurrent processes, (b) parallel processes, and (c) processes that share access to data

But most applications would be of little interest if there were no attempts to share access to data. Figure 2.2c illustrates a common model of concurrent and parallel processing. The two processes access the same data space, even though they may run on different target machines and execute different threads of control.

The model of Figure 2.2c can represent concurrent and parallel processes, because they both may share access to the data space. Thus, the problems of synchronization and control are very similar, but their solutions are often different.

In parallel processor systems, it is often difficult to match the hardware clocks of the processors, so it may be difficult to implement time-based synchronizations. Thus, we need to consider time-independent locks, and time-insensitive message-passing. These problems arise in typically small parts, called critical sections, of both parallel and concurrent programs. A *critical section* is a section of a program that accesses shared data.

In practice, there are two methods of sharing data: using *overlapped address spaces*, and *message-passing*. The method used is often determined by the hardware designer. Most distributed-memory target machines force the software designer to use message-passing, while most shared-memory target machines force the software designer to use overlapped address spaces. However, there are exceptions to this rule. For example, some target machines behave like shared-memory machines even though their hardware is implemented as distributed-memory machines.

This concludes a brief introduction to processes. The reader should know a few more definitions, however, that will be useful throughout this book:

1   Large-grained process. A process is said to be *large-grained* or *coarse-grained*, if it takes a long time to complete relative to the sum of the time it takes to initiate the process and the time it takes to send and receive its data.

2   Fine-grained process. A process is said to be *fine-grained* if it can complete its execution in less time than the total it takes to initiate it and send and receive its data.

3   Lightweight process. A process is considered to be *lightweight* if its setup and runtime overhead is small. It is also called *featherweight*.

4   Heavyweight process. A process is considered to be *heavyweight* if its setup and runtime overhead is large.

5   Threads and tasks versus processes. A process also has other names. A *thread* is sometimes used to denote a lightweight process. A *task* is sometimes used to denote a heavyweight process. *Task* is also sometimes used interchangeably with *process*.

2.2 PROPERTIES OF FLOW-CORRECT PROCESSES

We seek methods of analyzing concurrent and parallel processes to be sure they are flow-correct. There are three properties of large-grained flow that most concern us as designers of concurrent and parallel software: safety, liveness, and fairness. These three properties are usually associated with a *synchronization policy*, which dictates the behavior of processes when they attempt to interact through access to shared data. Synchronization policies are often implemented by a *synchronization mechanism*. A mechanism is any coding device for serialization of access to shared data. The difference between a policy and a mechanism is the difference between a law and its enforcement.

A safe policy guarantees safe access to shared data. That is, safety ensures that there is no indeterminism in the result.

A live policy guarantees that two or more processes cannot be permanently blocked by each other. That is, live processes are guaranteed to complete their threads of control without mutual interference. If such a configuration were to occur, the processes would be in *deadlock*.

A fair policy guarantees that one process is not starved by any other process. That is, an active process is not unfairly delayed in completing its threads of control.

Example 2.1

Consider the following pieces of code for three concurrent processes. In one thread of control, process 1 sets the value of x to 0, and in the other thread of control, process 2 sets the value of x to 1. Which value is obtained and printed by process 3?

Process 1	*Process 2*	*Process 3*
while TRUE **do**	**while** TRUE **do**	**while** TRUE **do**
$x := 0$;	$x := 1$;	print(x);

These three processes share access to the variable x in three distinct critical sections. The value of x depends on the order of execution of each critical section. Suppose, for example, process 1 always executes an iteration of its loop before process 2. Then, the value obtained by process 3 depends on the order of execution of process 3 relative to process 2.

The value of x is *indeterminate* as far as process 3 is concerned. That is, there is no way to guarantee the value of x that is printed. Each time the three processes are run together, the value of x is different. This is an example of a *race condition* on x.

Suppose we want to enforce a policy of safety, liveness, and fairness on these three processes. What would this mean?

Safety   There can be no race condition. To achieve this, we must serialize accesses to x using some delay mechanism. For example, a wait/signal pair can be used to serialize access. Recall that a wait delays a process until a corresponding signal is received. Let wait a,b delay a process until signal b arrives from process a. Thus, the signal/wait pair must match arguments:

Process 1	Process 2	Process 3
while TRUE **do**	**while** TRUE **do**	**while** TRUE **do**
x := 0;	wait 3,2;	wait 1,3;
signal 1,3;	x := 1;	print(x);
wait 2,1;	signal 2,1;	signal 3,2;

Process 1 sets $x := 0$ and then sends signal 1 to process 3. Process 3 waits until the signal is received before it prints 0. Then, process 3 signals process 2, which is waiting (wait 3,2) to set x to 1. After the value of x is set to 1, process 2 signals for process 1 to set $x := 0$ again. This pattern is repeated forever.

In this case, the effects of process 3 are ignored by the other two processes. Process 3 is delayed by process 1 to make sure the value of x does not change while it is being printed. The serialization is a safety mechanism, because indeterminism is eliminated.

Liveness: It is impossible for two or more processes to block each other forever. That is, there is no serialization mechanism that prevents a process from completing its thread of control. If there were, a deadlock would ensue. To illustrate this, we can modify the previous example in a manner that leads to a *deadlock* among the three processes. We change the placement of the wait in process 1 as follows:

Process 1	Process 2	Process 3
while TRUE **do**	**while** TRUE **do**	**while** TRUE **do**
wait 2,1;	wait 3,2;	wait 1,3;
x := 0;	x := 1;	print(x);
signal 1,3;	signal 2,1;	signal 3,2;

In this scenario, process 1 waits to get a signal from process 2, but process 2 is waiting to get a signal from process 3. Process 3 is also waiting for process 1. This cycle of waiting cannot be broken, so the processes are deadlocked. Does the following solution solve the deadlock problem and the safety problem? We have changed only the order of the signal/wait operations in process 3.

Process 1	Process 2	Process 3
while TRUE **do**	**while** TRUE **do**	**while** TRUE **do**
wait 2,1;	wait 3,2;	signal 3,2;
x := 0;	x := 1;	print(x);
signal 1,3;	signal 2,1;	wait 1,3;

The problem of indeterminism returns. Why?

Fairness   To enforce a fair policy, the serialization mechanism must guarantee that all processes have equal access to the shared data. This subtle property is often difficult to detect in safe and live systems. Yet, if access biases exist such that one process gets more frequent access than another, we call the result unfair. Unfair access is sometimes caused by *livelock*, which occurs when the processes are not deadlocked, but one or more processes starve another process by taking away all access.

The previous example restricts the output to 0. It might be more interesting to print the value of x regardless of whether it is 0 or 1. In this case, we want to give equal access to both processes, and then print both values of x. To do this, we replace the signal/wait pair with a lock/unlock pair. The lock(x) operation restricts access to mutual exclusion. Thus, when x is locked, only one process can access and change x. The process that locks x is allowed to change x; all other processes are prevented from making simultaneous access.

Process 1	*Process 2*	*Process 3*
while TRUE **do**	**while** TRUE **do**	**while** TRUE **do**
lock(x);	lock(x);	lock(x);
x := 0;	x := 1;	print(x);
unlock(x);	unlock(x);	unlock(x);

The lock/unlock pairs guarantee safety simply because they enforce mutual exclusion. But, these processes illustrate another property called *nondeterminism*. Nondeterminism is the inability to decide the order of process execution. In particular, process 3 is *nondeterministic*, because we cannot determine whether it prints 0 or 1.

Nondeterminism is different from indeterminism. A value may be indeterminate, but only processes can be nondeterministic. Nondeterminism is a property of processes, and indeterminism is a property of variables.

If the processes in the foregoing examples run at the same speed, and they all make equal access to x, the output from process 3 will be 0s approximately half the time and 1s the rest of the time. Each time x is changed or printed, its value is held determinate long enough to complete the operation.

But suppose process 2 is twice as fast as process 1. Then the outputs from process 3 would be biased toward 1s. In general, there would be twice as many 1s as 0s. The reason is that the faster process starves the slower process. *Starvation* is another word for unfair access.

In summary, parallel processes must be governed by safe, fair, and live policies in addition to the flow-correctness properties we have discussed, to be considered totally correct. But, how can we analyze a system of parallel processes to confirm their correctness?

2.3 TIMING DIAGRAMS

A *timing diagram* is a visual representation of a parallel processing scenario. It is used to analyze a system of parallel processes to determine if they are safe, fair, and live. The idea is simple: for each parallel process, we draw a line which assumes a high value when the process is active, and a low value when it is inactive. The elapsed time is indicated along the horizontal axis, and the processing step along the vertical axis. Vertical dotted lines are used to emphasize key events in the scenario, such as receiving a message, or setting a value.

Each timing diagram represents one possible outcome of a parallel program. These outcomes are called *scenarios*, and show the order of execution of the processes, message-passing, and key values of variables. All possible scenarios must be diagrammed to be sure that a parallel program is correct.

Example 2.2

How do we know that the configuration of the three processes described in the previous example are safe? Fair? Live? Figure 2.3 gives a timing diagram for one scenario, of the following:

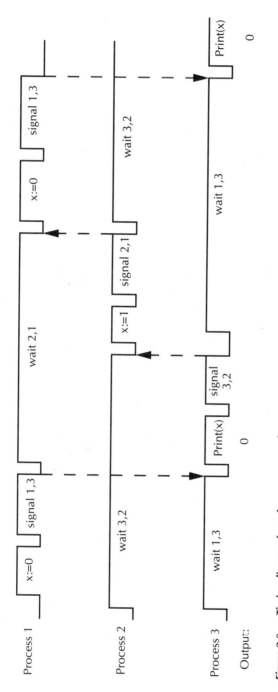

Figure 2.3   Timing diagram for safe access example

Process 1	Process 2	Process 3
while TRUE **do**	**while** TRUE **do**	**while** TRUE **do**
x := 0;	wait 3,2;	wait 1,3;
signal 1,3;	x := 1;	print(x);
wait 2,1;	signal 2,1;	signal 3,2;

The timing diagram shows time (left to right) and events (top to bottom). The vertical dotted lines indicate signal/wait pairs aligned in time. The rectangular waves indicate entry and exit from operations as labelled. Therefore, when process 1 sets x to 0, this is indicated by a rectangular wave whose width is proportional to the time it takes to perform the assignment.

The vertical dotted lines show how the wait/signal pair force processes to serialize in time. The arrow indicates the direction of the message flow. When a wait is terminated by a signal, we show this with a dotted line.

This diagram says the scenario is safe because x is always printed as 0; live, because all processes repeat forever; and fair, because all processes have equal access to x.

2.4 INTERLEAVE MATRIX ANALYSIS

The foregoing examples were brief but complex. It is not always clear how to determine if processes are properly accessing data through their critical sections by merely reading the textual code. An *interleave matrix* is used to visualize what can happen within such code.

Figure 2.4 shows how to construct an interleave matrix, which is a visualization of two processes. One process is shown as a Petri network across the top of the matrix, and the second process is shown as a Petri network down the left side of the matrix. Each square in the matrix corresponds to a combined state of the two processes. Lines represent transitions: a process crossing a vertical line corresponds to the execution of one transition of process 1; crossing a horizontal line corresponds to the execution of one transition of process 2.

Clearly, moving from one combined state to another corresponds to a change in the combined state of the two processes. In Figure 2.4a we have labelled the critical section transitions (CR) of each process to indicate where there may be a race condition. In addition, we have shaded the four states surrounding the intersection of the two critical section lines, to draw attention to these critical section states. The shaded area is called the *safety zone* of the interleave matrix, because it provides a protective buffer around the intersection. Any process that enters this safety zone is in danger of committing an error, because the outcome of executing one or both critical sections is indeterminate.

The interleave matrix allows us to visualize the effects of two processes on a critical section, and to analyze their behavior by drawing paths through the matrix representing possible executions of the code of the two process. Beginning in the upper left state, representing the initial state of both processes, we draw a path from square to square to model what can happen when the two processes execute. Concurrency dictates that the paths move horizontally or vertically,

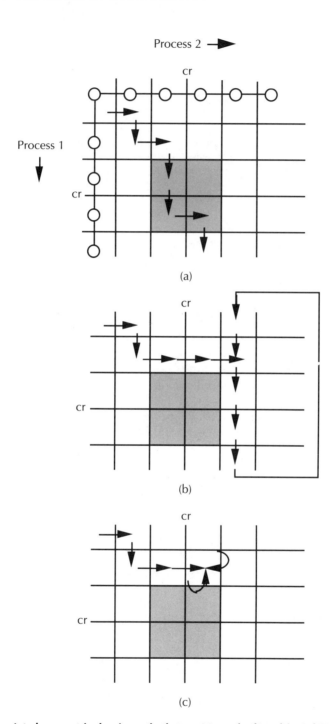

Figure 2.4   Interleave matrix showing paths that are (a) unsafe, (b) unfair, and (c) dead-lock prone. Lines represent indivisible operations, squares represent combined states, and arrows represent transitions of one process. Critical section transitions are labeled CR.

corresponding with execution of a statement in one process at a time. To move diagonally, a pair of processes would have to run on two processors.

A path from start to finish is called a *trajectory*. The trajectories of a process pair can be analyzed for flow-errors. In terms of the interleave matrix, the properties of safety, liveness, and fairness can be restated as follows:

Safety   A trajectory is said to be safe if it does not enter the safety zone. If all possible trajectories avoid the safety zone, the synchronization policy governing the process pair is said to be safe. Figure 2.4a illustrates an unsafe trajectory.

Fairness   A trajectory is said to be fair if it crosses the *cr* transition of process 1 as often as it crosses the *cr* transition of process 2. Figure 2.4b illustrates an unfair trajectory, because a faster process 2 is allowed to starve a slower process 1. If it is impossible for one process to repeatedly cross its cr transition while the other process waits, then the synchronization policy governing the process pair is said to be fair.

Liveness   A trajectory that enters a state which has no exit, e.g., a *deadlock state*, is said to be *deadlock prone*. Figure 2.4c illustrates a deadlock state and a deadlock prone trajectory. If all possible trajectories are examined, and none are deadlock prone, then the synchronization policy is said to be live. Otherwise, the policy is said to be deadlock prone. If such a process pair ever enters the deadlock state during program execution, we say the process pair has become *deadlocked*.

The interleave matrix can be made more useful if we label the states (squares) with the value of *state variables*. A state variable is any variable used to implement a mechanism for enforcing a synchronization policy. One of the most common low level mechanisms is called a *lock*. We used a simple lock/unlock mechanism in the previous section to solve the problem of indeterminism. The following examples illustrate the interplay between policy and mechanism, and shows how to use the interleave matrix to analyze and find errors in proposed mechanisms.

Example 2.3

Suppose we construct a lock using the famous test-and-set instruction found in most single cpu systems. The test-and-set instruction works as follows: a state variable, C, is used to store a Boolean value; i.e., C is either TRUE or FALSE. When the test-and-set instruction is issued on C, it has the following effect:

test-and-set(C) :-
    if not C **then begin** C := TRUE; **return** TRUE **end**
        else return FALSE;

The test-and-set operation returns TRUE only if the state variable C changes value as a side-effect of test-and-set. If C is not changed, the test-and-set returns FALSE.

When C is cleared using the complementary clear instruction, the value of C is always set to FALSE regardless of what it was previously. That is, C either changes from TRUE to FALSE, or else resets to FALSE:

Clear(C) :-
    C := FALSE;

The important thing to remember about the test-and-set(C) and clear(C) instruction pair, is that they perform their operations in one machine step. That is, they are *atomic*, i.e., indivisible, and rely on this indivisibility to work properly.

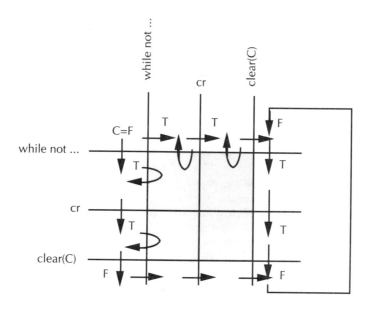

Figure 2.5   Interleave matrix of test-and-set lock

We can use these two instructions and state variable C to implement a simple *mutual exclusion lock* as follows. This kind of lock is called a *spin lock* because it repeatedly executes a test while waiting for access to the critical section (CR) of code:

while not test-and-set(C) **do**;	/* Spin until C = FALSE*/
CR;	
clear(C);	/* Set C to FALSE */

This is a very short section of code, but it is rather convoluted. The question is, does it enforce a policy of safety, liveness, and fairness? We will answer these questions using the interleave matrix.

Figure 2.5 shows the interleave matrix giving all possible trajectories for two processes. State variable C is shown as TRUE (T) or FALSE (F) in each accessible state. The mechanism is safe, because the spin lock repels access when the state variable is TRUE, indicating access by the other process. The mechanism is live because there are no deadlock states.

But, a faster process can starve a slower one, as indicated by the loop-back. A slightly faster vertical process can enter its critical section, clear C, and then quickly do a subsequent test-and-set(C) to force the horizontal process to wait, indefinitely. The same can be said for the horizontal process, if it is faster.

This example illustrates the interleave matrix visualization technique, but it also raises a question about parallel processes. If we use spin locking to synchronize two parallel processes, will the same result be obtained?

The synchronization of multiple processing units is made much more complex because there may be no atomic test-and-set operation that spans all processors.

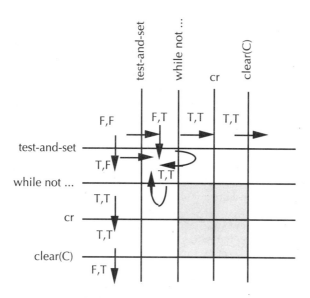

Figure 2.6 Interleave matrix for two-processor lock showing deadlock state

This added complexity is illustrated in the next example, where we attempt to use a test-and-set mechanism to synchronize processes on two separate processors.

Example 2.4

Suppose we use a test-and-set operation on each of two parallel processors to enforce a policy of mutual exclusion on access to data via critical sections. The two state variables are called $C[1]$ and $C[2]$ to indicate that they reside on processors 1 and 2, respectively.

Furthermore, to make things simple, we assume that the two processors share an address space, so it is easy to access each other's state variables. To make sure only one process is in its critical section at a time, each process sets its own state variable to TRUE, and then spin tests the other process's state variable to make sure it is FALSE, before entering its critical section. The code on each processor follows:

Process 1	*Process 2*
test-and-set(C[1]);	test-and-set(C[2]);
while not test-and-set(C[2]) **do**;	**while not** test-and-set(C[1]) **do**;
CR;	CR;
clear(C[1]);	clear(C[2]);

The interleave matrix for this mechanism is shown in Figure 2.6. In addition to the trajectories that we might expect from Figure 2.5, Figure 2.6 contains two deadlocked trajectories. The simple test-and-set mechanism fails for multiple processor systems!

The previous example shows that special care must be taken when developing locks for multiple processors. The standard techniques historically applied in single-processor operating systems do not always work in multiple-processor systems. The interleave matrix is one of several techniques we will employ to analyze synchronization mechanisms.

More elaborate mechanisms have been proposed to solve these problems. For example, Knuth proposed the use of a FIFO (first-in-first-out) queue and three simple atomic (noninterruptible) operations to solve the problems of safety, liveness, and fairness. The FIFO queue avoids starvation; the atomic operations guarantee safety, and the preemption avoids deadlock. However, Knuth's lock does not avoid system deadlock, whereby a system of interacting processes can deadlock regardless of the mechanism used by programmers to guarantee live synchronization.

Example 2.5

Knuth proposed a simple spin lock mechanism that can be extended to preemptive locking as shown below. Preemption means that the current process is halted so that some other process can run. Ultimately a preempted process is started again, so that no indefinite postponement takes place.

This mechanism assumes that the Add-to-queue(p), Remove-from-queue(p), and Head-of-queue(p) procedures are atomic; i.e., they cannot be interrupted, and complete their actions without delay. These procedures have obvious meanings, where p is the identifier of a process. For process p:

```
Add-to-queue(p);                        /* Lock and wait...   */
L1: if not Head-of-queue(p) then goto L1;
CR;
Remove-from-queue(p);                    /* Unlock   */
```

One can analyze this lock using the interleave matrix, and convince oneself that the mechanism is safe, live, and fair. The only drawback to this solution is the **goto** which spins on the test, Head-of-queue. This can be costly, and in some parallel systems, spinning can cause saturation of the interconnection network that holds the parallel processors together.

This mechanism is easily extended to a preemptive version as follows. The Supervisor(p) routine passes control to the local operating system so that another process can use the processor cycles. Rather than waste cycles on spinning, the supervisor trap permits preemption. Eventually, the local operating system returns control back to this process, so it can once again attempt to enter its critical section. For process p:

```
Add-to-queue(p);                        /* Lock and wait...   */
L1: if not Head-of-queue(p) then Supervisor(p);
    goto L1;
CR;
Remove-from-queue(p);                    /* Unlock   */
```

Note that the placement of the queue is not important, because of the atomic nature of queue operations. Thus, this solution works equally well on a multiple-processor system or a single-processor system. No deadlock state exists in the interleave matrix, because like a single test-and-set, the queue operations are indivisible.

Later, we will use the idea of a queue and atomic operations as building blocks for the control of large-grained parallel processes. This is the basis of a technique which solves the general problem of synchronized control of large-grained parallel programs.

2.5 BOUNDED BUFFERS

One of the most common problems of distributed and parallel programming is the so-called *bounded buffer problem*. This problem must be solved by nearly all parallel programs. In addition, some form of this problem is inherent to a large number of synchronization problems. A general solution to this problem will provide a basis for a general theory of synchronization in parallel programs.

Given a process P which produces elements and stores them at some sporadic rate into buffer $b[1..n]$, and another process Q which reads elements of the buffer $b[1..n]$ and consumes them at a different sporadic rate, what are safe, fair, and live policies and mechanisms for the synchronization of P and Q? Process P is called the *producer* and process Q is called the *consumer*.

The processes run at sporadic rates which is the reason for the buffer. We want to smooth the interface between these two processes by buffering the output from one and the input to the other. Thus, the two can run at their own rates and still communicate with one another.

The bounded buffer problem is important because it is the mechanism by which most parallel processes communicate. In a message-passing system, the producer is some process that wants to send a message to a receiver. The consumer is the receiver. The sender and receiver run at different rates, and thus we need to buffer the messages so that the receiver does not delay the sender.

Here is one possible way to code the producer and consumer processes. Assume that the message is stored in the message variable info:

Producer (sender)
while TRUE **do**
    Produce(info);

Consumer (receiver)
while TRUE **do**
    Consume(info);

The producer puts messages into a shared buffer, which typically holds many messages at once. The consumer copies messages from the shared buffer, typically in FIFO order. When the buffer is full, additional messages are blocked until space is made ready by the consumer. When the buffer is empty, the consumer must wait. Simultaneous access to the same message must be carefully synchronized to prevent indeterminism.

The buffer is circular. The producer puts data into elements buffer[1..n], and then cycles back to element buffer[1] after buffer[n] is filled. Similarly, the consumer takes data from elements buffer[1..n], wrapping around to element buffer[1] after taking buffer[n]. Variables p and q are indexes into the buffer; one for the consumer and the other for the producer.

```
Consume(info)  {
    while in ≤ 0 do;        /* Spin lock */
    q := q mod n + 1;       /* Access 1..n, 1..n, 1..n, etc */
    info := buffer[q];      /* Get */
    in := in − 1;           /* Keep track of number waiting to be taken */
    return };
```

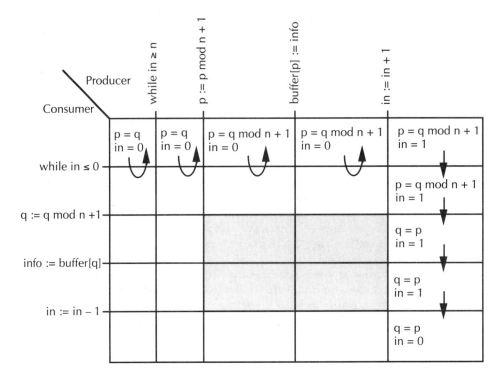

Figure 2.7   When *p* = *q*, *in* = 0 and no race condition occurs.

Produce(info) {
    while in ≥ n **do**;   /* Spin lock */
    p := p **mod** n + 1;   /* Access circular buffer */
    buffer[p] := info;   /* Put */
    in := in + 1;   /* Number in buffer */
    return }

The variable *in* records the number of elements in the buffer which have been put there by the producer, but which have yet to be copied out by the consumer. When *in* = 0, the buffer is empty; when *in* = *n*, the buffer is full.

Note that buffer overrun by producer is impossible, because the **while** loop guarantees that *in* < *n*. Similarly, buffer underrun by the consumer is impossible, because the **while** loop forces *in* > 0. The expression $x := x$ **mod** $n + 1$ mathematically guarantees that *p* and *q* are held within the range of buffer elements, 1..*n* for positive and zero *x*.

The **while** loops collectively force *in* to range from 1 to $n - 1$; i.e., $0 < in < n$. Therefore, we know the range of *p* and *q*: $1 \leq p, q \leq n$. The **while** loops are *spin locks* because they spin on their predicates, waiting for *in* to be changed by the other process.

The interleave matrix of Figure 2.7 considers the case when *p* = *q*; i.e., both processes attempt to access the same buffer element at the same time. This could lead to a race condition in the lock. But the trajectory of Figure 2.7 shows that the spin lock in the consumer safely locks out the producer until it produces a message that can be consumed.

Safety   Figure 2.7 shows an interleave analysis which proves that the spin locks guarantee safety on accesses to buffer[p], when $p = q$. That is, no path leads into the safety zone of the matrix. When we perform the timing diagram analysis of this mechanism, we will learn of a more subtle race condition. This race condition exists on state variable *in*, and will lead to a fix that is needed to guarantee proper updating of *in*.

Fairness   These processes are nondeterministic, meaning they can access the bounded buffer in any order. If the producer is faster than the consumer, the buffer eventually fills up, because it is bounded. Then additional producer access is blocked while the consumer removes messages. The reverse happens for the case when a consumer is faster than a producer. Thus, this solution may not be fair in the strict sense of our definition, but one process cannot starve the other indefinitely.

Liveness   No deadlock can occur because all states have exits. This is a consequence of the fact that the *in* counter is bounded and monotonic (strictly increasing or decreasing) in each process.

This solution is deceptive, because we are led to believe that the race condition of greatest concern is on buffer[$1..n$], but in reality, the race condition that we should be most concerned with is on *in*. That is, one of the state variables used to synchronize access to the bounded buffer is itself in danger of indeterminism. We need to synchronize access to the state variables themselves.

The timing diagram, as well as a modified interleave matrix, are shown in Figure 2.8, which reveal the possibility of unsafe access to *in*. This can happen when $p \neq q$ and $1 \leq in \leq n$, so that the producer and consumer simultaneously update *in*.

In Figure 2.8a the timing diagram scenario shows that the consumer is blocked until the producer places one message in the buffer. Then it is possible for both processes to simultaneously update *in*, leading to an indeterminacy.

Figure 2.8b reveals the same error, if we focus attention on the parallel updates of *in*. There is a trajectory that leads into the safety zone {$in := in - 1$} versus {$in := in + 1$}. What can we do to remove this race condition?

Clearly, placing a lock around the updates, in each case, prevents the race condition. The reader is invited to provide this solution, and prove it is flow-correct.

2.6 PATH EXPRESSIONS

The synchronization problems described in the previous sections of this chapter are major problems confronting the parallel programmer. Because synchronization is the responsibility of the programmer, and because the issues are so complex, we seek a method of large-grained parallel programming that is both powerful and yet simple. *Path expressions* offer this power and simplicity. Paths are simpler than locks and convoluted code, but they are also more powerful.

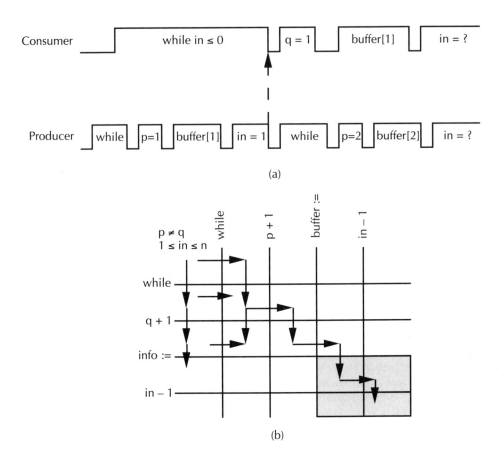

Figure 2.8   **Flow error in the bounded buffer synchronization mechanism, as revealed by (a) the timing diagram, and (b) the interleave matrix**

Campbell proposed path expressions as an alternative to low-level locks. A *path* is a regular expression that describes a finite state machine for specifying the order of activation of asynchronous processes. Each identifier in the regular expression is a process name. Each operator dictates the order of process activated relative to other processes in the expression. Thus, the expression tells how the parallel processes are to behave relative to one another. Indirectly, we can control data access patterns through these expressions.

Only four operators are needed to express the relative behavior of large-grained processes: *concatenation*, meaning parallel process activation; logical +, meaning sequential activation of processes; *exponentiation*, meaning concatenation of many processes operating in sequence; and [], meaning optional activation of processes (also called the *first right of refusal* operator). These operators are sufficient to express the most common policies of synchronization.

Concatenation   Parallel execution of processes is allowed
+   One or the other, but not both in parallel

^ (exponentiation)   Limited concurrency given by the value of the exponent

[]   Optional, meaning processes may be optionally activated

In addition, we will have occasion to use the arithmetic convenience of grouping terms using (), and expressing unbounded concatenation using *, a special constant denoting infinity.

()   Grouping, a shorthand for + processes

*   Special constant meaning infinity

Example 2.6

path A + B	/* Do process A, or process B, but not at same time */
path A B	/* Do A and B at the same time */
path A^1 + B^1	/* Same as A + B */
path A^2 + B^3	/* Two As in parallel, or three Bs in parallel */
path 2(A) + 3(B)	/* Same as A + A + B + B + B */

Path expressions are evaluated in relationship to a *request queue* containing the names of processes that are waiting to be activated. The request queue mechanism works very much like Knuth's lock. Serialization of requests through a queue prevents starvation and allows preemption, if desired.

The working mechanism of a path expression plus its request queue is quite simple, yet powerful. Requests for process activations are enqueued in FIFO order, and disposed of by a *scheduler* according to the path expression governing the processes. If the path expression restricts a process to sequential execution, it delays the process while another is allowed to run. On the other hand, if the path expression says that the two processes can run at the same time, the scheduler activates both simultaneously.

Example 2.7

Path expressions might be considered as restrictions or constraints placed on processes. For example, consider the following path expressions as constraints on processes A, B, C, and D.

path A + B;   /* Either one A or one B, but not both at same time */

If the request queue contains A A A B, then each process is activated in sequence in the same order: A followed by A again, followed by A, and then B.

path AB + CD;   /* Either one of the two pairs run in parallel */

If the request queue contains A B A B C D A B C D, then the activations are done as follows: A and B are run together, followed by a second run of A B. Then C and D are run in parallel after which the AB pair is run a third time. Finally, C and D are run in parallel. The AB pair never executes at the same time as CD.

path A^2 + B^3;   /* Up to 2 exclusive runs of A, or 3 runs of B, but not together */

The request queue containing A A B B B A B A B B B B is processed as follows: Two As are run in parallel, followed by B B B. Then, A is run by itself, followed by B alone. The remaining A is run by itself. Then, three Bs are run in parallel. The final B is run by itself, after the trio of Bs finish.

path A^* + B^* ;   /* Any number of As, any number of Bs, but not both */

The previous request queue A A B B B A B A B B B B is run as follows: A A, followed by B B, followed by A. Then B runs, followed by A, followed by all the remaining Bs, B B B B.

The request queue approach avoids starvation, which might occur when one or more processes prevent another process from executing. Activations are processed in the same order in which they appear in the request queue. Thus it is impossible for one process to execute more often than another process.

The path expression may or may not be safe, depending on the expression written by the programmer. For example, **path** AB, means that both processes may execute simultaneously, even if they produce an indeterminate value.

Example 2.8

Let R and W be *read* and *write* processes, respectively. R is benign, so we can permit as many R activations as requested. W is destructive, however, so we restrict its activation to one at a time. We want to be fair, however, so we handle the requests in FIFO order.

The following path expression and the serial nature of the request queue prevents starvation, unsafe, and deadlock prone behavior.

path W^1 + R^*;   /* One writer, many readers */

We can see that a request queue containing alternating Rs and Ws will be allowed to execute in the order of the requests. Actually, this path expression allows as many Rs as can be found in sequence to be executed. For R W R W R..., one R is found in sequence, so the reads alternate with the writes. If the queue contained R W R R R W R..., then the functions would be activated in order: R W R R R W R.... Had the queue contained W W R R R W..., the path expression would still have limited the number of writes to one at a time: W followed by another W, followed by three Rs, and so forth. This scenario is illustrated by a timing diagram (see Figure 2.9).

The timing diagram of Figure 2.9 shows three mutually exclusive accesses to the critical section by the W process, and three simultaneous accesses by the R process. The W processes must be done sequentially, but the R processes can access the critical section in parallel.

In some cases, the path expression conflicts with the ability of the process to execute. For example, when there are more requests waiting in the request queue than can be processed by the code, the path is deadlocked. This might happen whenever the processes have access to limited resources, such as in the bounded buffer problem. In this case, processes are given a *first right of refusal*, which they may choose not to exercise. The first right of refusal feature prevents starvation, but also prevents deadlock.

W W R R R W ...

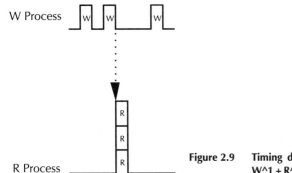

W Process

R Process

Figure 2.9   **Timing diagram of scenario for path expression**
$W^1 + R^*$ and request queue containing WWRRRW

Example 2.9

Path expressions can trivially express synchronization for producer/consumer process pairs in the bounded buffer problem. We need only mutual exclusion to guarantee safe access. So, we might use the mutual exclusion path given below:

path Producer + Consumer;

This solves the bounded buffer problem because it requires only mutual exclusion. But we can improve this solution if we restrict the number of messages placed in the buffer by Producer, using the added constraint, where n is the size of the buffer:

path n(Producer) + Consumer;

This is equivalent to:

path (Producer + Producer + ... + Producer) + Consumer

where *n* instances of Producer are logically added to form patterns to be matched against the request queue pattern.

Doing the same thing for Consumer, but noting that Consumer can only consume as many messages as there are in the buffer, and that Producer can only produce as many messages as there are empty elements in buffer[1..n], we obtain:

path (n − in)(Producer) + (in)(Consumer);

This path expression greatly simplifies the code, because it separates policy from process. This is a very powerful concept, which leads to enormous simplification of large-grained parallel programming. In fact, the synchronization code, such as a lock, need not be part of the implementation of either process. This allows changes to the policy without changes to the code—a most important benefit in software engineering.

Now we can give a path expression for the bounded buffer problem and simplify the code for each process. This solution has the added advantage of separation of synchronization policy from process code:

path (n − in)(Producer) + (in)(Consumer);   /* One at a time, with bounds */

```
Consume(info)  {
q := q mod n + 1;          /* Access 1..n, 1..n, 1..n, etc */
info := buffer[q];         /* Get */
in := in − 1;              /* Keep track of number waiting to be taken */
return };

Produce(info) {
p := p mod n + 1;          /* Access circular buffer */
buffer[p] := info;         /* Put */
in := in + 1;              /* Number in buffer */
return }
```

Unfortunately, this code has a problem that leads to deadlock as illustrated by the following example! Suppose the buffer size is $n = 3$, and the request queue initially contains P P P P C C C C P: The following scenario assumes $n = 3$, and $p = q = in = 0$, initially.

Request queue	*Path expression before processing queue*
P P P P C C C C P;	(3)(Producer) + (0)(Consumer)
P P P C C C C P;	(2)(Producer) + (1)(Consumer)
P P C C C C P;	(1)(Producer) + (2)(Consumer)
P C C C C P;	(0)(Producer) + (3)(Consumer)
	Deadlocked path

The queue contains requests for Consumer (C), but the path expression will not allow them to be activated because Producer (P) is next on the queue. The path expression is blocked by a request for Producer, and so it cannot be obeyed. No additional processes are processed.

This example illustrates why we need the [] operator. Processes bracketed by [] are made optional, and given first right of refusal. The bounded buffer problem can be solved in an elegant manner using the path expression shown in the next example.

Example 2.10

Using the first right of refusal operator, give a path expression for the bounded buffer problem, and show that it works. Recall that processes bracketed within [] can be bypassed to permit other processes to be activated out of order.

path [(n − in)(Producer)] + (in)(Consumer);   /* Same as [P+P+..+P] + C+C+..+C */

Consider the scenario with the initial request queue shown below:

Request queue	*Path expression before processing queue*
P P P P C C C C P;	[(3)(Producer)] + (0)(Consumer)
P P P C C C C P;	[(2)(Producer)] + (1)(Consumer)
P P C C C C P;	[(1)(Producer)] + (2)(Consumer)
P C C C C P;	[(0)(Producer)] + (3)(Consumer)
P C C C P;	[(1)(Producer)] + (2)(Consumer)
C C C P;	[(0)(Producer)] + (3)(Consumer)
C C P;	[(1)(Producer)] + (2)(Consumer)
C P;	[(2)(Producer)] + (1)(Consumer)
P;	[(3)(Producer)] + (0)(Consumer)
	[(2(Producer)] + (1)(Consumer)

The order of process activation for this example is P + P + P + C + P + C + C + C + P, or more compactly, (3)(P) + C + P + (3)(C) + P. Each process has exclusive access to the buffer, so the solution is safe. The order is changed, but because of the first right of refusal, no starvation occurs. And, because the first right of refusal is exercised, no deadlock occurs.

2.7 KEYWORDS AND CONCEPTS

The concepts of parallelism are borrowed largely from the concepts of operating systems, but with some important differences. In both kinds of systems the most useful principles are based on messages, locks, and path expressions. We have explored these mechanisms in detail, and applied them to several canonical problems of concurrency.

We have examined each concurrancy mechanism using three features common to all concurrent systems: safety, liveness, and fairness. These ideas are tied to the following keywords.

Atomic The notion of atomic action is central to all concurrent systems. At some level we must be able to perform a basic or primitve operation without interruption. Thus, an atomic action is indivisible. This is where a fundamental difference between time-multiplexed concurrency and true parallel systems arises. In a truly parallel system, atomic operations can be run in parallel; hence they are pseudoconcurrent. Two or more atomic test-and-set operations can be performed simultaneously. Thus, the principles of operating system concurrency must be carefully reexamined in the light of parallel processing.

Concurrent processes A concurrent process is a coroutine in a single processor system, and a parallel process in a parallel system. A coroutine is one that is time-shared with other processes. A parallel process can run at the same time as another parallel process.

Coarse-grained A process may be coarse- or fine-grained. A coarse grain is also known as a large grain. In either case, a grain is a process whose size is relative to the overhead of the parallel system. A 15 microsecond grain may be considered small, or fine, in one system, and large, or coarse in another one.

Deadlock prone Deadlock is one of the three dangers of parallel processing (the other two are safety failure and unfairness). A parallel program is deadlocked when two or more of the processes cannot continue because to do so would violate a synchronization mechanism such as a lock or message transfer. Deadlock prevents the program from completing. A deadlock state is any program state in which deadlock can occur. Even though the deadlock may be rare, the possibility of deadlock exists if a program contains one or more deadlock states.

Fairness Fairness is a property of parallelism which guarantees that all processes may gain equal access to shared data. A process may be starved by another process if access is unfair.

Fine-grained   A process is fine-grained if its completion time is small relative to the time it takes to create and send data to it. Grain size is relative to communication delay.

Interleave matrix   The interleave matrix is a visual tool for analyzing locks to see if they are safe, fair, and live. It is an exhaustive technique that becomes increasingly complex to use as the number of processes increases. Still, it can reveal subtle timing errors in parallel programs.

Liveness   A system of processes is live if it is impossible for deadlock to occur. Such a system must be devoid of any deadlock states. The mere existence of a deadlock state renders the system deadlock prone.

Livelock   Livelock is a subtle timing problem which is half-way between deadlock and unfairness. Two processes may postpone one another forever, without completely stopping one another, in a livelock state. This may occur, for example, if the two processes are allowed to execute, but they constantly conflict with one another to the detriment of both. Two humans are in livelock when they constantly interrupt one another, such that neither one can complete a sentence.

Lock   A lock is a synchronization mechanism which serializes access to shared variables by two or more processes. Locks can be preemtive, which means that a process is preempted by the lock. Alternatively, a spin lock continues to run a process until the lock is opened and the process is allowed to continue into its critical section. A mutual exclusion lock permits only one process to be active within a critical section at a time.

Path   In place of a lock, we can use a path. A path is a synchronization mechanism which serializes access to shared variables by two or more processes. Instead of an explicit lock, the path uses a path expression. All processes execute according to the path expression which constrains each process while attempting to enter a critical section.

Policy   All locks and paths attempt to carry out some policy. That is, the lock is a mechanism, separate from the policy. For example, a mutual exclusion policy states that only one process at a time can access a shared value. Another policy may allow multiple read accesses, but only a single write access at any time.

Race condition   Whenever two or more processes are allowed simultaneous access to a shared variable, a race condition may arise in which the value of the shared variable can become indeterminate. Thus, a race condition is the process that leads to an indeterminate value.

Readers/writer problem   The readers/writer problem is a canonical problem that is used to test the power of a lock. It is an example of a policy that allows many simultaneous reads, but only one write process at a time. The challenge that this problem poses is one of designing a lock that is safe, fair, and live, and yet permits more than a single process to make simultaneous access to some shared variable.

Safety   Safe access means there is no possibility of a race condition. This is one of the three features of a good lock (safety, fairness, liveness).

Starvation   Starvation occurs when one process prevents another process from ever accessing a shared variable. Starvation may occur, for example, in a parallel processing system when one processor is faster than another.

State variables   We define a program's state by the values of its shared variables. Thus, a state variable is any shared variable that is involved in a lock or critical section.

Timing diagram   We use a timing diagram to visualize the order of execution of parallel tasks. While it is not able to guarantee flow-correctness, a timing diagram can often reveal timing errors.

PROBLEMS

1   Show that the lock proposed by Knuth is safe, fair, and live. Use timing diagrams or interleave matrices, or both.

2   Give a safe, fair, and live, solution to the bounded buffer problem.

3   What is the difference between starvation and deadlock?

4   What is a locus of control? What is the relationship between locus of control and the Petri network model of a process?

5   What is a quantum of time? Where is it used?

6   What is the difference between a concurrent process and a parallel process?

7   What is a critical section? What is a safety zone? What is the relationship between these two?

8   What is the difference between a policy and a mechanism?

9   Give definitions of safety, liveness, and fairness.

10   Show that the following code has a slight bias toward starvation, when used to synchronize two processes. For process i:

```
b[i] := FALSE;
L1: if k <> i then begin
          c[i] := TRUE;
          if b[k] then k := i;
          goto L1;
          end                      /* Then */
     else begin
          c[i] := FALSE;
          for j := 1 to N do
          if j <> i and not c[j] then goto L1;
          end;                     /* Else */
CR;
c[i] := TRUE;
b[i] := TRUE;
```

11   Dekker's Algorithm was one of the first to claim to solve the problem of safe, fair, live mutual exclusion. Draw the interleave matrix for two processes, and then decide it this mechanism is flow-correct. For process me = 1 and other = 2:

```
Lock: flag[me] := TRUE;
while flag[other] do
    if turn<> me then begin
        flag[me] := FALSE;
        while turn <> me do;        /*Spin */
        flag[me] := TRUE;
        end;
CR;
Unlock: flag[me] := FALSE;
turn := other;
```

12   Give path expressions for two processes A and B and the following synchronization policies:

a   Mutual exclusion.
b   Multiple readers, one writer.
c   Bounded buffer problem.
d   Process A is allowed simultaneous access with B; B is allowed simultaneous access with itself and with one A; but A is not allowed access with itself.
e   At most, A can be activated 4 times, simultaneously, and B can be accessed 3 times simultaneously, but process A cannot run at the same time as process B.
f   Two As can run sequentially, and three Bs can run sequentially, but A and B processes cannot run together.

REFERENCES

R. H. Campbell and R. B. Kolstad, *A Practical Implementation of Path Pascal, TR*, Dept. of Computer Science, Univ. Illinois at Urbana-Champaign, UIUCDCS-R-80-1008, 1980.

R. H. Campbell and R. B. Kolstad, Path Pascal Users Manual, *ACM SigPlan Notices*, **15(9)**, 15–25, 1980.

Knuth D. E., Additional comments on a problem in concurrent programming control, *Communications of the ACM*, **9(5)**, 321–322, 1966.

Axioms of Flow-Correctness

This chapter gives methods for analyzing the correctness of the data-flow in a parallel program. First, we will develop a theory of parallel program correctness called *flow-correctness*. This kind of correctness applies only to the dependencies among variables, and does not assert the total or logical correctness of the program. We will show how to apply this theory to straightline code and loops. When found in loops, dataflow dependencies are called *loop-carried dependencies*. We use an *iteration space diagram* to show loop-carried dependencies.

Flow-correctness rests on three basic flow-dependency tests: FLOW, for testing dataflow dependency; ANTI, for testing antidependency; and OUT, for testing output dependency. For each data dependency that exists within a parallel program one of these axioms applies. To be sure that the program does what the programmer expects, the programmer must check the appropriate test for all variables in the program. If any test fails, we say the program is not flow-correct. If all tests pass, we say the program is flow-correct. (However, the program may still be logically flawed. Only flow-correctness is covered by these tests.)

The three fundamental axioms are expressed below in a succinct notation. In this chapter, we describe what each axiom means, and how it is applied.

FLOW(x, t) :-
    ($\exists \Delta t > 0 \mid$ DEF(x, t − Δt)),
    USE(x, t).

ANTI(x, t) :-
    ($\exists \Delta t > 0$ | USE(x, t − Δt)),
    DEF(x, t).
OUT(x, t) :-
    ($\exists \Delta t > 0$ | DEF(x, t − Δt)),
    DEF(x, t).

3.1 FLOW-CORRECTNESS IN PARALLEL CONSTRUCTS

Most everyday processes are sensitive to time. For example, when baking a cake it is important that the ingredients be mixed together before the cake is put into the oven. We often take the sequential nature of baking recipes for granted. Sequential programming automatically implies sequential ordering of the processing steps of the program, much like baking a cake. But what if we have more than one cook, all working at the same time to mix the ingredients and bake the cake? As soon as we remove the orderliness of sequential programming, we enter a combinatorially more complex set of concerns. These concerns become forms of *program correctness assertions* when applied to parallel programs, and correctness checking takes on a slightly different form.

We say a program is *logically correct* if it computes the correct output for its specified inputs. That is, each step of the program correctly transforms its data, incrementally leading to a valid output. We call this sequence of incremental transformations a *program path*. A program is *deterministic* if there is only one program path from input to output. Otherwise, it is *nondeterministic*. A program yields an *indeterminate value* for a variable if the program is nondeterministic and the value depends on which path was executed.

We say a program is *flow-correct* if, regardless of its logical correctness, the program's path coincides with its design specifications. In general, this means the program is either deterministic, or if it is nondeterministic, then no indeterminate values occur during execution along any path. Flow-correctness is achieved only if it is impossible for indeterminism to occur in any path. Because there may be a very large number of paths in a nondeterminate program, flow-correctness checking can be difficult, if not impractical.

Flow-correctness does not address the problem of total correctness checking. It is limited to the analysis of *data dependencies* among variables of the program. This is where parallel programs depart in behavior from serial programs. It is also one of the principle distinguishing features of parallel programming.

Parallel programs have synchronization requirements, particularly with respect to *dataflow*, i.e., the flow of values into and out of variables, among the simultaneously executing parallel parts of the program. The purpose of *synchronization* is to manage dataflow. These flows are time-sensitive because a parallel program might access and process a single piece of data two contradictory ways at the same instant in time. Such a clash of accesses is called a *race condition*.

The problem of race conditions, in turn, leads to the study of time-dependent dataflows. Fortunately, all dataflows of interest to us can be characterized by three temporal predicates—UNDEF, USE, and DEF—defined as follows:

UNDEF(x, t) is TRUE at time t when variable x is undefined at time t.

USE(x, t) is TRUE at time t when a value is copied from variable x at time t, e.g., $y := x$.

DEF(x, t) is TRUE at time t when a value is assigned to variable x at time t, e.g., $x := 3$.

UNDEF is TRUE for all variables when a parallel program begins execution at time $t = 0$. If a certain variable, x, is never assigned a value, then UNDEF(x, t) is TRUE for all values of $t \geq 0$. We write this as UNDEF(x, t) | $t \geq 0$, which is read "UNDEF(x, t) is TRUE when $t \geq 0$."

Most likely, x will be assigned a value, either by an input action, or by some calculation that takes place during program execution. When this occurs, the DEF(x, t) predicate becomes TRUE. Suppose x is assigned a value at time $t = 2$ then DEF(x, t) | $t \geq 2$; similarly, UNDEF(x, t) | $t < 2$, but not UNDEF(x, t) | $t \geq 2$.

The USE predicate is TRUE or FALSE depending on the reference pattern of a variable. For example, if variable x is defined at time $t = 2$, and referenced in a calculation at time $t = 3$, we say it is defined at time $t = 2$ and used at time $t = 3$; i.e., USE(x, t) | $t = 3$. Prior to this time, it is FALSE; i.e., USE(x, t) | $t < 3$ is FALSE.

We typically evaluate flow-correctness at some point in a parallel program based on the UNDEF, USE, and DEF patterns established at a previous point in time, $t - \Delta t$. This temporal dependency, in addition to flow dependency, is modelled as a *precondition* predicate PRE(x), and a *postcondition* predicate, POST(x). Let us see how this works.

Example 3.1

The statement S: $y := x + 1$ uses x at some time t, which assumes that x was defined prior to that time. Thus the precondition and postcondition for x are:

PRE(x) [S] POST(x) $\Rightarrow$ DEF(x, t – Δt) [y := x + 1] USE(x, t), where $\Delta t > 0$.

This formalism is read as follows: "Statement S has a precondition and a postcondition for variable x." The symbol $\Rightarrow$ means *becomes*, or *implies*, or *is*, so we say the precondition/postcondition pair is DEF at some time $(t - \Delta t)$, followed by USE at time t. Statement S is $y := x + 1$, so by substitution, we get DEF(x, t – Δt) [y := x + 1] USE(x, t). In simple words, the variable x is defined at time $(t - \Delta t)$, and used at time t.

To be even more specific, suppose x is defined as 10 at time $(t - \Delta t) = 2$; thus DEF(x, t – Δt)) | $(t - \Delta t) = 2$. Further, assume the assignment [y := x + 1] takes place at $t = 3$; thus USE(x, t) | $t = 3$. (See Figure 3.1a.) Therefore, at $t = 3$:

DEF(x, 3 – Δt) [y := x + 1] USE(x, 3) $\Rightarrow$ TRUE [y := x + 1] TRUE, when $\Delta t = 1$

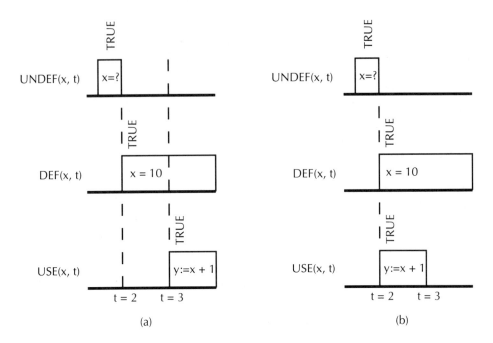

Figure 3.1   Timing diagrams for precondition/postcondition analysis: (a) DEF before USE, and (b) DEF at same time as USE

As a counterexample, suppose $[y := x + 1]$ occurs at time $t = 2$, so that USE(x,t) | $t = 2$. Then the situation is more interesting, because an indeterminacy is created when x is simultaneously used and defined. (See Figure 3.1b.) At $t = 2$:

DEF(x, 2 – Δt) $[y := x + 1]$ USE(x, 2) ⟹ TRUE [$y := x + 1$] TRUE, when Δt = 0

This says that x is simultaneously defined and used. Note that this occurs because Δt = 0. Had Δt = 1, 2, ..., the simultaneous use of a variable with its definition would not have occurred. We will be most interested in preconditions/postconditions that contain Δt = 0 as a consequence of the order in which statements are executed by one or more parallel processes.

We seek a property of parallel programs that we will call *flow-correctness*, meaning that the program is free from the kinds of anomalies illustrated above. But the language constructs needed in a parallel program may be more complex than the basic USE and DEF predicates are capable of representing. Thus, the following axioms are needed to model the fundamental flow anomalies of parallelism. Given these axioms, we can determine the flow-correctness of all parallel programs using simple logical deductions based on first-order logic.

3.2 AXIOMS OF DATA DEPENDENCY

The essential difference between a serial program and a parallel program is the potential for *race conditions* in data. A race condition is a state of a program where a variable can have more than one value, depending on the program paths leading to the variable. That is, the actual value stored in the variable depends on timing, not on the order in which the programmer wrote the statements or the sequence imposed on the program by the operating system.

There are several common forms of race conditions:

1   The value of a variable is copied before any value is stored in the variable.

2   The value of a variable is stored by two or more processes at the same time, thus leading to uncertainty as to the final value of the variable.

3   A variable's value is used, changed, and then used again, but the programmer's intent was that the variable's value be used, used, and then changed.

3.2.1 The Flow-Correctness Checking Strategy

All of the various forms of race conditions can be sorted into three kinds: *flow dependency, antidependency*, and *output dependency*. In the following discussion, we will illustrate each kind, and we will formalize all three by expressing them in terms of axioms. The axioms of flow-correctness are identical to the three axioms of data dependency. Thus, we will be able to analyze any parallel program by applying only these axioms.

Example 3.2

Output dependency   The following illustrates a very simple race condition:

x := 0; x := 1;

If these two statements are executed at the same instant by two different (shared-memory) processors, what is the resultant value of x? This is an example of an *output race condition*; hence this is called an output dependency.

Other forms of race condition arise because a value is taken from a variable "at the same time" that it is stored. For example:

y := x; x := 1;

We cannot know the value of y, unless we assume some ordering for when y := x and x := 1 are performed. If these two statements are executed on separate processors at the same time, they create one of two possible race conditions; either a flow dependency, or an antidependency. We will illustrate each of these below.

Flow dependency   Suppose the programmer intended y to be assigned before x is changed:

```
y := x;              /* Do this first  */
x := 1;              /* Followed by this  */
```

This illustrates a flow dependency, because we want to hold off reassigning x until y has copied its value.

Antidependency   Alternately, suppose the programmer intended x to be assigned a value before it is used:

```
x := 1;                /* Do this first  */
y := x;                /* Followed by this  */
```

This illustrates antidependency, because we want x to be defined before it is used.

Data dependencies are found in both serial and parallel programs, but due to the serial nature of sequential execution in a serial program, they pose no problem. When a serial program is converted into a parallel equivalent, however, the data dependencies surface as potential errors. Thus, we must be alert to dependencies that might lead to incorrect functioning of the parallel program.

We require a flow-correct parallel program to obey three synchronization predicates: *flow dependency, flow antidependency,* and *output dependency.* Actually, these predicates must be checked for every variable in the program. We must also know what the programmer intended, because sometimes the data dependency is intentional. So, our strategy is the following:

1   We propose a set of (three) predicates called axioms, which will be used to decide if a certain kind of data dependency exists within a parallel program.

2   We look at the parallel program in question, and determine if some form of data dependency exists. That is, we look for all the places in the program where a variable is undefined, defined, and used. Note that a dependency must exist before we suspect any anomaly.

3   When we apply the axiom to a variable in question, we try to solve the timing equations so that $\Delta t = 0$ instead of $\Delta t > 0$. If a solution is possible, we have an anomaly. If the programmer did not intend for this anomaly to exist in the program, we have a flow-correctness error.

3.2.2 The Axioms of Flow-Correctness

Now we can give the details of our technique. We start by listing the axioms in a formal notation:

```
FLOW(x, t) :-
    (∃ Δt >0 | DEF(x, t − Δt)),          e.g., x := 1; at t = 0
    USE(x, t).                                y := x; at t = 1
```

This notation is read "FLOW(x, t) is true if the following clauses are all true." Clauses are separated by commas, and the predicate is terminated by a period. The notation $\exists \Delta t > 0 \mid$ is read "there exists a Δt greater than zero such that." Therefore, the foregoing is read, "If a data dependency exists on variable x, then it is a flow dependency if there is a Δt greater than zero such that DEF(x, t − Δt) and USE(x, t) are both TRUE." That is, a variable is defined and then used.

ANTI(x, t) :-
    (∃ Δt > 0 | USE(x, t − Δt)),   e.g., y := x; at $t = 0$
    DEF(x, t).   x := 1; at $t = 1$

This is read as follows: "If a data dependency exists on variable x, then it is an antidependency if there is a Δt greater than zero such that USE(x, t-Δt) and DEF(x, t) are both TRUE." That is, a variable is used and then redefined.

OUT(x, t) :-
    (∃ Δt > 0 | DEF(x, t − Δt)),   e.g., x := 0; at $t = 0$
    DEF(x, t).   x := 1; at $t = 1$

This axiom is read as follows: "If a data dependency exists on variable x, then it is an output dependency if there is a Δt greater than zero such that DEF(x, t − Δt) and DEF(x, t) are both TRUE." That is, a variable is defined and then redefined.

How do we use these axioms? First, we need to determine if a flow dependency exists. This is done by observing the program, and looking for places where a variable is defined, used, and undefined. Thus, we must determine preconditions and postconditions on each variable that holds our interest. For a program containing thousands of variables, we would focus attention only on variables accessed from within a critical section of code.

We then apply the appropriate axiom. We are particularly interested when a dependency exists and Δt = 0, leading to potential race conditions; that is, when Δt = 0, and a dependency exists such that a variable is simultaneously used, defined, or doubly defined.

In general, a *flow anomaly* leads to an incorrect parallel program when Δt = 0. This indicates a *race condition*. Race conditions lead to indeterminism in the resulting value of a variable. The following example illustrates various potential race conditions.

Example 3.3

Check the assertion FLOW(x, t), in the code below:

```
read(x);              /* Happens at t = 1 */
y := x + 1;           /* Happens at t = 2 */
```

Clearly a data dependency exists on the variable x, so the precondition/postcondition pair applies to x:

PRE(x) [S] POST(x) ⇒ DEF(x, t − Δt) [y := x + 1] USE(x, t)

This matches the predicate for flow dependency:

FLOW(x, t) :-
    (∃ Δt > 0 | DEF(x, t − Δt)),
    USE(x, t).

Can we solve the timing equation for Δt? Simply using the information provided in the comments of the code, we note that $(t - \Delta t) = 1$ for DEF, and $t = 2$ for USE. Therefore, $t = 2$, leading to $(2 - \Delta t) = 1$, or $\Delta t = 1$. The condition that $\Delta t > 0$ is satisfied, so there is no anomaly.

Now consider a counterexample. The assertion would be FALSE if we attempted to execute both statements at the same time, say at $t = 1$. Therefore, $(1 - \Delta t) = 1$, leading to $\Delta t = 0$. Thus, a flow anomaly exists, and in this case, it is an error in the program.

Flow-correctness means that for every variable in the program, if one or more of the three predicates, FLOW, ANTI, and OUT apply, then they must assert $\Delta t > 0$. If any one of the predicates applies, and $\Delta t = 0$, a race condition exits.

How do we know when to apply a certain test? We look for data dependencies. They produce a USE/DEF pattern for each variable. These patterns are then matched up with the appropriate axiom. The table below summarizes these patterns and lists the appropriate axiom:

Pattern	Axiom
DEF–USE	FLOW
USE–DEF	ANTI
DEF–DEF	OUT

For each variable to be analyzed, we establish a precondition and postcondition pattern, check it against this table, and apply the appropriate test.

Example 3.4

An antidependency is flow-correct if a variable is used at some time $t - \Delta t$, and then defined (again) at some later time, t. In this example, we apply the ANTI test at $t = 3$, and find that $\Delta t > 0$, so the program is flow-correct with respect to variable y.

Suppose the programmer intended for y := x + 1 to be executed after x := y, say, leading to an antidependency on variable y. The variable y is used and then defined; hence the pattern is USE–DEF, so we must use the ANTI test. Specifically, at $t = 3$, we know that USE(y, 2) = TRUE, and DEF(y, 3) is TRUE:

ANTI(y, 3) :-
    $(\exists \Delta t > 0 \mid$ USE(y, $3 - \Delta t$)),
    DEF(y, 3).
$\Rightarrow$ $(\exists \Delta t > 0 \mid$ USE(y, 2)),
    DEF(y, 3).
$\Rightarrow$ $(3 - \Delta t) = 2$
$\Rightarrow$ $\Delta t = 1$.

Because $\Delta t > 0$ assures passage of the ANTI test, this is a flow-correct program segment, relative to variable y.

One way to remove output dependency problems is to restrict assignment of a value to a variable to only once within a program. A programming language that forbids output dependency in this way is called a *single-assignment language*. Programming language constructs that restrict output variables to single-assignment are naturally called *single-assignment constructs*. Later on, we show that a construct called **par** is guaranteed to be flow-correct if it is single-assignment.

Example 3.5

An output dependency exists when variable x is defined, then defined a second time later on. This might occur, for example, when variable x is used for two different purposes, as shown below. This gives a DEF–DEF pattern, so we must use the OUT test:

```
x := 1;              /* DEF(x, t) at t = 1  */
write(x);            /* USE(x, t) at t = 2  */
x := 2;              /* DEF(x, t) at t = 3  */
```

$$\text{OUT}(x, 3) :-$$
$$(\exists \, \Delta t > 0 \mid \text{DEF}(x, 3 - \Delta t)),$$
$$\text{DEF}(x, 3).$$
$$\Rightarrow \quad 3 - \Delta t = 1$$
$$\Rightarrow \quad \Delta t = 2$$

Again, because $\Delta t > 0$, this is a flow-correct program segment.

This dependency could be avoided by forcing single assignment. A single-assignment version of this code would be the following:

```
x := 1;
write(x);
y := 2;
```

The DEF–DEF pattern has been removed, leaving only a DEF–USE pattern. No output-dependency exists in a single-assignment program.

3.3 ITERATION SPACE

In a program containing arrays, a dependency can be established within the iterations of a loop. Such a dependency is called a *loop-carried dependency*, because the iterations of the loop create a flow-dependency among subscripted expressions.

When the subscripts of an array establish a dependency between an early loop iteration and a later iteration, we say the loop-carried dependency is *forward*. Conversely, a loop-carried dependency between a later iteration and an early iteration is called a *backward dependency*. *Forward* and *backward* refer to the *direction* of the dependency, and not to the kind of dependency.

An iteration space diagram like the one shown in Figure 3.2 is used to visualize loop-carried dependencies and their directions. Figure 3.2a shows a forward dependency between successive iterations. Figure 3.2b shows a backward dependency between pairs of iterations. The iteration space shown in Figure 3.2 is linear, because it runs in only one dimension. This corresponds to a single loop with the loop counter i.

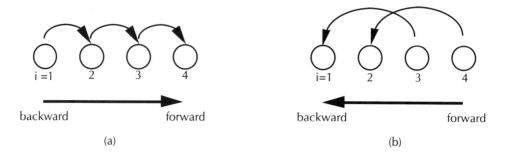

Figure 3.2   Linear iteration space diagrams: (a) forward dependency, and (b) backward dependency

Example 3.6

Consider the following loop that processes elements of arrays $A[1..N]$ and $B[1..N]$. The loop index iterates from $i := 2$ to $N - 1$. The iteration space diagram for this loop is shown in Figure 3.2a:

for (i := 2; i ≤ N; i++) {
   A[i] := A[i − 1] + B[i + 1] }

We might be tempted to rewrite this loop in parallel form so that each iteration of the loop is executed simultaneously by different processes. For example, if we did this for $N = 5$, using parallel processes P1, P2, P3, and P4:

P1: A[2] := A[1] + B[3]
P2: A[3] := A[2] + B[4]
P3: A[4] := A[3] + B[5]
P4: A[5] := A[4] + B[6]

But now that the iterations are listed, we can clearly see a DEF–USE pattern between $A[2]$ in processes P1 and P2; between $A[3]$ in processes P2 and P3; between $A[4]$ in processes P3 and P4; and between $A[5]$ in processes P3 and P4. This pattern of forward dependencies is shown in Figure 3.2a, where each bubble corresponds to a single statement in the loop body, and the arrows correspond to the dependency.

This kind of flow-correctness problem is called a *loop-carried dependency* between iteration i and iteration $i − 1$. That is, iteration i cannot be computed until iteration $i − 1$ is done. Furthermore, the dependency pattern matches the FLOW axiom, so we have a flow dependency problem that is loop-carried.

To be more rigorous, we must check for the flow-correctness error as follows. Let the time we perform the ith iteration be denoted by t_i:

FLOW(A[i], t_i) :-   /* Iteration i at time t_i */
      (∃ Δt_i > 0 | DEF(A[i], t_i − Δt_i)),
      USE(A[i], t_i).

Then, if we perform all iterations at the same time, $t_i − \Delta t_i = t_i$, we have

$\Rightarrow \quad t_i - \Delta t_i = t_i$
$\Rightarrow \quad \Delta t_i = 0$

If the loop is performed sequentially, and iterations take $t_i > 0$ time units, then $\Delta t_i > 0$. This example illustrates how a flow dependency in a sequential program becomes a problem in the parallel program equivalent.

A loop-carried dependency can occur between future and past iterations of a loop. The backward dependency shown in Figure 3.2b is illustrated by the next example.

Example 3.7

Consider the backward dependency established by the following loop:

for (i := 2; i < N; i++) {
A[i] := A[i + 2] + B[i + 1] }

Again, considering the first few iterations (see Figure 3.2b):

A[2] := A[4] + B[3] }
A[3] := A[5] + B[4] }
A[4] := A[6] + B[5] }

In this loop, iteration i depends on the original value of $A[i + 2]$. This means that we must use $A[i + 2]$ before we define it in iteration $i + 2$. The USE–DEF pattern also means that an antidependency exists:

ANTI(A[i], t_i) :-
$\quad (\exists\, \Delta t_i > 0 \mid$ USE(A[i], $t_i + \Delta t_i$)),
$\quad$ DEF(A[i], t_i).

Assuming the sequential loop takes one time unit to execute each iteration, then two time units are used to execute two iterations following iteration i:

$\Rightarrow \quad t_i + \Delta t_i = t_i + 2$
$\Rightarrow \quad \Delta t_i = 2$

The sequential loop is flow-correct. The reader is invited to show that a parallel version of the loop is flow-correct, only if the dependency is somehow removed.

In general, when looking for a loop-carried dependency, we must find a solution to a *Diophantine equation* which falls within the bounds of the loop counter. A Diophantine equation is a linear equation whose solutions are integers. For example, $x + y = 3$ has integer solutions $(x, y) = (1, 2), (3, 0), (4, -1)$, etc.

We derive the Diophantine equation by setting the subscript expressions involved in the dependency equal to one another, as illustrated in the next example. Note that we create a variable for each loop iteration, and then solve for all integers which satisfy the multivariable equation.

Example 3.8

The dependency between $A[i]$ and $A[i-1]$ occurs whenever $A[i]$ and $A[i-1]$ reference the same storage location. Let storage location $A[i]$ be indicated by variable A_j and storage location $A[i-1]$ be indicated by A_{i-1}. Then, a dependency exists when $j = i - 1$. This Diophantine equation has solutions $(j, i) = (1, 2), (2, 3), (3, 4), ..., (k, k + 1)$, for all pairs of integers in the interval $[1..N]$.

Similarly, dependency between $A[i]$ and $A[i + 2]$ occurs for solutions to $j = i + 2$. That is, $(j, i) = (3, 1), (4, 2), (5, 3), ..., (k, k - 2)$, for all pairs of integers in $[1..N]$.

The iteration space diagram becomes more interesting when nested loops are analyzed. Two nested loops result in a two-dimensional iteration space diagram; three nested loops result in a three-dimensional diagram, and so forth.

The result of loop-carried dependency analysis in the following example is shown as a two-dimensional iteration space diagram in Figure 3.3. The visualization in Figure 3.3 is clearly much easier to understand than the Diophantine equation, but of course the equation can be used to automate the dependency check.

Example 3.9

Suppose we diagram the dependencies of the following 2-nested loops.

```
for (i := 2; i < N; i++) {
    for (j := 2; j < N; j++) {
    A[i, j] := A[i – 1, j + 1] * B[i + 1, j – 1] }
}
```

Let reference to $A[i, *]$ be denoted by i, and reference to $A[i-1, *]$ be denoted by $(k-1)$. For the second subscript, let $A[*, j]$ be denoted by j, and let $A[*, j + 1]$ be denoted by $(m + 1)$. The Diophantine equations for this nested pair are:

$$i = k - 1$$
$$j = m + 1$$

These equations have solutions $(i, k) = (2, 3), (3, 4), ...,$ for the first subscript and $(j, m) = (3, 2), (4, 3), ...,$ for the second subscript. We are concerned only with a race condition on a single storage cell; thus, we look for matches in the two subscripts at the same time. The match occurs between iteration $i = k - 1$ in the outer loop, and iteration $j = m + 1$ in the inner loop (see Figure 3.3). For example, when computing $A[6, 4]$, we note the dependency on $A[5, 5]$, because $A[5, 5]$ cannot be computed in iteration $(i = 5, j = 5)$ until used in iteration $(i = 6, j = 4)$.

3.4 KEYWORDS AND CONCEPTS

The correctness of an arbitrary program is in general undecidable, but we can prove certain assertions about specific programs. In the world of sequential programming, correctness checking assertions assume that statements are executed one following the other. There is never any question about the execution

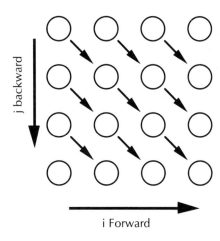

i Forward

Figure 3.3   Iteration space for 2-nested loops

order. In particular, it is not possible to execute two or more statements at exactly the same time. Therefore, techniques that may apply to sequential programs become inadequate when applied to parallel programs.

Flow-correctness assertion checking is a supplement to sequential program assertion checking. It focuses on the heart of the problem: data dependency. A parallel program differs from a sequential program largely because of data dependencies. Indeed, we can identify three kinds of dependency: flow, anti-, and output.

We have shown that the conversion of sequential loops to parallel constructs can be dangerous. The iteration diagram was used to reveal dependencies called loop-carried dependencies. We will need to carefully analyze the various parallel programming constructs to make sure that no loop-carried dependencies are carried over from the sequential program.

In summary, every parallel program contains dataflow dependencies. To be sure that these dependencies do not result in race conditions on one or more program variables, we must check the flow-correctness of every variable. This involves a check for flow, anti-, and output dependencies, both in straightline code, and in loops.

The following keywords summarize the concepts of this chapter.

Data dependencies   Three data dependencies can lead to errors in parallel programs: flow, anti-, and output. In addition, anyone of these three can exist within a loop, in which case they are called loop-carried dependencies.

Diophantine equations   We use Diophantine equations to analyze loop-carried dependencies. If the equation has a solution within the range of the loop, a loop-carried dependency exists.

Direction   Dependencies can flow in either forward or backward directions. The direction of flow can be visualized in an iteration diagram. Depending on the direction of the dependency, we can select the appropriate parallel construct to safely implement a sequential loop as a parallel construct.

Flow-correct   We say a parallel program is flow-correct if no flow, anti-, or output dependency errors exist. Flow-correctness does not imply total correctness, but it does point out possible timing errors. A flow-anomaly means there is an unusual dataflow pattern, which may or may not be a timing error.

Iteration space diagram   An iteration space diagram is a visualization of the data dependencies in a loop.

Program correctness assertions   We use preconditions and postconditions to assert the flow-correctness of parallel programs. A precondition asserts the state of the program before a statement is executed, and a postcondition asserts the state after the statement is executed. When used to express the dependencies before and after each statement, we can assert flow-correctness properties for each variable in the program.

Single-assignment language   One way to guarantee that no output dependencies exist is to limit the programming language to single assignment. This means that each variable can be assigned a value at most once during the life of the variable.

PROBLEMS

1   List the forms of flow dependencies in the following serial code:

```
S := 0;
for (i := 1; i ≤ N; i++) {
  S := S + X[i];
  PUT(S);
  }
S := S / N;
PUT (S)
```

2   What forms of loop-carried dependencies occur in the following serial loop?

for $(i := 1; i \leq K; i++) \{ A[i] := (A[i-1] + A[i+1]) / 2.0 \}$

3   Apply the ANTI test to the following code to show under which conditions it is flow-correct. Do not assume that the statements are executed in the order they arc listed.

```
x := 0;
y := 1;
z := x + y;
y := z + 1;
x := y / z;
```

4   Under what conditions is the following code flow-correct? What assumptions does one have to make? Once again, do not assume the statements execute in their listed order.

x := 2;
x := y + 1;
y := x * 5;

5   Is the following code FLOW correct? Under what conditions? Show why or why not.

GET(x);
GET(y);
while(x ≠ y) {
    if x > y **then** x := x − y **else** y := y − x }
OUT(y)

6   Draw the iteration space diagrams for the following 2-nested loops.

a   **for** (j := 2; j ≤ N; j++) {
        for (i := 1; i < N; i++) { A[i + 1, j] := A[i, j] + A[i, j − 1] }}

b   **for** (j := 2; j ≤ N; j++) {
        for (i := 4; i ≤ N; i += 2) { A[i, j] := A[i − 3, j − 1] }}

c   **for** (j := 1; j < N/2; j++) {
        for (i := 1; i < N/2; i++) { A[i + j] := A[i − j + 1] }}

REFERENCES

U. Banerjee, *Dependence Analysis For Supercomputing*, Kluwer Academic Publishing, Boston, 1988.

Z. Li, P.C. Yew, and C. Q. Zhu, Data Dependence Analysis on Multidimensional Array References, ACM Int'l Conf. on Supercomputing, 1989.

M. Wolfe, *Optimizing Supercompilers for Supercomputers*, Research Monographs in Parallel and Distributed Computing, MIT Press, Cambridge, 1989.

CHAPTER 4

Performance Analysis

In this chapter we will develop performance formulas for parallel programs modelled as modified Petri networks called *program graphs*. Program graphs consist of *transitions*, *places*, and *arcs*, where a transition corresponds to a sequential action, a place corresponds to a program counter belonging to a single parallel process, and an arc corresponds to a control path from a place to a transition, or from a transition to a place. Imaginary tokens move from place to place, each along an arc, and through a transition, thus imitating the execution of the parallel program.

Tokens correspond to the state of a process, transitions correspond to one or more sequential statements, and arcs correspond to paths through the program. The program starts with a single token, representing the initial process. Then, as processes are forked, the number of tokens increases, one new token for each new process. Each parallel process is modelled by a token, so that N tokens model N parallel processes.

A program graph is annotated with timing information (labels) designating estimates of the execution time of each transition and message delay times along each arc. For example, a transition that takes 10 microseconds to execute is labelled "10." An arc that takes 25 microseconds to send a message is labelled "25." We can simply add these time delays, along a path from the initial place to the final place, to get a time estimate for the entire program graph.

In the following, we will develop formulas for sequential and parallel program constructs modelled as pieces of a program graph. In particular, we will develop

68

performance formulas for sequence, branching, and looping within sequential programs, and message-distribution patterns (rings and trees) within parallel programs. We will show that the optimal degree for a message-passing tree is $M = 2$; i.e., binary distribution trees are better than ternary or higher order trees. We will use these results later to estimate the execution time of real parallel programs.

4.1 SEQUENTIAL PROGRAM GRAPHS

A program graph is a form of Petri network consisting of two kinds of nodes: places, drawn as round bubbles, and transitions, drawn as straight horizontal lines. In addition, a program graph contains arcs which connect places to transitions and transitions to places. Arcs never connect places to places, or transitions to transitions. More precisely,

PN   {s, P, T, A, Map} = program graph
- s   Start node
- P   Set of places (bubbles)
- T   Set of transitions (straight lines)
- A   Set of arcs
- Map   Mapping of arcs to place–transition pairs

The idea of a PN is to model the essential behavior of a program. We call this model the program graph of a program. The formal PN definition becomes:

- s   Start of the program
- P   Set of states where the program counter rests between instructions
- T   Set of sequential code segments; one or more instructions
- A   Control-flow flowchart of the program
- Map   Connectivity of the flowchart

A program graph can model any program at its lowest level, i.e., instruction by instruction, or at its highest level, i.e., procedure by procedure. Depending on the level of the model, a transition can be an instruction or an entire procedure. An arc is a control flow path from a state to a block of code, or from a block of code to a state. A state is an imaginary resting place for the program counter between instructions.

Figure 4.1 shows the program graph sections for the three fundamental constructs of sequential programming: sequence, if-then-else, and for looping. Each bubble is numbered to indicate the process assigned to the sequential code represented by the transition. A transition is labeled with the action it represents, a timing estimate, and in the case of branching transitions, a probability estimate, p, of the branch predicate being TRUE.

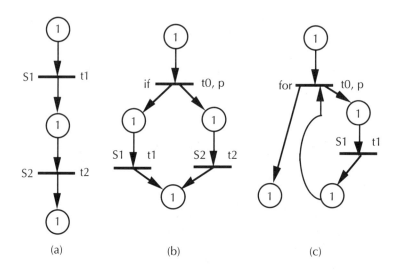

Figure 4.1   Network graphs of (a) sequence, (b) if-then-else, and (c) for loop constructs

The constructs of Figure 4.1 are the basic building blocks of any sequential program. *Sequence* means that statements are performed sequentially, one after another; branching is done by the if-then-else; and looping is done by the for loop.

In terms of text, the meanings of the graphs in Figure 4.1 are:

a	S1;	/* Do this... */
	S2;	/* Then do this */
b	**if** Pred **then** S1 **else** S2;	/* Do one, but not both */
c	**for** (Pred) {S1};	/* Repeat S1 until **not** Pred */

The meaning of a sequential statement is easily determined by following a *token* through the places and transitions of Figure 4.1a. For example, starting at the first place, we can move a token through the S1 transition in time $t1$, and then through the S2 transition in time $t2$. The total elapsed time to traverse the sequential graph is $t1 + t2$.

When branches are involved, the execution time is a function of the probability of each branch. That is, the time delay is $t0$ plus either $t1$ or $t2$ (see Figure 4.1b). Note that S1 is executed a fraction p of the time, and S2 is executed a fraction $(1-p)$ of the time. Thus, the expected elapsed time is $t0 + (p)t1 + (1-p)t2$, and we have

Elapsed time (if-then-else) = $t0 + p(t1 - t2) + t2$

The loop is executed each time Pred is evaluated and found to be TRUE, with probability p, but p changes with each iteration. Suppose we assign to the jth iteration the probability p_j. Then, the expected duration of the loop is an average:

$$\text{Ave } T = \sum_{j=1}^{N} (t0 + t1)p_j = (t0 + t1) \sum_{j=1}^{N} p_j$$

Assuming a declining probability, the loop is guaranteed to eventually terminate, we have

$$p_j = \frac{N - j + 1}{N} \qquad j = 1, 2, \ldots, N$$

Substituting into the summation, we obtain the estimated elapsed time for a loop, given the assumptions of declining probability:

Elapsed time = $(t0 + t1)(N + 1)/2$

where N is the number of loop iterations.

In summary, sequential execution time is additive, if-then-else execution time is $O(p)$, and for-loop execution time is $O(N)$. This is not surprising, but illustrates the technique we use to analyze any program.

Example 4.1

A simple program for computing the greatest common divisor (GCD) is given below, and its program graph is shown in Figure 4.2a. What is the estimated execution time of this program?

```
read(x, y)
while x <> y do begin
    if x > y then x := x − y
            else y := y − x
    end
write(x)
```

The timing information given in Figure 4.2a is used to derive the estimate, but where do we begin? We use the *reduction principle* of structured programming, which means that we start at the innermost level of the program graph, estimate its execution time, replace it with a single transition, and repeat the reduction process over again. Looking at Figure 4.2a, we find the innermost level to be the if-then-else construct. We use the if-then-else formula to estimate the time to do the entire if-then-else subgraph:

tif = $t3 + t4(p3) + t5(1 - p3)$

Now we can replace the if-then-else subgraph with a single transition, as shown in Figure 4.2b. The innermost subgraph now becomes the loop. Recall that we had to know the number of iterations to estimate the time to execute a loop, but this is a while-loop, and the number of iterations is not known in advance:

twhile = $(t2 + \text{tif} + t6)(N + 1)/2$

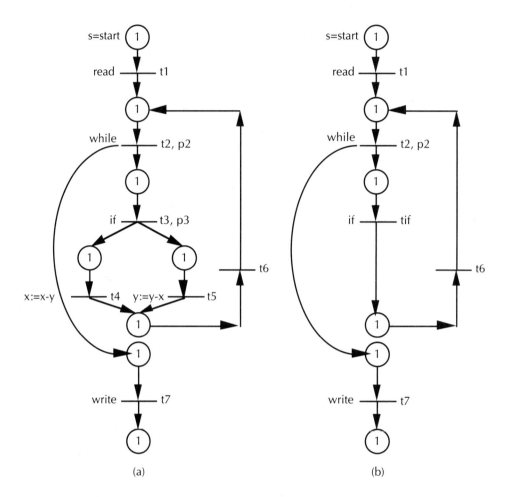

Figure 4.2 Reduction technique applied to the GCD program: (a) complete program, (b) reduce if statement

where N is not known. Substituting for tif,

$t\text{while} = (t2 + t3 + t4(p3) + t5(1 - p3) + t6)(N + 1)/2$

Again, the program graph is reduced by replacing the while-loop with a single transition (see Figure 4.2c). The next step is to reduce the graph one more time, to obtain Figure 4.2d.

$t\text{GCD} = t1 + t7 + t\text{while}$
$= t1 + t7 + (t2 + t3 + t4(p3) + t5(1 - p3) + t6)(N + 1)/2$

Suppose, for purposes of illustration, we estimate N, $t1$, $t2$, $t3$, $t4$, $t5$, $t6$, $t7$, and $p3$ as follows:

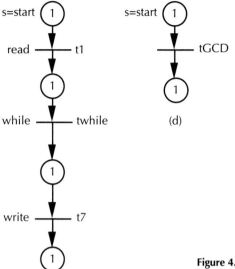

Figure 4.2   (Continued) Reduction technique applied to the GCD program: (c) reduce while statement, (d) reduce sequential statements

$t1 = t2 = t3 = t4 = t5 = t6 = t7 = 10$
$p3 = 0.5$
$N = |x-y|$

Then, the time to execute GCD is, approximately,

$$t\text{GCD} = 20 + 40\,(\frac{|x-y|}{2}) = 20\,(1+|x-y|)$$

The reduction principle works for any *structured program graph*, which means that the program graph must be free from *knots*. A program contains a knot if its program graph cannot be drawn on a semi-infinite plane without crossing control flow lines.

Example 4.2

The following program contains a control flow knot because the if-then-goto makes it impossible to reduce the program from the inside out.

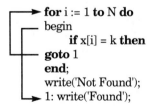

```
for i := 1 to N do
    begin
        if x[i] = k then
    goto 1
    end;
    write('Not Found');
1: write('Found');
```

The for-loop cannot be replaced by a single transition because the goto provides a second exit path out of the loop. The if-then-goto cannot be reduced because it is already a basic construct. Hence, the program cannot be reduced.

A program graph describes the execution time delays for a program, but in our current formulation it ignores the time it might take to copy data from one place to another. This detail is not important for precise modelling of sequential programs, but for parallel programs we take into account the time needed to move data. This is done by labelling arcs with time delays.

4.2 PARALLEL PROGRAM GRAPHS

The simple sequence, loop, and branch constructs of sequential programming are not sufficient for modelling parallel programs. We need to represent processes spawned by forking a parent process, model a message-passing operation, and describe the joining together of processes. This is usually done by a fork/ join pair of operating system commands. A *fork* command is executed by a parent process and creates sibling processes. A *join* command waits for all siblings to complete, and then destroys all but the parent process.

In addition, we must model the message-passing that typically occurs after a fork, and before a join. The PN model of the previous section is not suitable for modelling sends and receives, because it becomes too detailed and obscures important information. For this reason, we propose a modification of Petri networks to simplify the representation of the send and receive mechanisms. The resulting program graphs are no longer pure Petri networks. Rather, program graphs are simplified PN graphs.

Example 4.3

The fork and join constructs illustrated in Figure 4.3a, show send and receive message-passing time delays, as well as the sequential nature of the fork-send-send-join branch. From this detailed PN, we can derive a time delay for the entire fork/join graph. The Gantt chart (see Figure 4.3b) shows that a *critical path* exists through the PN, as indicated by the bold arcs. This critical path determines the overall execution time of three parallel processes, as they all perform the same SPMD operation, designated $f(d/3)$. The execution time may be calculated:

$$T_{\text{fork/join}} = T_{\text{fork}} + 2(w_0 + w_1(d/3)) + r_0 + r_1 f(d/3) + w_0 + w_1 + T_{\text{join}}$$

where $f()$ is the computational time-complexity of the SPMD operation; T_{fork} is the time to fork the processes; w_0, w_1, r_0, r_1 are the target machine parameters; and d is the size of data to be distributed. The time to join processes is given by T_{join}.

In general, for k processes:

$$T(k)_{\text{fork/join}} = T_{\text{fork}} + (k-1)(w_0 + w_1(d/k)) + r_0 + r_1 f(d/k) + w_0 + w_1 + T_{\text{join}}$$

(a)

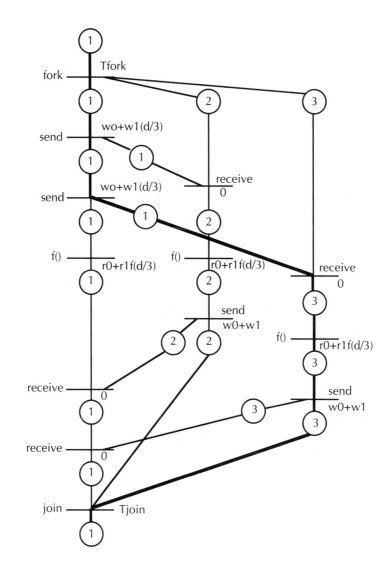

(b) Tfork + w0+w1(d/3) + w0+w1(d/3) + r0+r1f(d/3) + w0+w1 + Tjoin

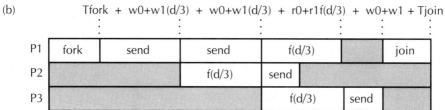

Figure 4.3 **Program graph of the fork/join operation: (a) full PN graph and (b) Gantt chart schedule for fork/join of three processes**

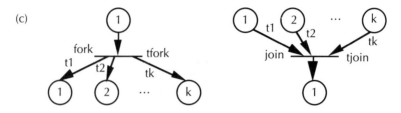

Figure 4.3   (Continued) Program graph of the fork/join operation: (c) simplified program graph model of fork/join of k processes

Figure 4.3c shows the same pattern of fork and join operations, but in a simplified program graph form. In this form, message-passing is combined with the fork operation, as shown by a single fork transition. But there is a subtle difference in the interpretation of the fork transition: we assume the messages are sequential; hence the outgoing arcs are weighted by the appropriate delays such that the Gantt chart in Figure 4.3b is honored. That is, we retain the same critical path through the simplified program graph as we had in the detailed PN graph.

In Figure 4.3c, the time to send a message along each arc is given as $t1, t2, t3, ..., tk$. These times will include start-up, transmission times, and sequential delays assumed by the model in Figure 4.3a. We assume throughout this book that messages are initiated and sent in series. Therefore, the time delay for a fork is:

$$T_f = t\text{fork} + t1 + t2 + t3 + ... + tk$$

Typically, a fork takes some time, $t\text{fork}$, and the messages each take time to send. We will further assume that the messages are buffered by the sender; hence the time is charged to the sender process. But at the other end, the receiver does not have to pay for message setup time, because we assume that the message is buffered at the receiving end. (This may be a poor assumption for some systems.) The receive time is shown in Figure 4.3a as a receive transition with zero time delay.

The time to do a join is:

$$T_j = t\text{join} + \text{Max}(t1, t2, t3, ..., tk)$$

The maximum delay always lies along the critical path. Hence, in our formulation, the time delay is always tk. In the three-process example, this delay is simply $w_0 + w_1$.

The assumptions of this example may be lifted, and the formulas adjusted accordingly, if they do not represent reality. For the remainder of this book, however, we assume that a sender takes the sum of all message-passing times to send, and the receiver merely waits for the slowest message to arrive. Clearly, it is possible that the receiver need not wait at all, or that the sender will buffer all messages, thus taking very little time to send a series of messages.

In addition, the reader is reminded that the linear model of the target machine may also be a gross simplification. The message delay given by $(w_0 + w_1(d / k))$ is only a model. Real machines often exhibit nonlinear behaviors.

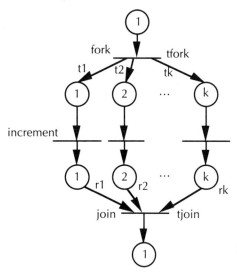

Figure 4.4   Program graph of a simple fork/join parallel program

Example 4.4

To illustrate this point further, we use the simplified program graph notation to model a SPMD calculation. Consider the simple fork/join program graph of Figure 4.4 representing the code shown below:

fork 3 processes
send a[1] to process 1; a[2] to process 2; a[3] to process 3;
{ Increment a[i] in process i}
receive increment in a[1]; increment in a[2]; increment in a[3];
join

This code splits into three parallel processes, and then runs identical code in each process. The SPMD code increments each value received, and then returns the incremented value to the parent process. Another way to interpret this piece of parallel program is to simulate it using a sequential program. The parallel code performs the same function as the following sequential loop:

for i := 1,3 **do** a[i] := a[i] + 1;

The serial version ignores message-passing costs, but the parallel version cannot. The parallel program adds overhead in the form of message-passing delays. Any performance estimate must consider these delays.

From Figure 4.4, and the assumptions made earlier, we can estimate the cost of the parallel version as follows:

$$T = T_f + T_{\text{increment}} + T_j$$

$$= t\text{fork} + \sum_{i=1}^{3} t_i + T_{\text{increment}} + T_{\text{join}} + \sum_{i=1}^{3} r_i$$

Assuming the following parameters and time estimates, $k = 3$, $t1 = t2 = t3 = 10$, $r1 = r2 = r3 = 1$, and $t\text{fork} = t\text{join} = 100$, we have

$$T = 100 + 30 + T_{\text{increment}} + 100 + 1 = 231 + T_{\text{increment}}$$

Assuming that the time to do an increment is the same for both serial and parallel versions of the program, we estimate the speedup as follows:

$$T(1) = 3T_{\text{increment}}$$

because the loop executes $k = 3$ iterations, and

$$T(3) = 231 + T_{\text{increment}}$$

because the parallel version incurs overhead. Finally,

$$S = \frac{T(1)}{T(3)} = \frac{3T_{\text{increment}}}{231 + T_{\text{increment}}}$$

Notice that the speedup is less than unity, unless the time to increment is greater than 115.5 time units. This is a classic example of the central problem of parallel programming. How can we guarantee a speedup in every case?

4.3 COMMUNICATION PATTERNS IN PARALLEL PROGRAMS

From the foregoing, it is clear that the performance of a parallel program is heavily influenced by communication patterns. The fork/join pattern is only one of many possible distribution patterns. What other communication patterns are there, and what are the performance implications of these patterns?

In the following, we examine the communication patterns of some common parallel programs. The overall goal of these patterns is to distribute data in an efficient manner. But as it will be shown, the performances of these patterns vary widely, leading one to rightfully conclude that parallel program performance is greatly influenced by communication algorithms.

The ring distribution pattern is explored first, because of its simplicity and usefulness when data must be broadcast to all processes in an orderly fashion. Then we look at the binary tree distribution pattern, which attempts to parallelize the broadcast pattern. The m-ary tree method is a variant on the binary tree method, and may offer advantages over the simple binary tree pattern. Finally, we attempt to find the best possible broadcast pattern by optimizing a general tree pattern.

4.3.1 Ring Pattern

A collection of N processes form a *ring* pattern whenever they are connected in sequence, 1, 2, 3, ..., N, 1, 2, 3, ..., such that the last process, N, is connected to the first process, 1, as shown in Figure 4.5. Thus, a message is sent from a source node in the program graph to some sink node by hopping between intermediate nodes. The number of hops is equal to the number of intermediate nodes through which a message must pass to get to the sink node.

A message takes the shortest route between the source and the sink. Thus, the tables in Figure 4.5 show the smallest number of hops necessary to traverse the ring from one node to another. The table of hops reveals patterns for even and odd N. The average number of hops between an arbitrary source node and an arbitrary sink node, both selected at random, is given by dividing the total over the entire table, by N:

Avg Hops = Total$/N$

We compute the total in each table by noting that the rows contain the sums of the first k integers, up to approximately $N/2$, depending on whether N is odd or even. For odd N:

$$\text{Total} = 2 \sum_{i=1}^{N-1} i = \frac{N^2 - 1}{4}$$

For even N:

$$\text{Total} = \sum_{i=1}^{N/2} i + \sum_{i=1}^{N/2-1} i = \frac{N^2}{4}$$

Thus, the average number of hops in a ring pattern is given by:

Avg Hops = $(N^2 - 1)/4N$ if N is odd; $N/4$ if N is even.

Example 4.5

What is the average number of hops a message must make to go from one node to another in the $N = 5$ and $N = 6$ ring patterns of Figure 4.5?

$N = 5$ (odd); Avg Hops = $(5^2 - 1)/4(5) = 1.2$ hops
$N = 6$ (even); Avg Hops = $6/4 = 1.5$ hops

The average number of hops in a ring pattern is $O(N/4)$, instead of $O(N/2)$, because the ring is bidirectional; i.e., messages can pass in either direction. In fact, messages are sent along the shortest path from the source to the sink. Given

Program graph   Number of hops

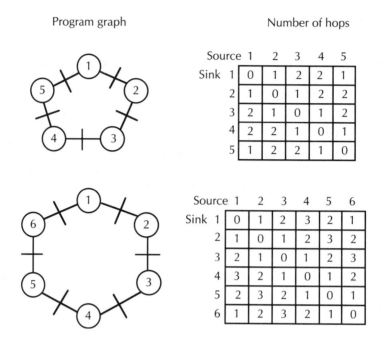

Figure 4.5   Two rings, one of size $N = 5$ and the other of size $N = 6$. Tables list the number of hops between source and sink processes.

that each message hop involves a start-up and transmission, we get the performance of the message-passing portion only as follows:

$$T(N, d) = (w_0 + w_1 d)\, O(N/4)$$

where d is the size of data, and N is the size of the ring pattern. That is, message-passing is linear in the number of nodes and the size of the messages being passed. If we were to evenly distribute the data across the segment of the ring lying between the source and the sink, we would obtain the following estimate of the communication time delay, assuming Avg Hops $= N/4$:

$$T(N, d) = \sum_{i=1}^{N/4} (w_0 + w_1 \frac{(N-i)\,d}{N/4}) = (w_0 \frac{N}{4} - w_1 d\,(\frac{N}{8} - 3.5)) = O(N)$$

The ring pattern, while simple, is slow.

Example 4.6

What is the expected time delay to distribute a character array of size $d = 10{,}000$ character array over one-fourth of a ring of $N = 100$ processes, assuming a message start-up delay of 250, and a transmission parameter of 0.005? Using the formula above:

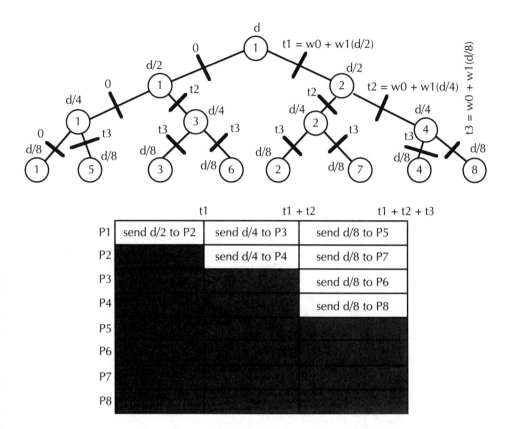

Figure 4.6   **Program graph and Gantt chart schedule for a binary tree pattern**

$T(100, 10000) = (250(25) - .005(10000)(128/8 - 3.5) = 5625$

The distribution takes place in stages; first $(10,000 - 400)$ characters are sent to process 2; then $(10,000 - 800)$ characters are sent from process 3, and so forth, until process $(N/4) = 25$ receives $(10,000 - 9,600)$ characters. Each time the remaining characters are forwarded, we pay a penalty in starting up the message-passing mechanism.

4.3.2 Binary Tree Pattern

The linear performance of the ring stems from the sequential nature of the ring message-passing pattern. Might there be a way to parallelize the message-passing, itself? The answer is a definite "yes," and the most obvious method is the *binary tree pattern* as shown in Figure 4.6.

The binary tree pattern begins in parent process P1, and proceeds by sending $d/2$ data elements to the adjacent processor P2, keeping the remaining $d/2$ data elements for itself. The initial steps take $t1$ and zero time units, respectively. Thus far, this is a sequential process.

Next, a parallel distribution is performed at the same time by P1 and P2, but the amount of data moved to adjacent processes is one-half of the remaining data, i.e., $d/4$. That is, P1 keeps $d/4$ data elements and passes the remaining $d/4$ elements to P3. Simultaneously, P2 keeps $d/4$ elements and passes $d/4$ elements to P4. This phase takes $t2$ time units.

Finally, Figure 4.6 shows the 4-way parallel pattern of passing $d/8$ elements to processes P1, P5, P3, P6, P2, P7, P4, and P8. That is, all eight processes get one-eighth of the data. This phase takes $t3$ time units.

At each phase of the binary distribution pattern, one-half of the remaining data is sent to adjacent processes. Thus, the message-passing times are:

$$t_1 = w_0 + w_1(d/2)$$
$$t_2 = w_0 + w_1(d/4)$$
$$t_3 = w_0 + w_1(d/8)$$

In general, $t_i = w_0 + w_1(d/2^i)$, and there are $k = \log_2 d$ levels in the tree. Therefore,

$$T(k) \;=\; \sum_{i=1}^{k} t_i \;=\; \sum_{i=1}^{\log_2 d} w_0 + w_1\frac{d}{2^i} \;=\; w_0\log_2 d + w_1 d\left(\frac{\log_2 d - 1}{\log_2 d}\right) \;=\; T(d)$$

Approximating, $(\log_2 d - 1)/\log_2 d = 1$,

$$T(d) = w_0\log_2 d + w_1 d$$

Assuming we want to distribute d data elements to d parallel processes, we require $\log_2 d$ phases. But, what is the computational complexity of this pattern?

Example 4.7

What is the expected time delay to distribute a character array of size $d = 10{,}000$ over a binary tree of $N = \log_2 d = 14$ processes, assuming message startup delay of 250, and transmission parameter of 0.005? Using the formula above:

$$T(d) = w_0\log_2 d + w_1 d = 250(14) + 0.005(10000) = 3550$$

What is the time delay if the transmission parameter is 0.5?

$$T(d) = w_0\log_2 d + w_1 d = 250(14) + 0.5(10000) = 8500$$

Note that the formula for time delay involves both $O(d)$ and $O(\log_2 d)$ terms. Does this pattern run in linear or logarithmic time?

The binary tree pattern generally performs better than the ring pattern because of the parallelism in trees. The question naturally arises: What is the best tree pattern for distribution of messages to all processes? Can we increase the degree of the tree and obtain even better performance results?

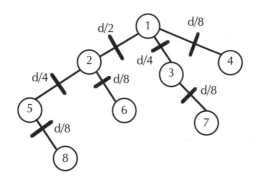

	w0+w1(d/2) +	w0+w1(d/4) +	w0+w1(d/8) +	w0+w1
P1	send d/2 to P2	send d/4 to P3	send d/8 to P4	
P2		send d/4 to P5	send d/8 to P6	send R to P1
P3			send d/8 to P7	send R to P1
P4				send R to P1
P5			send d/8 to P8	send R to P1
P6				send R to P1
P7				send R to P1
P8				send R to P1

Figure 4.7   *M-ary tree pattern and Gantt chart schedule of message-passing*

4.3.3 *M*-ary Tree Patterns

The binary tree pattern is natural because of its simplicity and symmetry. But is it the best tree structure for distribution of data from a parent process to all other processes? Can we gain greater speed by selecting an M-ary tree pattern for $M > 2$?

An example of a 3-ary tree distribution pattern is shown in Figure 4.7. In this pattern process P1 keeps $d/8$ data elements, and then sequentially sends $d/2$ elements to P2, $d/4$ elements to P3, and $d/8$ elements to P4.

At the second level, P2 keeps $d/8$ elements and sends $d/4$ elements to P5 and $d/8$ elements. This process continues until all processes have $d/8$ elements. That is, all 8 processes ultimately have $d/8$ data elements, and they can begin to process their data as shown in the Gantt chart of Figure 4.7.

We have also shown the aggregation phase of this distribution pattern in the Gantt chart. This is the phase following parallel computation where the result is returned to the parent process P1. We assume the result is only one element in size, hence the simplified estimate for the time to send a reply.

The question is whether this is better than the binary pattern shown previously. Clearly, the distribution time is the same as for the binary tree:

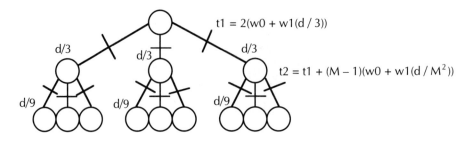

Figure 4.8   *M*-ary tree for *M* = 3, *d* = 27, and 2 levels

$$T(k) = \sum_{i=1}^{k} w_0 + w_1 \frac{d}{2^i} = w_0 \log_2 d + w_1 d = T(d)$$

This illustrates an idea we might pursue. Is it possible to increase the degree of the *M*-ary tree, thereby decreasing the level of the tree? Reduction of levels means fewer delays, and so the total delay time is decreased.

If we increase *M*, we also increase the sequential message-passing, which increases the delay! This becomes an optimization problem. How large should the degree of an *M*-ary tree be such that the least delay is guaranteed?

Using a similar analysis to the ones shown in Figures 4.6 and 4.7 the reader can show that the time delay of an *M*-ary tree is approximated by *T*(*M*) (see Figure 4.8):

$$T(M) \approx M(\log_M d) w_0 + w_1 d$$

What is an optimal value of *M*?

Note that $\log_M d = (\log_2 d / \log_2 M)$, so that *T*(*M*) becomes

$$T(M) = M \frac{\log_2 d}{\log_2 M} w_0 + w_1 d = \frac{M}{\log_2 M} (\log_2 d) w_0 + w_1 d$$

Differentiating *T*(*M*) with respect to *M* and setting the result to zero yields an optimal value for *M*:

$$\frac{DT}{DM} = 0 = \frac{\log_2 M - \log_2 e}{(\log_2 M)^2} w_0$$

because

$$\log_2 M = (\log_2 e)(\log_e M)$$

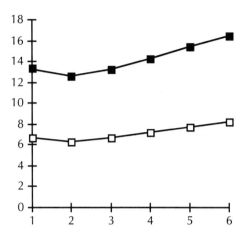

Figure 4.9 $T(M)$ versus M. The optimal M is near 2.

and

$$\frac{D \log_2 M}{DM} = \frac{\log_2 e}{M}$$

Solving for M:

$$0 = \log_2 M - \log_2 e$$

which means $M = e$ is optimal!

M must be an integer, so should we choose 2 or 3? This argument is exactly the one used in the 1950s to convince hardware designers to use the binary system as the basis for computer arithmetic. We will follow this ancient tradition and use $M = 2$. Therefore, the optimal data distribution tree is a binary tree.

Example 4.8

Let $w_0 = 100$. What is the optimal value of M for an M-ary tree? The value of M is not influenced by w_0. Figure 4.9 shows the graph of $T(M)$ versus M for $w_0 = 100$ and $w_0 = 10$. Note that the optimal value of M is unchanged. (Figure 4.9 is a plot of the integer values of M. If the real values of M had been used, the optimum point would have been $M = e$.)

4.4 KEYWORDS AND CONCEPTS

We have used the traditional Petri network graph as a basis for a parallel program graph so that we can model a parallel program as a control-flow graph. This provides a mechanical means of estimating the performance of any parallel program. Such a program graph is annotated with timing information (labels) designating estimates of the execution time of each transition and message delay along each arc. By simply adding these time delays along a path from start to end, we can estimate the execution time for the entire program.

We easily obtain formulas for both sequential and parallel program constructs. In particular, we have developed performance formulas for sequence, branching, and looping within sequential programs, and message-distribution patterns (rings and trees) within parallel programs. We have shown that the optimal degree for a message-passing tree is $M = 2$; i.e., binary distribution trees are better than ternary or higher order trees.

The following keywords and concepts summarize the ideas developed in this chapter:

Arcs   An arc connects program states (called places) to program actions (called transitions), or transitions to places. Arcs represent the flow of control through a parallel program, but they also model the performance of message-passing. An arc is labeled with the communication delay corresponding to the data distribution in a parallel program.

Binary tree pattern   A large message can be efficiently distributed to a large number of processors through a divide-and-conquer algorithm which conforms to a binary tree pattern. We have shown that the optimal distribution pattern is such a tree.

Fork and join   Processes are created by a fork in the flow of control, and destroyed later on by a join. These two operations are modelled as a special kind of transition in the program graph notation. When a fork takes place, we must remember to account for the time it takes to create new processes, and also for the communication costs associated with sending messages to all new processes.

Knots   The program graph model works very well for structured programs, i.e., programs containing only single-entry-single-exit constructs. However, not all programs are structured in this way. For example, a program knot is a control flow pattern that cannot be reduced to a simple single-entry–single-exit flow through the program. Therefore, the program graph proposed here cannot model such convoluted programs.

Places   A place in a program graph corresponds to a program state, i.e., to the value of all process variables and the position of the program counter for the specific process corresponding to the place. To help keep track of processes, we number the places of a program graph to indicate which process state is modelled by the place.

Reduction principle   A program graph is reducible to a single-entry–single-exit construct by repeated application of reduction. That is, a subgraph that is devoid of a knot can be replaced by a single transition. We repeat the replacement until only one single-entry-single-exit transition remains, or until it is impossible to find a subgraph that is devoid of a knot. If the final replacement reduces the graph to a single transition, we say the program graph is reducible. The reduction principle is equivalent to the structured programming principle. Thus, a reducible parallel program is a structured parallel program.

Transitions   A program graph transition models any action we want the program to carry out when it executes. Sometimes a transition represents a single statement, and other times it models an entire procedure. Regardless, we label the transition with a number which represents the execution time of the statement or entire procedure. This number is an estimate that we need in order to analyze the performance of the entire graph.

PROBLEMS

1   Show that

$$(t0 + t1) \sum_{j=1}^{N} p_j = (t0 + t1) \frac{(N + 1)}{2}$$

when

$$p_j = \frac{M - j + 1}{N}; \quad j = 1, 2, ..., N$$

2   Draw the Petri network graph of the sequential program below. What is its performance?
```
begin
read(x,y,z);
if x > y then repeat
            if x > z then x := x div z
            until x < z
        else x := z – y;
write(x,y,z)
end.
```

3   Is it possible to model any arbitrary parallel or serial program as a Petri network? As a program graph? Explain you answer.

4   What are the functions of the three program graphs in Figure 4.10? For each graph, give a pseudocode program that performs the function modelled by the program graph. Explain the differences between Figures 4.10b and 4.10c.

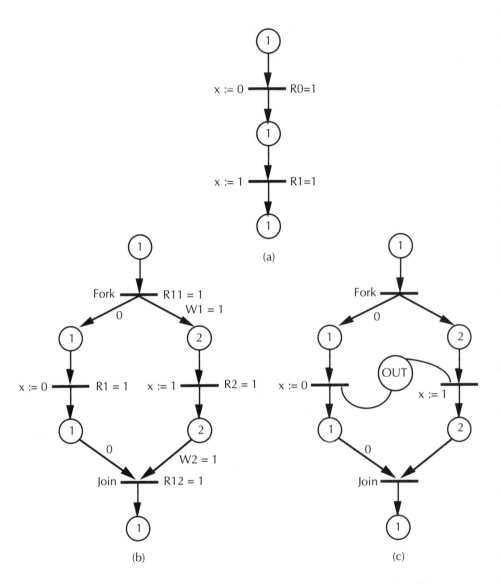

Figure 4.10   Three program graphs: (a) simple, (b) fork/join, and (c) synchronized fork/join

5   Calculate the expected time delays in the following communication patterns, given the parameters $d = 2^{20}$, $w_0 = 256$, $w_1 = .0001$:

a   Ring structure, $N = 128$ nodes, with data evenly distributed to all 128 nodes.

b   Binary tree structure, $N = 128$ nodes, with d/N data elements per node.

c M-ary tree structure, $N = 128$ nodes, and d/N data elements per node.

d   Same as a–c, above, except that $N = 512$.

6   Derive performance formulas for assignment, if-then-else, and while-loop (serial) programming constructs assuming that the branch probabilities are $p = (1 - p) = 0.5$, and that the loop body execution probabilities are 0.9, in all cases.

7   Derive a performance formula for the program modelled by Figure 4.10c. List your assumptions.

8   Show that $T(M)$ is approximated by $T(M) \approx M(\log_M d)w_0 + w_1 d$ for the M-ary tree. *Hint:* Use the same approximation as in the binary tree estimate.

9   Show that

$$\frac{DT}{DM} = 0 = \frac{\log_2 M - \log_2 e}{(\log_2 M)^2} w_0$$

CHAPTER 5

The Data Parallel Fan

We will present the data-parallel **fan** for expressing SIMD/SPMD algorithms. The body of a **fan** consists of a function that performs identical operations on all processes, each processing its own data. This is the classic *broadcast-compute-aggregate* form of all data-parallel calculations. In the broadcast phase, data is mapped from one process into N duplicate processes. In the compute phase, all processes perform exactly the same operations but on different data. In the aggregate phase, all results are mapped back to the parent process.

We will present the **fan** construct, which consists of a **mapin** clause for broadcasting (distributing) data; a function body for defining duplicate routines to be executed by all processes; and a **mapout** clause for aggregation of the results back to the parent process.

A **fan** implements a structured fork/join control flow operation. In addition, a **fan** can constrain the SIMD calculation, using a **with** clause, and can terminate the calculation phase early, using the **exit** statement. We will show that for certain applications, constraints and early termination are essential. Applications to matrix, searching, sorting, and nearest-neighbor overrelaxation algorithms illustrate these ideas.

We will also analyze the performance of a **fan** and show that there is an optimum number of duplicate processes that minimizes its elapsed execution time. This optimum will depend on the communication and process creation overhead as well as on the grain size of the compute phase.

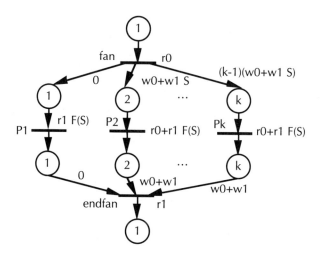

Figure 5.1   **Graph representation of parallel fan construct**

5.1 THE FAN

We begin with the **fan**, which is, perhaps, the easiest of the parallel programming constructs. The code for each process is identical, but each process works on different data. Fans follow a three-phase broadcast-compute-aggregate form of control whereby data and code are broadcast to identical processes, all processes execute the code using the broadcast data as inputs, and the results are collected. This is sometimes called the *supervisor/worker model*, because a supervisor process distributes the jobs to processes, waits for them to complete their work, and then collects the results. In our formulation, the supervisor will also perform work, thus keeping all processes busy all the time.

The program graph of this construction is shown in Figure 5.1. The **fan** is initiated on parent process 1. First, $k - 1$ additional processes are instantiated, assuming process 1 does work as one of the parallel processes. Parent process 1 sequentially creates processes 2, 3, ..., k, each one on its own parallel processing element. These processes are furnished with data which are sent in serial fashion, first to P1, which takes zero time because it is on the same process, then to P2 on processing element 2, and ultimately to Pk on processing element k. When each process executes its identical code on its copied data, it returns a value to process P1 as shown in Figure 5.1.

The communication time delays shown in the program graph are the machine parameters w_0, w_1, r_0, and r_1. The size of the data to be distributed is S, and $F(S)$ is the time complexity of the processing routine. The program graph of Figure 5.1 shows cumulative communication time delays; i.e., the time to send data to P1 is zero; the time to send data to P2 is $w_0 + w_1 S$; and the time to send data to Pk is the sum of all the other times: $(k - 1)(w_0 + w_1 S)$.

Because they receive their data at different times, each duplicate process completes at a slightly different time. All processes meet at **endfan**; any process reaching **endfan** early waits until all processes arrive. Thus, **endfan** is a *barrier lock*. But if one of the identical processes executes an **exit** before the others, it forces all others to terminate early. We will describe early termination using the **exit** statement later in greater detail.

Data are returned to the supervisor or parent process as they are computed by each process. The returned data are copied into local variables according to an aggregation phase. Because we charge all message-passing time to the sender, and none to the receiver, the **endfan** barrier introduces a time delay equal to the latest completion time of all parallel processes.

The broadcast-compute-aggregate phases are specified by a programmer as follows:

fan <counter>
with <Boolean-constraint>
mapin <distribution-list>
{<SPMD-routine>}
mapout <aggregate-list>
endfan

One process is created on a processor for each <counter> value; elements of the <distribution-list> are sent to each process; <SPMD-routine> is duplicated on each processor; and elements from the duplicated processes are collected according to <aggregate-list>. The Boolean constraint is an optional clause which may be used to restrict the number of duplicates, based on some test.

Example 5.1

A simple example of incrementing the elements of vector $x[1..N]$ is shown below:

```
fan i := 1..N              /* Make N duplicates, numbered 1..N   */
mapin x[i] to elem;        /* Copy x[1] to P1, x[2] to P2, ..., x[N] to PN */
{ float elem;              /* Duplicate this code N times...   */
    elem += 1}             /* Increment each x[i] by one   */
mapout elem to x[i]        /* Copy all N elem's to corresponding x[i]   */
endfan
```

This fan distributes the elements of the vector to N processes, one element per processor, and then simultaneously increments each element by 1. Then, each process returns its incremented element to $x[i]$. If we ignore communication overhead, the entire vector is incremented in one time step, using N processes.

5.2 PERFORMANCE ANALYSIS

In Figure 5.1, processes P1, P2, ..., Pk perform identical routines on processing elements 1, 2, ..., k, respectively. The **fan** initiates the supervisor task, using r_0 time units, and then sends each message to 2, 3, ..., k in sequence. That is, process P1 must send $(k-1)$ messages, using $(k-1)(w_0 + w_1 S)$ time units to distribute S characters to each process.

We assume a small (one character) result is returned by each process; thus each process uses $(w_0 + w_1)$ time units to send a return message. Furthermore, we assume the barrier at **endfan** waits for the last return message to arrive.

The source of the speedup is data parallelism. Thus, each parallel process manipulates only a portion of the data given by S/k, where S is the size of the original data. To obtain an accurate representation of **fan** parallelism, we must replace S in Figure 5.1 by S/k. Therefore, each process takes exactly the same length of time, given by the formula $r_0 + r_1 F(S/k)$, where $F(S/k)$ is the estimated computation time of each routine in terms of the length of its input data.

The function $F(S)$ depends on the computational complexity of the SPMD routine. A linear algorithm takes time proportional to (S/k); a polynomial time algorithm is modelled as $(S/k)^n$, and so forth.

In fact, the performance of a **fan** is easy to compute, given the labeled graph of Figure 5.1. The *critical path* in Figure 5.1 is clearly the path through process Pk. This path yields the elapsed time of the entire **fan**:

$$T_k = (r_0 + r_1 + w_0 + w_1) + r_1 F(S/k) + (k-1)(w_0 + w_1 S/k)$$

Also note that this same program segment executes as a single process in time:

$$T_1 = r_0 + r_1 F(S)$$

Hence, the speedup of a **fan** is given by

$$\text{Speedup} = \frac{r_0 + r_1 F(S)}{(r_0 + r_1 + w_0 + w_1) + r_1 F(S/k) + (k-1)(w_0 + w_1 S/k)}$$

The question naturally arises, "what value of k yields the smallest elapsed execution time of a **fan**?" That is, what is the minimum value of T_k? We can find a k that yields the optimal value of T_k by assuming some reasonable function for F. Suppose $F(S/k) = (S/k)^n$. What is the smallest elapsed time for $n = 1$, and $n = 2$?

Case 1: Linear Algorithm

When $n = 1$, substitute $F(S/k) = S/k$ into the equation for T_k and set its first derivative to zero:

$$0 = -r_1 S + w_0 k^2 + w_1 S$$

Solving for k yields

$$k = \sqrt{\frac{S\,(r_1 - w_1)}{w_0}}; \qquad r_1 > w_1; \qquad F\left(\frac{S}{k}\right) = \frac{S}{k}$$

Case 2: Quadratic Algorithm

When $n = 2$, the solution requires solving a cubic polynomial for k. Two of the roots are imaginary, and one is real. Let A and B be factors in the solution:

$$A = \sqrt{\frac{S^4 r_1^2}{w_0^2} + \frac{S^3 w_1^3}{27 w_0^3}}; \qquad B = \frac{S^2 r_1}{w_0}$$

Then the optimal solution is given by the cube root expression:

$$k = \sqrt[3]{B + A} + \sqrt[3]{B - A}$$

Note that $(k - 1)$ is approximately equal to k for $k \gg 1$. This assumption greatly simplifies the mathematics, so the equation can be more easily solved:

$$k \approx \sqrt[3]{\frac{2 S^2 r_1}{w_0}}; \qquad F\left(\frac{S}{k}\right) = \left(\frac{S}{k}\right)^2$$

Example 5.2

Suppose the **fan** routine and the machine it runs on have the following characteristics: $S = 1{,}000$ characters, $w_0 = 10$ ms, $w_1 = 0.001$ ms/character, $r_0 = 100$ ms, and $r_1 = 10$ ms/operation, where ms is milliseconds, and an operation is roughly equivalent to a multiplication. What is the optimum number of processes to use, and what is the expected speedup? Substitution into the formula for $n = 1$ yields $k = 33$ processes (approximately). And substitution into the approximation formula for $n = 2$ yields $k = 126$ processes (approximately).

To compute speedup we substitute these values into the formula:

$$\text{Speedup} = \frac{r_0 + r_1 F(S)}{(r_0 + r_1 + w_0 + w_1) + r_1 F(S\,/\,k) + (k - 1)\,(w_0 + w_1 S\,/\,k)}$$

≈ 14 linear case
≈ 19 quadratic case

Thus, using 33 processes we get a fourteenfold speedup, and using 126 processes we get a nineteenfold speedup. These are efficiencies of 42% and 15%, respectively. Keep in mind that the 33-process solution assumes linear time complexity of the duplicate routines, while the 126-process solution assumes quadratic time complexity at each process. What happens if we use more processes?

We will use the values $r_0 = 100$, $r_1 = 10$, $w_0 = 10$, and $w_1 = 0.001$ in later examples. Substituting these parameters into the appropriate formulas yields orders of complexity for the number of processes and the speedup:

Linear time complexity $k = O(\sqrt{S})$;   Speedup $= O(\sqrt{S})$

Quadratic time complexity $k = O(\sqrt[3]{S^2})$;   Speedup $= O(\sqrt[3]{S^4})$

5.3 FLOW-CORRECTNESS ANALYSIS

Is the **fan** flow-correct? When used in combination with other parallel constructs, does the combination retain flow-correctness? To answer these questions, we apply the FLOW, ANTI, and OUT predicates to the construct shown in Figure 5.1.

The **fan** distributes data to identical processes, each of which takes an input, say x, and uses it, redefines it, or both. Thus for each identical parallel process P_i in the **fan**,

PRE(x) [P_i] POST(x) = PRE(x) [P_i] {USE(x) **or** DEF(x)}

Furthermore, the value of x can be undefined, used, or defined before entering the **fan**; thus the possible preconditions and postconditions of a **fan** are:

{UNDEF(x) **or** DEF(x) **or** USE(x)} [P_i] {USE(x) **or** DEF(x)}

Enumerating, and giving names to each case:

1	UNDEF(x) [P_i] USE(x)	Undefined x
2	DEF(x) [P_i] USE(x)	Single reference x
3	USE(x) [P_i] USE(x)	Double reference x
4	UNDEF(x) [P_i] DEF(x)	Define x
5	DEF(x) [P_i] DEF(x)	Double define x
6	USE(x) [P_i] DEF(x)	Redefine x

We shall examine each case in turn.

    1   UNDEF(x) [P_i] USE(x)   Undefined x

This case is clearly an error, regardless of synchronization problems.

    2   DEF(x) [P_i] USE(x)   Single reference x

This is the most commonly encountered case in practice. It corresponds to a **fan** taking as input a defined variable x, and using it. The **fan** does not change the value of x; therefore, it may be subject to a FLOW incorrectness. We check it using the FLOW predicate.

Let the clock read $t - \Delta t$ prior to entry into the **fan**, and t at exit from the **fan**. Then, the FLOW predicate for x is

FLOW(x, t) :-
    ($\exists \Delta t > 0$ | DEF(x, t – Δt)),
    USE(x, t).

The **fan** takes a finite time to execute, so this predicate is TRUE across all parallel processes, because $\Delta t > 0$. In addition, because all parallel processes execute the same code, it is impossible for one process to change x, another to use it, and so forth. All processes are constrained to behave the same.

However, the parallel processes of a **fan** may execute at the same time as another **fan** or some other statement. In this case, we must check for a flow-correctness problem whenever $\Delta t = 0$. This may occur when another construct defines a new value of x while the **fan** is executing.

3   USE(x) [P_i] USE(x)   Double reference x

In this case, the value of x is used either prior to entry into the **fan**, or at the same time as the **fan**. In either case, multiple references to variables are benign, because no destructive writes occur. So regardless of the placement of the references, internal or external to the **fan**, this construct is flow-correct.

4   UNDEF(x) [P_i] DEF(x)   Define x

The **fan** may define an undefined variable x only once. Otherwise, two or more P_i would cause an output dependency if they simultaneously stored a value in x. Because all P_i do the same thing, this can happen when x is an array of distributed elements. Thus, we must demand that

OUT(x[i], t) :-
    ($\forall i \neq j$ | DEF(x[i], t)),
    DEF(x[j], t).

This is usually the case when using a **fan**, because each element of the array is assigned to a unique process, thus each element is changed by only one P_i. However, should $i = j$, an output dependency would result. We will see a case of this in the early termination example given later.

In addition, another **fan** or some other parallel construct may execute at the same time as the **fan**. This also gives rise to an output dependency. Hence, we must demand that no double defines occur anywhere in the parallel program.

5   DEF(x) [P_i] DEF(x)   Double define x

This case is identical to the previous one, if the DEFs occur within the **fan**. However, this precondition and postcondition expression may also refer to the effects of a **fan** used in combination with another statement which also defines x.

Assuming that the **fan** is internally flow-correct according to the previous case, we must still check for an output dependency as follows:

OUT(x, t) :-
    ($\exists \Delta t > 0$ | DEF(x, $t - \Delta t$)),
    DEF(x, t)

This will be guaranteed only if $\Delta t > 0$, which depends on the behavior of the other statement. Thus, we cannot assert this condition in general. Even if this predicate is satisfied relative to other parts of the parallel program, we must still check for internal consistency, using the previous case. We want to be sure that no duplicates clash, and that there are no clashes between the **fan** and any other part of the program.

  6   USE(x) [P_i] DEF(x)   Redefine x

This case raises the specter of an antidependency either internally, or due to a combination with some other statement. Both cases must be checked. First, we examine the possibility of an array antidependency among the parallel routines of the **fan**:

ANTI(x[i], t) :-
    ($\forall$ i $\neq$ j | USE(x[i], t),
    DEF(x[j], t).

This might occur, for example, if two processes access the same two elements of x, and both processes change both elements. This must be checked for each use of **fan**.

    Externally, we must check:

ANTI(x, t) :-
    ($\exists \Delta t > 0$ | USE(x, $t - \Delta t$)),
    DEF(x, t).

The **fan** takes $\Delta t > 0$ time, but some other statement running in parallel with the **fan** may violate this predicate, so the restriction on the **fan** is not sufficient. Again, we must check this condition in combination with other statements.

Example 5.3

Suppose we create two fans in a program: fan1 inputs $x[1..4]$ and outputs elements $x[1..2]$, while fan2 inputs the same $x[1..4]$, but outputs $x[2..3]$. Furthermore, assume that fan1 is executed before fan2; i.e., fan1 executes in time interval $[0..1]$, and fan2 executes in time interval $[2..5]$. Is there a flow-correctness problem, here?

    Restating the program in terms of the following precondition and postconditions for the two fans:

{UNDEF(x[1..4])} [fan1] {DEF(x[1..2]) **and** UNDEF(x[3..4])}
{DEF(x[1..2]) **and** UNDEF(x[3..4]) } [fan2] DEF(x[2..3]) **and** UNDEF(x[4])}

The assertion for fan1 says that fan1 defines values for only two of the four elements, leaving $x[3..4]$ undefined. The assertion for fan2 says that the results of fan1 are assumed as preconditions, and that fan2 defines $x[2..3]$, but not $x[4]$.

We examine each of these assertions in turn:

{UNDEF($x[1..4]$)} [fan1] {DEF($x[1..2]$) **and** UNDEF($x[3..4]$)}

From the analysis given above, fan1 is allowed to define an undefined $x[i]$ only once. Otherwise, two or more P_i would cause an output dependency if they simultaneously stored a value in x. Thus, we must demand that

OUT($x[i]$, t) :-
    ($\forall$ i $\neq$ j | DEF($x[i]$, t)),
    DEF($x[j]$, t).

This means each P_i of the fan must operate on a different $x[i]$.

{DEF($x[1..2]$) **and** UNDEF($x[3..4]$) } [fan2] DEF($x[2..3]$) **and** UNDEF($x[4]$)}

The UNDEF($x[3..4]$) [fan2] DEF($x[2..3]$) portion of this assertion is similar to the previous situation, and is left to the reader to ponder. The DEF($x[1..2]$) [fan2] DEF($x[2..3]$) portion is more interesting. First we check for internal out-correctness, followed by a check for external out-correctness:

Internally, we check for output dependencies among the P_i routines:

$\forall$ i **in** [2..3], j **in** [2..3] | OUT($x[i]$, t) :-
    ($\forall$ i $\neq$ j | DEF($x[i]$, t),
    DEF($x[j]$, t).
$\Rightarrow$ OUT($x[2..3]$, t) :-
    DEF($x[2]$, t),
    DEF($x[3]$, t).

This means that one process defines $x[2]$, and the other defines $x[3]$. This is flow-correct. Next we check for external output dependency as follows:

OUT($x[2]$, t) :-
    ($\exists$ $\Delta t > 0$ | DEF($x[2]$, t $- \Delta t$)),
    DEF($x[2]$, t)

This is guaranteed only if $\Delta t > 0$, which is TRUE in this application because fan2 executes after fan1.

5.4 APPLICATIONS OF FAN

Nearly all applications that can be solved by SIMD or SPMD algorithms use some form of a **fan**. The following sample applications are taken from matrix algebra, searching, and numerical solution of the wave equation. There are many other fields of science where a **fan** can be used, but these three illustrate the concepts of SPMD supervisor/worker parallelism, early termination of an SPMD calculation, and constraints in fans.

5.4.1 Matrix Calculations

Matrix algebra is one of the most obvious applications of a **fan**. We begin with simple processing cliches and end with a program segment that solves a linear system of equations by a modified form of parallel *LU decomposition*. First, a simple case.

Two vectors, $x[1..N]$ and $y[1..N]$, can be added together in one step, using k processes, as follows. We assume the result is stored in vector x; thus in vector notation, $X = X + Y$, element by element:

```
fan i:= 1..N                /* Distribute N processes   */
mapin x[i] to X;            /* Copy to local X   */
      y[i] to Y;            /* Copy to local Y   */
{ float  X, Y;              /* Duplicate routines   */
        X := X + Y;         /* All do the same thing   */
}
mapout X to x[i];           /* Send the result back   */
endfan                      /* Barrier   */
```

This **fan** establishes a USE–DEF relationship on x, and a USE–USE relationship on y. From the foregoing analysis we know to check only for antidependencies. That is, we show that the **fan** is flow-correct by showing that $\Delta t > 0$. Externally,

```
ANTI(x, t) :-
    (∃ Δt > 0 | USE(x, t − Δt)),
    DEF(x, t).
```

This assertion holds because there is no other parallel activity. Thus, the **fan** is the only activity that is using and changing x. Internally,

```
ANTI(x[i], t) :-
    (∀ i ≠ j | USE(x[i], t),
    DEF(x[j], t).
```

This holds because each **fan** process works on an entirely different element of x. The same argument holds for the elements of y.

Now, consider a more complex matrix calculation. We want to compute the product of two matrices, $x[1..N, 1..N]$ and $y[1..N, 1..N]$, to obtain a third matrix, $z[1..N, 1..N]$. In matrix algebra notation, $Z = X \times Y$.

Matrix multiplication involves many inner product calculations:

```
fan  i := 1..N;                    /* N × N duplicates   */
     j := 1..N
mapin x[i, 1..N] to A;             /* Row i to A[1..N]   */
      y[1..N, j] to B;             /* Column j to B[1..N]   */
{float A[1..N], B[1..N], Sum;      /* O(N) summations   */
      Sum := 0.0;
      for(k := 1; k ≤ N; k++) Sum += A[k] * B[k];        /* N × N of these...   */
}
mapout Sum to z[i,j];              /* Return N × N results   */
endfan
```

Each duplicate **fan** process computes a sum using $O(N)$ steps. Thus, we might ask, what is the optimum number of processes needed to maximize speedup?

Suppose we use $N = 100$ for concreteness. Further, we assume that each $x[i, j]$, $y[i, j]$, and $z[i, j]$ occupies 4 characters of storage. Then, 400 characters of x and 400 characters of y are mapped into each duplicate process. Only 4 characters are mapped back from each process, but we ignore the time to map back.

Using the linear time complexity formulas developed above,

$$S = \text{size of } x, y \text{ matrices} = 4 \times 2 \times N^2 = 80000$$

$$k = \sqrt{S} = 280$$

$$\text{Speedup} = \frac{100 + 10S}{120 + 10S/k + (k - 1)(10 + 0.001S/k)} = 137$$

That is, a speedup of 137 is achievable using 280 processes. This is an efficiency of $137/280 = 0.489$, or 48.9%. But, the **fan** specifies $N^2 = 10,000$ processes! If we allocate each of these duplicates to one processor, we would need 10,000 processors. Instead, the optimization formula requires only 280 processors to run all 10,000 processes. This means that we must pack approximately 36 processes onto each processor.

This illustrates the importance of *grain packing* to achieve a balance between communication overhead and computation time. Each grain consists of 36 duplicate processes, each computing a sum. The matrix multiplication algorithm has a potential speedup of 10,000. Yet only a fraction of this speedup can be realized, due to the practical limits of machinery.

Of course, we could have increased the performance of this solution using a parallel summation. This topic will have to wait until we discuss the *tree* construct, which uses divide-and-conquer techniques to compute sums in $O(\log_2 N)$ time rather than $O(N)$ time.

5.4.2 Gaussian Elimination

A **fan** can be used to speed up a major portion of the Gaussian elimination algorithm, using a modified lower-upper-decomposition (LUD) strategy. We want to find the solution vector $x[1..n]$ in $Ax = b$, where A is an $n \times n$ coefficient matrix, and $b[1..n]$ is the right-hand side vector. Along the way, we want to produce a matrix $m[1..n,1..n]$ containing the multipliers needed to convert any right-hand side b, into a new solution, without having to repeat the elimination step.

We will give a serial version of the program, followed by a parallel version. The serial version is useful for understanding the parallel version. This code converts A into LUD form. To obtain a solution to $Ax = b$, this code must be followed by a back substitution phase.

```
/* Gauss elimination—serial version   */
/* No partial pivoting, no row interchange   */
/* Modified LUD: produces multiplier array m[n, n] instead   */
/* System: Ax = b. Inputs: n, A, b. Outputs: m, modified A, b.   */
```

```
for t:= 1 to (n − 1) do                                  /* t = row number   */
  begin
    pivot := A[t, t];                                    /* Assumes A[t, t] ≠ 0   */
    for i := (t + 1) to n do m[i, t] := A[i, t] / pivot;  /* m is the multiplier   */
    for i := (t + 1) to n do                             /* Keep it around   */
      begin
        for j := t to n do A[i, j] := A[i, j] − m[i, t] * A[t, j];  /* Modify A into LUD */
        b[i] := b[i] − m[i, t] * b[t];                   /* And b, also   */
      end
  end
```

This solution takes $O(n^3)$ time to compute, because of the 3-nested loops, each taking $O(n)$ steps. If we could simply parallelize some of these loops, we could get a much better time. But, is this possible?

One parallel version goes like this:

```
/* Gauss elimination—parallel version   */
/* Modelled after serial version   */
/* Uses 2 data-parallel fans to reduce O(n) calculations to O(1).   */
/* Uses 1 data-parallel fan to reduce O(n**2) calculations to O(1).   */
```

```
for(t := 1; t < n; t++)                            /* Flow-dependencies exist in loop   */
{/*f1*/ fan i := (t + 1)..n                         /* Calculate multipliers   */
      mapin  A[t, t] to pivot;                      /* Replace O(n) loop with O(1) fan   */
             A[i, t] to ColElem;
      {float pivot, ColElem;
             ColElem := ColElem / pivot}
      mapout ColElem to m[i, t]
      endfan;

/*f2*/ fan i := (t + 1)..n                          /* Calculate modified b[i]   */
      mapin m[i, t] to mpy;                          /* Distribute to (n − t) processes   */
            b[i] to rhs;
            b[t] to bt;
      { float  mpy, rhs, bt;                         /* Local variables at each process   */
             rhs −= mpy * bt }                       /* SIMD decrement   */
      mapout rhs to b[i]                             /* Aggregate solution   */
      endfan;                                        /* (n − t) processes take 1 time unit   */

/*f3*/ fan i := (t + 1)..n;                          /* O(n**2) processes take 1 time step   */
            j := t..n                                /* One process for each (i, j)   */
```

```
      mapin m[i, t] to mpy;
            A[i, j] to RowElem;
            A[t, j] to ColElem
      {float  mpy, ColElem, RowElem;
            RowElem -= mpy * ColElem }  /* SIMD decrement   */
      mapout RowElem to A[i, j]
      endfan;                          /* Mesh of procs compute upper A[i,j]   */
}
```

This version implements three fans in sequence, designated by comments /*f1*/, /*f2*/, and /*f3*/. These three fans establish preconditions and postconditions as follows:

{USE(A[t, t], A[i, t] | i ≠ t)} [f1] {DEF(m[i, t] | i ≠ t)}
{USE(m[i, t] | i ≠ t, b[i] | i ≠ t, b[t])} [f2] {DEF(b[i] | i ≠ t)}
{USE(m[i, t] | i ≠ t, A[i, j] | i ≠ t, A[t, j])} [f3] {DEF(A[i, j])}

No flow-errors exist due to USE–DEF patterns as long as f1 is done before f2 and f3. In fact, f2 and f3 can be done in parallel, because there are no dependencies at all! The outer for-loop is serial, so all of these USE–DEF patterns are flow-correct. In other words, there are no antidependency problems.

Internally, all three fans are flow-correct because $i ≠ t$. This is largely due to the fact that we stored the lower portion of the LUD in an ancillary array m. Had we stored m back in A, the dependencies would have been more complex.

Example 5.4

Suppose we step through this version for a 3 × 3 example. Let the inputs A and b be:

$$A = \begin{bmatrix} 3 & -2 & 5 \\ 6 & 8 & 2 \\ 1 & -4 & 7 \end{bmatrix} \quad b = \begin{bmatrix} 8 \\ 20 \\ 12 \end{bmatrix} \quad m = \begin{bmatrix} ? & ? & ? \\ ? & ? & ? \\ ? & ? & ? \end{bmatrix}$$

Because $n = 3$, the outer loop is executed only twice, once for $t = 1$ and then for $t = 2$. The following table lists the assignments of each fan for $t = 1$:

fan f1

i	pivot	ColElem	m
2	3	6	m[2,1] = 2
3	3	1	m[3,1] = 1/3

fan f2

i	mpy	rhs	bt	b
2	2	20	8	b[i] = 4
3	1/3	12	8	b[3] = 28/3

fan f3

i, j	mpy	ColElem	RowElem	A
2, 1	2	3	6	$A[2, 1] = 0$
2, 2	2	-2	8	$A[2, 2] = 12$
2, 3	2	5	2	$A[2, 3] = -8$
3, 1	1/3	3	1	$A[3, 1] = 0$
3, 2	1/3	-2	-4	$A[3, 2] = -10/3$
3, 3	1/3	5	7	$A[3, 3] = 16/3$

This completes the first iteration through all three fans. At this stage, the results are:

$$A = \begin{bmatrix} 3 & -2 & 5 \\ 0 & 12 & -8 \\ 0 & -\dfrac{10}{3} & \dfrac{16}{3} \end{bmatrix} \quad b = \begin{bmatrix} 8 \\ 4 \\ \dfrac{28}{3} \end{bmatrix} \quad m = \begin{bmatrix} ? & ? & ? \\ 2 & ? & ? \\ \dfrac{1}{3} & ? & ? \end{bmatrix}$$

The second, and final iteration completes the elimination, $t = 2$:

fan f1

i	pivot	ColElem	m
3	12	-10/3	$m[3, 2] = -5/18$

fan f2

i	mpy	rhs	bt	b
3	-5/18	28/3	4	$b[3] = 94/9$

fan f3

i, j	mpy	ColElem	RowElem	A
3, 2	-5/18	12	-10/3	$A[3, 2] = 0$
3, 3	-5/18	-8	16/3	$A[3, 3] = 28/9$

The result of this iteration is:

$$A = \begin{bmatrix} 3 & -2 & 5 \\ 0 & 12 & -8 \\ 0 & 0 & \dfrac{28}{9} \end{bmatrix} \quad b = \begin{bmatrix} 8 \\ 4 \\ \dfrac{94}{9} \end{bmatrix} \quad m = \begin{bmatrix} ? & ? & ? \\ 2 & ? & ? \\ \dfrac{1}{3} & -\dfrac{5}{18} & ? \end{bmatrix}$$

We can check this result by completing the back substitution, and then substituting the solution into the original matrix:

$$x[3] = \frac{\dfrac{94}{9}}{\dfrac{28}{9}} = 3.36$$

$$x[2] = \frac{4 + 8\,(3.36)}{12} = 2.57$$

$$x[1] = \frac{8 - 5\,(3.36) + 2\,(2.57)}{3} = -1.22$$

For the first row, $6x[1] + 8x[2] + 2x[3] \approx 20$. The second and third rows produce a similar verification. Thus, the parallel version works as expected.

The time complexity of this highly parallel version of LUD is $O(n)$ because the outer loop is serial and each of the fans takes $O(1)$ time. But, what is the actual performance? Once again, using the formulas developed earlier in this chapter, we can estimate optimal execution times for each **fan**, add them together to get the time for one loop iteration, and then compute the overall speedup.

Fan f1

We use $n = 100$ for concreteness. Using the linear time complexity formulas developed above, and noting the size of input data, iteration t takes the following time:

$$S\,(t) \; = \; \text{size of pivot plus } (n - t) \text{ RowElems} \; = \; 4\,(n - t + 1) \; = \; 4\,(101 - t)$$

$$k\,(t) \; = \; \sqrt{S\,(t)} \; = \; \sqrt{4\,(101 - t)} \;\mid\; t \; = \; 1..99$$

$$\text{Elapsed time } T\,(k, t) \; = \; 120 + 10\frac{S\,(t)}{k\,(t)} + (k\,(t) - 1)\,(10 + 0.001\frac{S\,(t)}{k\,(t)})$$

The worst-case elapsed time occurs when $t = 1$, and the best-case occurs when $t = 99$:

$S(1) = 400$	$S(99) = 8$
$k(1) = 20$	$k(99) = 57$
$T(k, 1) = 510$	$T(k, 99) \approx 176$

As an approximation, we fit $T(k, t)$ to a straight line using $T(k, 1)$ and $T(k, 99)$ as endpoints, and drop the parameter k. Thus, $T(t) \approx 513.4 - 3.4t \mid t = 1..99$, for fan f1.

Fan f2

A similar argument holds for fan f2.

$S(t) = \text{size of } (n - t)\ (m[i, t], b[i]) \text{ pairs plus } b[t] = 8(n - t) + 4 = 8(101 - t) + 4$

$S(1) = 804$	$S(99) = 20$
$T(1) \approx 676$	$T(99) \approx 200$

Thus, fitting the endpoints to a straight line, we once again get an estimate of the elapsed time of the second fan, $T(t) \approx 681 - 5t \mid t = 1..99$.

Fan f3

Once again, we estimate the elapsed time over all values of t as follows:

$S(t) = 4(n - t)(n - t + 1) = 4(100 - t)(101 - t)$
$S(1) = 39{,}600$ $\qquad\qquad\qquad\qquad$ $S(99) = 8$

$k(1) = \sqrt{39600} = 199$ $\qquad\qquad\quad$ $k(99) = \sqrt{8} = 2$
$T(1) \approx 4090$ $\qquad\qquad\qquad\qquad\quad$ $T(99) \approx 167$

Again, approximating by a straight line, $T(t) = 4130 - 40t \mid t = 1..99$. We add these elapsed times for the tth iteration through the outer loop:

$T(t) \approx 5324 - 48t \mid t = 1..99$.

The total elapsed time over all values of t is the sum

$$T_p = \sum_{t=1}^{99} (5324 - 48t) = 289476$$

Keep in mind that the serial version takes $O(n^3)$ time. But this looks like $O(n^2)$ time complexity, even though the program design suggests an $O(n)$ complexity using n^2 processes. So, why is the elapsed time estimate so high? The answer lies in the actual parallelism obtained, i.e., the actual number of processors used. This number is k. Recall the optimal values of k for $t = 1$: $k(1) = 199$ processes, when the algorithm specifies 9,800 processes! At the other extreme, $k(99) = 2$, which is appropriate because only two processes are needed. Therefore, the cause of the poor performance is the relatively low number of processors used to run the large number of processes.

At $t = 1$, we pack $9800/199 = 49$ processes onto each processor. This is nearly 50% of the 100 vectors involved in the $n = 100$ system. The corresponding speedup is what we might have expected given the parallelism specified by the program:

$$\text{Speedup} = \frac{100 + 10F(39600)}{120 + 10F(39600/199) + 198(10 + 0.001/199)}$$

Remembering that $F(S) = S = 39{,}600$ in this case:

$$\text{Speedup} = \frac{100 + 10(39600)}{120 + 10(39600/199) + 198(10 + 0.001/199)} = \frac{396100}{4090} = 97$$

Therefore, using 199 processors to run 9,800 processes, we obtain a speedup of 97, or an efficiency rating of $97/199 = 49\%$. While this is not bad, the effect of fan f3 is to deliver $O(n)$ performance in place of the expected $O(1)$ performance. When the $O(n)$ fan is nested inside of the $O(n)$ outer loop, the resulting performance behaves as $O(n^2)$ instead of $O(n)$.

We can compare this performance with the serial version. Once again, we use $n = 100$, $r_0 = 100$, and $r_1 = 10$, and note that only one process is initiated, so we need count only the following number of operations:

Inside the outer loop over t, the first serial loop executes $(100 - t)$ operations. The next two loops are nested, so together they take $(100 - t)(100 - t)$ iterations. Being generous, we estimate 4 operations per iteration, so the total is

$$T_s = 100 + 10 \sum_{t=1}^{99} (4(100 - t)^2 + (100 - t)) \approx 13183600 = O(n^3)$$

Then computed speedup is simply T_s / T_p:

$$\text{Speedup} = \frac{13183600}{289476} = 46$$

We used at most 199 processors to achieve a factor of 46 speedup. The overall efficiency of this version is $46 / 199 = 23\%$. Thus, an $O(n^3)$ algorithm is computed in $O(n^2)$ time, using $O(n)$ processors with 23% efficiency.

5.4.3 Applications with Early Termination

The foregoing examples obey a strict discipline of parallel processes executing to completion, and then waiting at the **endfan** barrier for all peers to arrive before terminating the **fan**. This assumes that all duplicate processes take roughly the same time regardless of nondeterminism in their routines. That is, because the code is identical, we have assumed that all duplicates take the same time to complete.

There are two exceptions to this rule that we will now consider. First, the duplicate processes may not execute in lockstep, due to branches or loops that take varying lengths of time. Second, there are algorithms whereby only one duplicate returns a value, while all others must terminate without returning a value.

For example, consider the case of a parallel search. Let the variable *key* hold an integer identifier and let *list*[1..N] be an array of integers to be searched. We want to compute the index i such that $key = List[i]$, or return a zero. To do this, we must use an **exit** statement to terminate the entire fan when one process finds a match. The match-maker process returns the value and executes the **exit**.

A speedup is achieved by partitioning the list into k sublists such that $List[1..N/k]$ is distributed to process 1, $List[N/k + 1..2N/k)]$ is distributed to process 2, and so on. The search is done simultaneously over each sublist of length k, but only one process is expected to find a match. If more than one match exists, the first process to find a match terminates the entire fan.

```
index := 0;                              /* Assume NOT FOUND    */
fan i := 1, (N div k+1)..(N–N div k+1)   /* E.g., N=100, k=5;  i := 1,21,41,61,..81 */
mapin List[i..i–1+N div k] to SubList;   /* Sublists of size N div k   */
        key to key
```

```
{ int i, SubList[1..N div k], key;
   for( i := 1; (i ≤ N div k) && (key ≠ SubList[i]); i++){};    /* Empty loop body  */
   exit }                                          /* Exit terminates all processes  */
mapout if key = SubList[i] then i + (N div k)*(this − 1) to index;
endfan
```

The returned index is offset by **this**, plus the local index, i. This offset maps $[1..N$ **div** $k]$ onto $[1..N]$.

Example 5.5

Consider the 12-element array, List = [5, 4, 2, 7, 6, 8, 0, 3, 1, 9, 12, 10], and a three-process solution, as follows. Using key = 0, initially distribute the sublists:

P1(this = 1)	P2(this = 2)	P3(this = 3)
[5, 4, 2, 7]	[6, 8, 0, 3]	[1, 9, 12, 10]

This table shows the mapping of List onto SubList[1..4]. That is, three SubList[1..4] arrays exist; one for each process. The parallel comparisons are done on elements 1, 2, 3, ..., 4 in all three processes. After the first parallel comparisons, the processes have the following values of i, and the remaining elements to compare:

P1(this = 1)	P2(this = 2)	P3(this = 3)
[i = 1: 4, 2, 7]	[i = 1: 8, 0, 3]	[i = 1: 9, 12, 10]

Parallel searching continues for i = 2, and i = 3. At the third comparison, i = 3 in each process, and the search is terminated by process **this** = 2, because of the match:

P1(this = 1)	P2(this = 2)	P3(this = 3)
[i = 3: 7]	[i = 3: 3]	[i = 3: 10]

Then, according to the mapout, i + (N **div** k) * (**this** − 1) **to** index, becomes 3 + (4) × (2 − 1) **to** index, and returns the value 7 to index.

The **mapout** list is conditional. That is, i is mapped to index only if key = SubList[i]. Otherwise, no message is returned to the parent process. This merits a closer examination. The preconditions and postconditions contain USE–DEF patterns:

{DEF(index, t − Δt) **and** USE(List[i] | i = [1..N], key, t − Δt)} [fan] {DEF(index, t)}

Because of the DEF–DEF pattern we suspect a possible output dependency on the variable index. That is, we should do an OUT test:

OUT(index, t) :-
    (∃ Δt > 0 | DEF(index, t − Δt)),
    DEF(index, t)

This is assured by the fact that the fan executes after the assignment. Thus, Δt > 0. But, what about double definitions of the variable index?

OUT(index, t) :-
    ($\forall$ i $\neq$ j | DEF(index, t)),
    DEF(index, t).

This predicate is violated if two or more duplicate processes find a match and simultaneously terminate. This is possible whenever the list contains multiple keys such that $i = j$, which leads to multiple definitions of the variable index.

Example 5.6

The array list = [1, 2, 3, 4, 2, 5, 2, 6] contains duplicate elements; thus it is possible that more than one process will return a value of index.

    The result is indeterminate, because we do not know which process will define index first, only to be redefined by a subsequent process. For example, if key = 2, and the search is over two sublists, [1, 2, 3, 4] and [2, 5, 2, 6], both processes locate a match key = 2, but process 1 returns $i + (N$ **div** $k) *$ (**this** $- 1) = 2$, and process 2 returns $1 + 4(2 - 1) = 5$. We cannot discern which process will win this race. However, one process will exit before the others, thus terminating the fan. One value will be returned to index. But which one?

Why did we select $(N$ **div** $k) > 1$ as the size of each grain, when we could allocate one element to each parallel processor? If we distribute a single element of the list to each of N processors, then greater parallelism is realized. Such a **fan** returns nothing, or the value of the index which matches. The **fan** code is much simpler in appearance, and the mapping is straightforward.

Each parallel process makes a comparison and returns nothing, or else returns its identifier, **this**. In the case of multiple matches, the result is indeterminate, which is no better than the earlier solution.

```
index := 0;
fan i := 1..N                      /* Distribute one element per process   */
mapin List[i] to L;                /* Element i goes to process i   */
    key to key                     /* Everyone gets a key   */
{ int L, key ;                     /* Comparison is in mapout   */
    i := this}                     /* this is the process' identifier   */
mapout if key = L then i to index  /* Either i or nothing is passed back   */
endfan
```

This simplification raises the question of finding an optimum value for k. Each routine computes in $O(N$ **div** $k)$ time, so we can use the performance estimates established earlier. Assuming $N = 100$:

Linear time complexity $k = \sqrt{S}$

$$\text{Speedup} = \frac{100 + 10\,(S)}{120 + 10\,(S/k) + (k - 1)\,(10 + 0.001S/k)}$$

S = List of size N + key = $4\,(N + 1)$ = 404

$k = \sqrt{404} \approx 20$

This means that each process searches 5 elements. So,

$$\frac{S}{k} = 20.2$$

$$\text{Speedup} = \frac{100 + 10\,(404)}{120 + 10\,(20.2) + 19\,(10 + 0.001\,(20.2))} = 8$$

Had we used $k = 5$, the speedup for a nonoptimal k is computed from:

$$T_k = (r_0 + r_1 + w_0 + w_1) + r_1 F(S) + (k - 1)\,(w_0 + w_1 S)$$

$$= (100 + 10 + 10 + 0.001) + 10S + (5 - 1)\,(10 + 0.001S)$$

where

S is replaced by $\dfrac{S}{k} = \dfrac{404}{5} \approx 81$

$$\text{Speedup} = \frac{4140}{970} = 4.3$$

Similarly, had we used $k = 100$, the speedup would be:

$$\text{Speedup} = \frac{4140}{1150} = 3.6$$

Clearly, $k = 1$ or 5 is not optimal. Instead, $k = 20$ gives the best performance.

5.4.4 Applications of the Constrained Fan

Many problems in mechanics and physics can be solved by a *finite element* technique, which we will illustrate next. In this technique, a metal plate, bar, or other physical object is modelled by a computer program which simulates some phenomena, such as the flow of heat, electricity, or fluid. The object is partitioned into a grid of points and the temperature, say, is computed at each grid point. Figure 5.2 illustrates this idea using a simple rectangular grid shown as 16 points in a 4×4 grid.

For purposes of concreteness, suppose we study the classical successive overrelaxation (SOR) solution to the wave equation in two dimensions. This problem is considered a classic one because it has been studied for hundreds of years by mathematicians. Mathematically, we must find a function which satisfies the

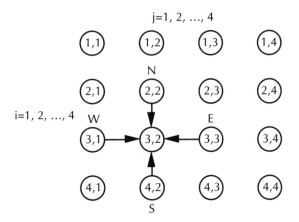

Figure 5.2   A 2-D 4 × 4 mesh nearest-neighbor calculation problem

equation. However, the wave equation is often difficult to solve, so modern mathematicians often resort to approximate numerical solutions performed by computer.

In a computerized approach, we use a form of relaxation in which the temperature at each grid point is computed by repeated averaging. This replaces the wave equation formulation by a simple numerical formulation. But, the number of simple calculations can be enormous. This appears to be a perfect problem for parallel computers.

Here is how the computer version of the solution works. Temperature values are distributed to an array of grid points arranged at constant intervals over the 2-D region, see Figure 5.2. Then, each grid point value is replaced by the average of its north, east, west, and south (NEWS) neighbors. The averaging is repeated until successive values differ by less than some error bound. This is called *successive overrelaxation*, because the averages are only relaxed approximations, and they are repeated over and over again.

This problem appears to be very simple until we examine the data dependencies in a parallel version of the algorithm. Simplified, the algorithm copies the four nearest neighbors' values, computes a sum, waits for all neighbors to do the same thing, and then repeats the process. But, problems arise when attempting to gain the maximum speedup by making as many calculations in parallel as possible. For example, can all averages be computed at the same time using N^2 processes? Can the iterations be overlapped as well? What happens on the boundaries of the mesh?

Assuming a square mesh as shown in Figure 5.2, the fan construct for one iteration is given below. Note the conditional **mapin** pattern. The function *boundary* returns boundary values at the edges of the grid. The input parameters are placed on the left side of the function name, and the output variables are placed on the right side.

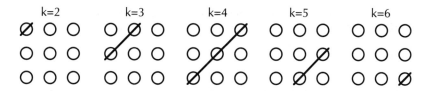

Figure 5.3   Synchronization of the SOR algorithm for N = 3 showing wavefront

```
fan i := 1,2..N;
    j := 1,2..N
mapin a[i, j] to Current;
    if j < N then a[i, j+1] to N else boundary(i, j+1) to N;
    if i < N then a[i+1, j] to E else boundary(i+1, j) to E;
    if j > 1 then a[i, j–1] to W else boundary(i, j–1) to W;
    if i > 1 then a[i–1, j] to S else boundary(i–1, j) to S;
{
    float  er, avg, N, E, W, S, Current ;
    avg := (N + E + W + S) / 4.0;
    er := abs((avg – Current) / Current)              /* Relative error   */
}
mapout avg to a[i, j];
    er to Err[i, j]
endfan
```

The Err array is an array of error values, which will be used to terminate the iterative solution. The average value replaces each grid point $a[i, j]$. This suggests a USE–DEF pattern on grid point $a[i, j]$. But, because $\Delta t > 0$, and each duplicate process takes a different $a[i, j]$, there are no race conditions in this fan.

How can this fan be incorporated into an iteration that sweeps over the entire mesh? We might let all grid points be replaced in parallel, but then how do we guarantee flow-correctness? The solution is to constrain each iteration to lie on a wavefront defined by $k = (i + j)$. This leads to the *constrained fan*, which code is given below. The solution for $N = 3$ is shown in Figure 5.3.

The **with** clause is needed to constrain the number of duplicates to those lying on the wavefront given by $(i + j) = k$. Without this constraint, grid points might be simultaneously used, and defined, leading to a race condition.

```
for(k := 2; k ≤ 2*N; k++)                /* k := 2,3, ..., 2*N   */
{
fan i := 1,2..N;
    j := 1,2..N
with  (i + j) = k                        /* Constraint   */
mapin a[i, j] to Current;
    if j < N then a[i, j+1] to N else boundary(i, j+1) to N;
    if i < N then a[i+1, j] to E else boundary(i+1, j) to E;
```

```
        if j > 1 then a[i, j–1] to W else boundary(i, j–1) to W;
        if i > 1 then a[i–1, j] to S else boundary(i–1, j) to S;
    {
        float er, avg, N, E, W, S, Current ;
        avg := (N + E + W + S) / 4.0;
        er := abs((avg – Current) / Current)            /* Relative error   */
    }
    mapout  avg to a[i, j];
        er to Err[i, j]
    endfan
```

The mapping of duplicate tasks to processes is assumed to be ordered according to <counter> = (i, j) = (1, 1), (1, 2), (1, 3), (2, 1), (2, 2), (2, 3), (3, 1), (3, 2), (3, 3). But, parallelism is constrained to $(i + j)$ = 2, 3, 4, 5, 6. Thus, only $P = N = 3$ processes are needed to compute the corresponding averages along the wavefront:

loop	Allocation	DEF
$k = 2$	$p = 1$	$a[1, 1]$
$k = 3$	$p = 1$	$a[1, 2]$
	$p = 2$	$a[2, 1]$
$k = 4$	$p = 1$	$a[1, 3]$
	$p = 2$	$a[2, 2]$
	$p = 3$	$a[3, 1]$
$k = 5$	$p = 1$	$a[2, 3]$
	$p = 2$	$a[3, 2]$
$k = 6$	$p = 1$	$a[3, 3]$

The wavefront sweeps over all grid points each time the loop is executed. But this does not yield the final solution, because we must make multiple sweeps over the grid until the maximum error is below some limit. This solution is left to the reader to discover.

Another approach to the SOR program is to alternate the averaging so that the even-numbered grid points are simultaneously updated, followed by the odd-numbered points. The even–odd sweeps alternate in time, thus avoiding race conditions. This solution is also left to the reader.

5.4.5 Parallel Sorting

Another example illustrates how an inefficient sequential algorithm can often be turned into an efficient parallel algorithm. What may be considered to be a brute-force method on a single processor, often is the best way to design a parallel program. This concept is illustrated by a simple parallel *sort* followed by a more sophisticated sort.

On a single process system, most *comparative sorts* take $O(N\log_2 N)$ time to rearrange a list of N elements into ascending order. In addition, such sorts often take extra storage space on the order of $O(\log_2 N)$ to hold temporary values. For example, *quicksort* uses up to $\log_2 N$ extra elements to record subscripts of sublists in a pushdown stack. Is it possible to sort in $O(\log_2 N)$ time using N processors? There is no known $O(\log_2 N)$ time parallel sort algorithm.

In the next section we will describe two sorting techniques, one which runs in $O(N^2)$ time on one processor, and $O(N)$ time on N processors; and another algorithm which runs in $O(N\log_2^2 N)$ time as a sequential algorithm, and $O(\log_2^2 N)$ time on N processors. *Rank sort* takes $O(N)$ computation steps and $O(N^2)$ communication steps; while the *bitonic sort* takes $O(\log_2^2 N)$ computation steps, but $O(N\log_2^2 N)$ communication steps to complete the sort. Both techniques sort in place; hence, they take $O(N)$ memory space.

5.4.5.1 Rank Sort

An optimal parallel sort would take $O(\log_2 N)$ time to sort $x[1..N]$ using N processes. But, this is unrealistic if we keep the storage space complexity down to $O(1)$. Instead, it may be possible to sort in $O(N)$ time using a parallel version of an $O(N^2)$ algorithm. Here is how.

Let each of N fan processes compare one element of $x[1..N]$ against all others, and count the number of elements that are less than that element. This computes the rank of each element, in parallel, and uses this rank as the new subscript (location) of the sorted element.

```
fan j := 1,2..N
mapin x to List;                    /* Copy entire list   */
      x[j] to Key;                  /* Find the rank of this one   */
{     int List[1..N], Key, Rank;
      Rank := 0;
      for(i := 1; i ≤ N; i++){
            if List[i] ≤ key then Rank += 1}
}
mapout Key to x[Rank]
endfan
```

All N duplicate processes simultaneously scan the entire list in $O(N)$ time to compute the new location of each element.

Example 5.7

Consider a list of odd numbers in reverse order: x = [17, 15, 13, 11, 9, 7, 5, 3]. The first process of the fan compares 17 against all other elements, and finds that its rank is 8, because $17 \le 17$, $15 \le 17$, $13 \le 17$, $11 \le 17$, $9 \le 17$, ..., $3 \le 17$. The second process compares 15 against all others and finds 7 instances where it is less than or equal to an element, $15 \le 15$, down to $3 \le 15$. Continuing, we obtain a rank for each element; thus, 17 is placed in x[8], 15 is placed in x[7], and so on, until 3 is placed in x[1]. That is, the elements are replaced in order.

This example raises the question of a DEF–DEF pattern of output dependencies. Is it possible for one element of x to be defined by two or more simultaneous processes? If this were to happen, the sort would not be flow-correct. Checking the OUT predicate:

$\forall$ i, j | {OUT(x[i], x[j]) :-
    ($\exists$ i $\neq$ j | {(DEF(x[i]) **and** (DEF(x[j], t)}}

This will not occur as long as Rank is distinct for all processes. Conversely, if two or more processes compute the same value of Rank, then this predicate is TRUE, and we have a problem. So, the proof depends on showing that Rank is distinct.

As it turns out, this sort is not flow-correct, because it is possible for two or more fan processes to compute the same value of Rank. This happens when the list contains duplicate elements.

Example 5.8

Consider the list with duplicate 3s as follows: $x = [8, 3, 6, 5, 3, 3, 7, 2]$. Now, the **fan** computes identical Ranks for all 3s in the list, and simultaneously sets $x[4]$ to 3, but leaves $x[1]$, $x[2]$, and $x[3]$ as they were before the sort., e.g., $x = [8, 3, 6, 3, 5, 6, 7, 8]$.

We can fix this problem with a simple modification. The flow-correct fan below uses the original position in the list to advantage. The Rank of a duplicate such as 3 is incremented whenever the duplicate is to the right of other duplicates in the list.

```
fan j := 1,2..N
mapin x to List;                /* Copy entire list   */
    x[j] to Key;                /* Find the rank of this one   */
    j to Index                  /* Could also have used this   */
{      int List[1..N], Key, Index, Rank;
       Rank := 0;
       for(i := 1; i ≤ N; i++){
              if List[i] < key then Rank += 1;
              if (List[i] = Key) & (i ≤ Index) then Rank += 1}
}
mapout Key to x[Rank]
endfan
```

The flow-correctness of this version is left as an exercise for the reader, but the effect of this change on the previous example is shown in the following example.

Example 5.9

Consider once again the list $x = [8, 3, 6, 5, 3, 3, 7, 2]$. Use the modified sort fan to compute the ranks, and hence the locations of all elements in the sorted list.

Original list	8, 3, 6, 5, 3, 3, 7, 2
Ranks	8, 2, 6, 5, 3, 4, 7, 1
Output list	2, 3, 3, 3, 5, 6, 7, 8

Note that all ranks are distinct, and that the destruction of x takes place at some time $\Delta t > 0$ after it is copied into all processes. Thus, the flow predicate below is TRUE:

$\forall$ i, j | {OUT(x[i], x[j]) :-
    ($\exists$ i $\neq$ j | {(DEF(x[i]) **and** (DEF(x[j], t)}}

This use of a **fan** does not partition and distribute the data evenly across all processes; hence, we cannot use the performance formula derived earlier:

$$T_k = (r_0 + r_1 + w_0 + w_1) + r_1 F(S) + (k - 1)(w_0 + w_1 S)$$

The value of S is N, and the complexity of each process is $F(S) = N$. Furthermore, there is no optimal value of k, because $k = N$ is determined by the problem. Thus,

$$T_k = (r_0 + r_1 + w_0 + w_1) + r_1 N + (N - 1)(w_0 + w_1 N) = O(N) + O(N^2)$$

That is, the execution time of this parallel sort grows as $O(N)$ in terms of the computation, but grows as $O(N^2)$ in terms of the communication component! The validity of this algorithm depends heavily on the characteristics of the target machine. Using the same parameters as before, we get:

$$T_k \approx 120 + 20N + 0.001N^2$$

Keep in mind that the $O(N)$ term in this expression is due to computation; i.e., $(110 + 10N)$, while the communication part is $10.001 + (N - 1)(10 + 0.001N)$. For what value of N does communication become dominant?

5.4.5.2 Bitonic Sort

The rank sort example suggests it may be better to adapt a poor rather than a good sequential algorithm to a parallel computer. If so, perhaps it is possible to find a nonoptimal sequential algorithm that will run in $O(\log_2 N)$ in parallel. *Bitonic sort* comes close, but still requires $O(\log_2^2 N)$ computation steps, and $O(N \log_2^2 N)$ communication steps. However, it is the best known parallel sorting algorithm when communication overhead is ignored.

Figure 5.4 illustrates the bitonic sort algorithm on a list of $N = 16$ elements. Each row in Figure 5.4 shows an array of exchanges, in which pairs of elements are exchanged if they compare as less than or greater than, depending on the phase and exchange pattern. The parallel exchanges start at the bottom of Figure 5.4, using the pattern of exchanges $B = 01101001$, where 0 means to sort the pair in ascending order, and 1 means to sort the pair in descending order. Then, the algorithm moves up one row and performs another array of parallel exchanges based on the pattern $B = 00111100$, and so forth.

There are $\log_2 N = 4$ phases in the sort, and each phase contains i passes, thus there is a total of $1 + 2 + 3 + \ldots + \log_2 N$ passes to be done in parallel. This gives a total of $\log N(1 + \log N)/2$ passes over the list. Each pass performs $N/2$ exchanges which can be done in parallel. But first, we will study the sequential version of bitonic sort to understand how it might be parallelized.

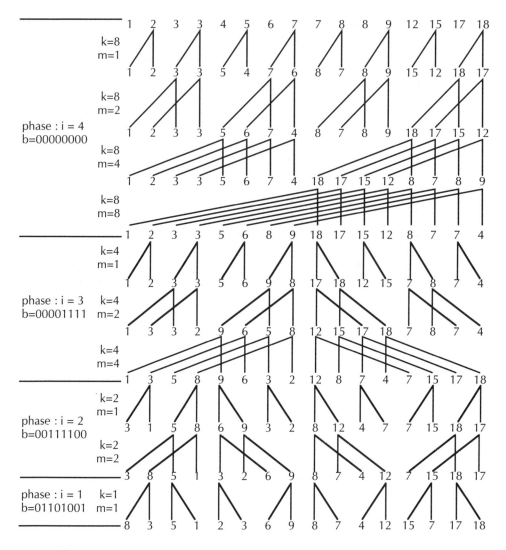

Figure 5.4   Bitonic sort pattern for N = 16

Without further explanation, the sequential bitonic sort is:

```
program bitonic;
const
  n = 16;                              { Change These   }
  n2 = 8;                              { n2 means n div 2   }
type
  list = array[1..n] of integer;      { Sort list of this type   }
```

```
var
 i, j, k, t, p, q, m, logn, logn4, updn: integer;
 d: list;                                { Data list   }
 b: array[1..n2] of boolean;             { Up or down flag   }
 fn, flogn: real;                        { Float versions of n and logn   }
 bitfile: text;                          { This is where the list is stored   }
 fname: string;                          { This is the name of the list file   }

procedure showlist (d: list);            { Display data   }
 var
  i: integer;
begin
 for i := 1 to n do
  begin
   write(d[i] : 3);                      { Write out 3 digit numbers   }
  end;
end;


procedure Exchange (var left, right: integer;
                                  bit: boolean);
 procedure swap (var l, r: integer);
  var
   temp: integer;
 begin
  temp := l;                             { Swap left and right   }
  left := r;
  right := temp;
 end;

begin
 if bit then                             { Up or down order of exchange?   }
  begin
   if left < right then
    begin                                { Assert down order   }
     swap(left, right)                   { Swap only if out of order   }
    end;
  end
 else if left > right then               { Assert up order   }
  swap(left, right)                      { Swap only if out of order   }
end;

function comp (b: boolean): boolean;
begin                                    { Complement bits: T → F, F → T   }
 if b then
  comp := false
 else
  comp := true;
end;
```

```
function power2 (b: integer): integer;
  var                                    { Compute the bth power of 2    }
   p, i: integer;
  begin
  p := 1;
  for i := 1 to b do
   p := 2 * p;
  power2 := p;
  end;

begin                                    { Start main program here   }
  writeln('Enter file name : ');         { List is taken from file    }
  readln(fname);
  reset(bitfile, fname);
  for i := 1 to n do
   begin
    readln(bitfile, d[i]);
   end;
  showlist(d);                           { Display original list   }
  fn := n;                               { Get around Pascal Limits    }
  flogn := ln(fn) / ln(2.0);             { Convert from natural logs    }
  logn := trunc(flogn);
  flogn := ln(fn / 4) / ln(2.0);         { log(N/4)   }
  logn4 := trunc(flogn);

  for i := 1 to logn do                  { Make logn passes over list    }
   begin
    k := power2(i - 1);                  { k = 2^{i-1}   }
    for t := 1 to k do
     begin
      b[t] := false;                     { Initialize the up/down bit pattern   }
     end;

    for t := (i - 1) to logn4 do         { Compute B pattern    }
     for j := 1 to power2(t) do
      begin                              { Compute up/down bit pattern    }
       b[j + power2(t)] := comp(b[j]);    end;

    for j := i downto 1 do
     begin                               { The exchanging starts here    }
      m := power2(j - 1);                { Number of pairs to exchange    }
      updn := 1;                         { Up/down bit pattern index    }
      p := 1;                            { Offset of pair to exchange    }
      repeat
       for q := 1 to m do                { Exchange up to m pairs    }
        begin
         Exchange(d[p + q - 1], d[p + q - 1 + m], b[updn]);
         updn := updn + 1;
        end;
```

```
    p := p + 2 * m;                        { Offset to next pair   }
  until p >= n;
  showlist(d);                             { Display sorted list    }
  end;
 end;
end.
```

This program uses a Boolean array, $b[1..N/2]$ to store the up/down exchange pattern instead of a bit string. FALSE means the exchange should maintain an ascending order, whereas TRUE setting means the exchange should maintain a descending order between the pair of elements.

Careful study of the loops in the sequential version reveals several independent loops which can be converted into fans. Turning the independent loops into fans speeds up the computation of exchange pattern $b[]$. But most importantly, the inner loop for performing an entire row of exchanges can be converted into one **fan**. Thus, an $O(N)$ loop is converted into an $O(1)$ **fan**.

The parallel equivalent is shown below (we show only the part of the program that has changed). We use the same support functions as before to compute 2^i, logical complement, and list display. The resulting parallel program is modestly different than the serial version, but because the **fan** speeds up the innermost part of the program, the **fan** has a dramatic impact on the overall speedup.

```
for i := 1..logn
{
    k := power2(i – 1);
    fan t := 1..k                          { Initialize b[]   }
    {}
    mapout False to b[t]
    endfan;

    for t := (i – 1)..logn4                 { Compute b[] Pattern }
{        fan j := 1..power2(t)
        mapin b[j] to RHS;
        { int RHS;
        RHS := comp( RHS )}
        mapout RHS to b[j + power2(t)]
        endfan;
    };
    for j := i..1
    {
        m := power2(j – 1);
    fan p := 1, 2*m..N;                      { Array of fans }
            q := 1..m
        mapin d[p + q – 1] to Left;
                d[p + q – 1 + m] to Right;
                b[this] to bit
```

```
    { int Left, Right, bit;
        if bit = False
        then if Left < Right then swap(Left, Right)
        else if Right > Left then swap(Left, Right)
    }
    mapout Left to d[p + q − 1];
             Right to d[p + q − 1 + m]
    endfan;
}
showlist(d);
}
```

The final **fan** in the parallel program maps $b[\text{this}]$ to each parallel process, without regard for which process carries out the exchange. Assuming the processes are numbered **this** $= 1..N / 2$, process **this** performs exchange number **this**.

5.5 KEYWORDS AND CONCEPTS

A **fan** implements a SIMD/SPMD fork/join control flow operation that is needed to perform most data-parallel operations. In addition, we have shown that a **fan** often needs to be constrained (using the **with** clause), and terminated (using the **exit** statement) to carry out real-world data-parallel operations.

We have analyzed the performance of a **fan** and shown that there is an optimum number of duplicate processes that minimizes the elapsed execution time of a fan. The optimum will depend on the communication and process creation overhead, as well as on the grain size of the compute phase.

Finding an optimal number of fan processes is not a solved problem, even though we can give closed-form formulas. The formulas determine how many processes to grain-pack onto each processor. However, once the packing is done, the program graph used to analyze performance is no longer valid, because communication delays have been eliminated and processing times increased for each new grain. The new model can be analyzed, but there is no guarantee that the new model will converge to the desired optimum. This is the min–max problem described earlier.

An interesting point was made by careful analysis of sorting. The sequentially inefficient bitonic sort becomes extremely efficient when run on multiple processors. But, the sequentially efficient quicksort becomes extremely inefficient when run on a parallel processor. This illustrates the importance of good algorithm design, and points out the difficulty encountered when attempting to convert a sequential program into an equivalent parallel program.

The following keywords and concepts summarize the ideas in this chapter:

Bitonic sort   A bitonic sort is a very efficient parallel sorting algorithm because it reduces sorting to a sequence of parallel comparisons. In contrast to a sequential sort algorithm, the number of comparisons is extremely high, but the algorithm is efficient on a parallel system because large numbers of comparisons can be done in parallel.

Finite element   The **fan** is particularly useful for finite element algorithms, where some region is divided into a grid of points and a numerical quantity is calculated at each point. The number of points may be very large, but because they are often arranged in some regular pattern, a **fan** can be used to accelerate the overall computation.

Grain packing   As pointed out, the grain packing problem exists for **fans**. The optimum grain size can be computed by balancing the amount of communication with the degree of parallelism. But, when we change the degree of parallelism, we correspondingly change the communication, and vice verse.

LUD decomposition   The Lower-Upper-Diagonal technique for solving a linear system of equations is well suited to SPMD calculation because of the regularity of matrix data. However, we have assumed a dense matrix, which may not always be true. When the matrix is sparse, is the **fan** the best choice?

Sort, quicksort, and rank sort   Sorting on a parallel machine can be done by parallelizing a sequential sort like quicksort, or reinventing sorting altogether, such as suggested by the rank sort. Quicksort is not very parallelizable, but rank sort and bitonic sort are. Therefore, to get the most out of a parallel machine, it may be necessary to completely redesign the algorithms used by the application program.

Successive overrelaxation   The wave equation can be solved using an iterative technique and relaxation. Relaxation techniques are used to estimate the solution to an equation, and then improve the estimate through iterative refinement. Such direct techniques require enormous computational power. The **fan** is often used because of the regular structure of the application's data.

PROBLEMS

1   Derive the formulas for optimal k in the **fan** construction. Draw a graph of speedup versus k for the parameters given in Example 5.2.

2   What happens to fan speedup when k is twice its optimal value? One-half of its optimal value?

3   Draw a graph of speedup versus k using the formula derived in Section 5.2:

$$\text{Speedup} = \frac{r_0 + r_1 F(S)}{(r_0 + r_1 + w_0 + w_1) + r_1 F(S / k) + (k - 1)(w_0 + w_1 S / k)}$$

What value of k yields the greatest speedup?

4   Check the flow-correctness of the following parallel program. Two **fans** execute in parallel, that is, fan1 and fan2 both execute in the time interval [1..2]. In addition, fan1 inputs $x[1..4]$ and outputs $x[1..2]$; fan2 inputs the same $x[1..4]$, but outputs $x[2..3]$. Identify all flow-correctness problems.

5   Modify the Gaussian elimination program to handle partial pivoting and row interchange. Modify the serial version first, then the parallel version. How do you know your parallel version is correct?

6   Write a fan statement to solve $Ux = b$, assuming U is an upper triangular matrix. Your fan will perform the missing back substitution step in $Ax = b$ described in Section 5.4.1.

7   Show that the constrained fan of the SOR application is flow-correct. Enumerate all USE–DEF patterns.

8   What is the performance of the SOR example? What is the optimum number of processes?

9   Recompute the optimum k for the search **fan** when $r_0 = 200$, $r_1 = 20$, $w_0 = 50$, $r_1 = 0.001$, and $N = 100$. Compare your answer with the results given in this chapter.

10   Give a fan algorithm for searching an ordered list of integers using duplicate binary search routines.

11   Give an alternative solution to the SOR problem. *Hint*: use the even-odd method outlined in the text.

12   Show that the modified fan for rank sorting is flow-correct. That is, show that rank is distinct even when the list contains duplicates.

13   For what size of lists does the value of N in rank sort cause the target machine to spend more time on communication that computation, assuming the target machine parameters used throughout this chapter?

14   Derive the complexity formula for the number of communication steps needed to perform the bitonic sort in parallel.

15   Derive the algorithm for exchange patterns $B[1..N/2]$ in the bitonic sort. Consider the following example for $N = 16$:

In phase $i = 1$: $b[1] = 0$; $t = 1..1$
   $t = 1..1$; $b[t + 1] = \text{comp}(b[t])$
   $t = 1..2$; $b[t + 2] = \text{comp}(b[t])$
   $t = 1..4$; $b[t + 4] = \text{comp}(b[t])$

In phase $i = 2$: $b[1] = 0$; $t = 1..2$
   $t = 1..2$; $b[t + 2] = \text{comp}(b[t])$
   $t = 1..4$; $b[t + 4] = \text{comp}(b[t])$

In phase $i = 3$: $b[t] = 0$; $t = 1..4$
   $t = 1..4$; $b[t + 4] = \text{comp}(b[t])$

CHAPTER 6

The Reduction Tree

Many algorithms in computer science lend themselves to classic divide-and-conquer solutions. That is, an $O(N)$ problem can be solved in $O(\log_2 N)$ time by subdividing a large problem into smaller problems and applying a *base function* to each subproblem. When we adapt this strategy to parallel processing, the result is a tree of processes which is useful for parallel *reduction*. Reduction operators apply an operation to many data values to obtain a single returned value. Therefore, reduction is a special–purpose data-parallel operation.

In this chapter we will study the flow-correctness and performance properties of the **tree** construct which implements reduction using parallel processors. The **tree** construct achieves data-parallel reduction on partitioned data by repeatedly invoking identical tasks over a binary tree of processes. The body of the **tree** construct is executed $\log_2 N$ times, each step repeatedly invoking the body of the **tree** with modified values obtained from the previous phase. This construct has the following features:

- The reduction operation must be amenable to recursion.
- The input data is destroyed by the reduction.
- The tree of processes is binary.

We will show, mostly by example, how the **tree** construct is implemented on a parallel computer. Applications in statistics, searching and matching, and other basic data processing functions will be illustrated to show that trees are a necessary fundamental construct.

6.1 DIVIDE-AND-CONQUER PARALLELISM

Many divide-and-conquer algorithms lend themselves to parallel execution even though divide-and-conquer is intrinsically a serial process. In *divide-and-conquer*, a problem is solved by dividing it into two subproblems, and then (recursively) solving each subproblem. That is, the subproblems are solved in turn by divide-and-conquer. This process of divide followed by subsequent divide-and-conquer is repeated until some *basic* problem-solving algorithm can be used to solve the *base problem*. Basic solutions are passed back up the chain of recursively called problem solvers, until the original problem level is reached.

A divide-and-conquer algorithm consists of a *base function* for solving the basic problem, and a policy for dividing problems into subproblems. This is where parallelism comes in. Duplicate copies of the base function can be applied in parallel at each stage of the process. Instead of iteratively calling the base function as in a sequential computer, we can run parallel duplicates of the base function, thus gaining speed. This has the effect of changing an $O(N)$ time-complex problem into an $O(\log_2 N)$ time-complex problem. Unfortunately, we cannot reduce time complexity further using N processes because of the sequential nature of divide-and-conquer. Yet, converting an $O(N)$ problem into an $O(\log_2 N)$ problem can lead to significant performance for large N.

Typical algorithms which lend themselves to divide-and-conquer are *reduction operations* such as summation, maximum, minimum, inner product of vectors, π-product, and certain kinds of searches and sorts. All forms of reduction apply to N values stored as a vector or as a list of N values. Reduction earns its name from the fact that it collapses N values into a single value. For example, summation takes N numbers and returns a single sum as a result of *addition reduction*. A maximum reduction operation takes N numbers as arguments, and returns a single number.

To optimize the parallelism, the calculations of a reduction operation are organized as a tree; hence we call this the tree *construct*. The general form of a tree is given below.

tree <counter>
mapin <mapping>
{ <base-function> }
mapout <mapping>
endtree

The tree distributes data to all processes enumerated by the counter, much as in a **fan**. In fact, the program graph of a tree looks like a **fan** with a feedback loop, as shown in Figure 6.1. Each parallel step of the **tree** is called a *phase*. Therefore, a **tree** is a sequence of fan-like phases, organized into a binary tree. Early phases use twice as many parallel processes as subsequent phases.

A **fan** of base functions performs one phase of a tree. The result of a phase is a partial reduction value, e.g., a partial sum, or a current maximum. The reduction value is aggregated by the **mapout** clause, and then the next phase is begun. On the final phase, the result is the total reduction over all data.

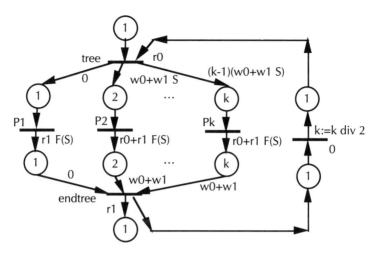

Figure 6.1   Program graph of tree construct

To obtain the binary tree shape, the upper bound on the counter is cut in half prior to each new phase. The tree of parallel processes is once again performed; data is distributed to all processes according to the **mapin** clause; the base function is performed in parallel; and the partial reduction is distributed back through the **mapout** clause. This sequence of halving the upper bound on counter, broadcasting followed by parallel execution of the base function, and aggregation of the result, is repeated until no more halving of the upper-bound is possible. That is, the *broadcast-compute-aggregate* cycle is applied $\log_2 N$ times.

The **tree** appears very similar to the **fan** construct, but **trees** carry out their computations in $\log_2 N$ *sequential* steps, each consisting of a broadcast-compute-aggregate cycle, while **fans** carry out their calculations in one parallel step. **Fans** attempt to convert $O(N)$ time algorithms into $O(1)$ algorithms; whereas **trees** attempt to convert $O(N)$ time algorithms into $O(\log_2 N)$ algorithms. (Note that the distribution of data at the start of each phase is performed sequentially, as in the **fan**. The time to complete a phase is greatly influenced by this assumption.)

In addition, **trees** destructively use their broadcast data, because each phase passes its result on to the next phase through the broadcast data. This means that a **tree** creates a USE–DEF pattern followed by a DEF–USE pattern between phases. We must check each **tree** construct for possible flow- and antidependency errors.

Finally, **trees** must process vectors and arrays containing exactly 2^k elements, where $k > 0$. If the vector or array mapped into a tree does not contain 2^k elements, it must be padded to round out its length to a power of 2. We will illustrate this padding in the examples which follow.

Example 6.1

The semantics of the **tree** are best illustrated by a parallel algorithm to compute the maximum element of vector $a[1..N]$. This algorithm uses $N/2$ processes, each of which compute a pairwise maximum, then passes its reduced value on to the next level in the **tree** which once again computes the maximum of two values, etc., until the final maximum value is found in $O(\log_2 N)$ steps (see Figure 6.2).

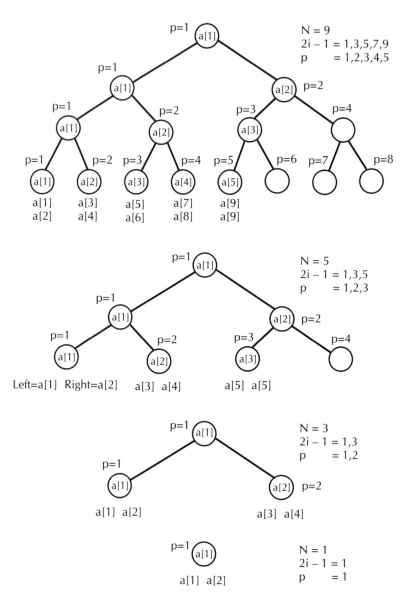

Figure 6.2   Tree execution phases for maximum example, N = 9

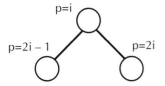

Figure 6.3   **Mapping of task *i* to process *p* in the tree construct**

We want to compute

$$\overset{N}{\underset{i=1}{\mathbf{M}}} x_i$$

where we have abbreviated the maximum reduction operator as

$$\overset{N}{\underset{i=1}{\mathbf{M}}}$$

with arguments $x[1..N]$. That is, we want to reduce N arguments to one maximum value. The construct for the execution pattern shown in Figure 6.2 is:

```
tree i := 1,2..top(N / 2)                           /* Top = greatest integer of N / 2  */
mapin a[2*i – 1] to Left;
      if i < top(N / 2) then a[2*i] to Right        /* Padding  */
                        else a[2*i – 1] to Right;
{                                                    /* Base Function  */
      int Left, Right ;
      if Left < Right then Left := Right
}
mapout Left to a[i]                                  /* Destroy half of a[1..N / 2]  */
endtree;
maxi := a[1];                                        /* The answer  */
```

Figure 6.3 shows how to map the binary tree of tasks onto a linear array of processes. At each assignment, the left subtree of process i is $2i - 1$, and the right subtree is $2i$. Thus in Figure 6.2, process 1 performs all tasks associated with task 1. This correspondence is general; later we will show how to do the correspondence for multiple index counters.

This **tree** repeats the following steps until only one process remains:

1   Duplicate the base function in all leaf nodes as per Figure 6.2.

2   Distribute the data to all leaf nodes of the tree, as shown in Figure 6.2.

3   In parallel, compute the pairwise maximums in $N / 2$ parallel processes.

4   Collect the results, as per the mapout correspondence.

5   Cut the number of processes by one-half.

This iteration stops as soon as the final process completes its calculation, as shown in Figure 6.2. Each phase processes half as many data as the previous one.

In Figure 6.2 we have marked the tree node with a process number, p, to show the assignment of a process to a base function. The interior of each node is labelled with the returned element, showing how the tree destructively changes its input data. Thus, $a[1]$, $a[2]$, ..., $a[N/4]$ are changed by the first phase; $a[1]$, ..., $a[N/8]$, are changed by the next phase; and so on, until the final result is computed and stored in $a[1]$, only.

$Log_2 9 \approx 4$ sequential phases are needed. The first phase distributes to $top(9/2) = 5$ processes (the function top gives the smallest integer that is greater than or equal to $N/2$); the second, to $top(5/2) = 3$ processes; the third, to $top(3/2) = 2$ processes; and finally the fourth phase, to $top(2/2) = 1$ process. But, each phase does k parallel base functions in parallel.

6.1.1 Flow-Correctness of Tree

The flow-correctness of **tree** follows from the fact that each phase of the reduction is performed at one level of a **tree** of processes. That is, the **tree** calculation proceeds level–by–level until the root is reached. There are $\log_2 N$ levels, hence the **tree** takes $\log_2 N$ sequential time steps to complete.

Second, the **tree** destroys half of its input data at each level. Thus, the sequential nature of level-by-level processing, combined with destructive writes over its input data, leads to USE–DEF patterns followed by DEF–USE patterns that must be checked with the ANTI and FLOW predicates.

Example 6.2

The preconditions and postconditions for the maximum **tree** of the previous example are:

PRE(a) = ($\forall$ i = 1,2..N) (USE(a[i], t $-$ Δt))
POST(a) = ($\forall$ i = 1,2,N) (DEF(a[i], t))

Because of the destructiveness of **tree**, we must be sure that the modifications on the elements of $a[1..N]$ are flow-correct within the **tree**. That is, how do we know that successive iterations (phases) do not violate an antidependency as we march up the **tree**?

ANTI(a[2i $-$ 1], t) :-
    ($\exists$ Δt > 0 | USE(a[2i $-$ 1], t $-$ Δt)),
    DEF(a[i], t).

ANTI(a[2i], t) :-
    ($\exists$ Δt > 0 | USE(a[2i], t $-$ Δt)),
    DEF(a[i], t).

Given i = 1, 2, ..., top($N/2$), the ANTI property follows because $2i - 1 \neq i$, and $2i \neq i$ are guaranteed. Similar arguments can be made for FLOW.

The following, more comprehensive proof shows the flow-correctness of the parallel maximum algorithm without loss of generality. We set out to show:

$$a[1] = \overset{N}{\underset{i=1}{\mathbf{M}}} a[i]$$

where we have abbreviated the maximum as M. In addition, let k denote the kth phase (level) of the calculation. Thus, $a^k[i]$ is the resulting value of $a[i]$ after phase k. We will ignore the endcondition handled by the **if** statement in **mapin**, to simplify the proof.

Finally, we use

$$\bigcup_{i=1}^{N} \{\ldots\}$$

to enumerate the elements of a set, using index i.

Thus, in the first phase, when $k = 1$ the precondition on the **tree** is given as the pairwise maximum of adjacent elements of $a[1..N]$:

$$\bigcup_{i=1}^{N/2} \{a^1[i] = \max(a[2i-1], a[2i])\}$$

Again, we have simplified top($N/2$) by using the form $N/2$. Throughout the following, we assume $N/2$ means top($N/2$) and that the **mapin** function duplicates the final array element as shown in Figure 6.2.

In general, we can define a tree *invariant* given by the kth phase expression as follows:

$$P_k = \bigcup_{i=1}^{N/2^k} \{a^k[i] = \max(a^{k-1}[2i-1], a^{k-1}[2i])\}$$

That is, P_k is a set of maximum values obtained by computing the pairwise maximum of even-odd pairs. At level k, a^k is the value of the list.

Assuming P_k is correct, we show that

$$P_{k+1} = \underset{R}{M} P_k$$

which is the inductive step needed to prove the postcondition, P_k & ($k \leq$ top($\log_2 N$)). The proof depends on noting that the maximum of maxima is also a maximum.

$$P_{k+1} = \underset{R}{M} P_k$$

$$= M\{\bigcup_{i=1}^{N/2^k} \{a^k[i] = \max(a^{k-1}[2i-1], a^{k-1}[2i])\}\}$$

$$= M\{\bigcup_{i=1}^{N/2^{k+1}} \{a^k[2i-1] = \ldots a^k[2i] = \ldots\}\}$$

$$= \mathbf{M}\{ \bigcup_{i=1}^{N/2^{k+1}} \{ a^{k+1}[i] = \dots \} \}$$

$$= P_{k+1}$$

Then, the postcondition is simply

$$P_{\log N} = \{ a^{\log N}[1] = \mathbf{M}\{ a^{(\log N)-1}[1], a^{(\log N)-1}[2] \} \}$$

where we have used $\log N$ as a simplification of top($\log N$). The induction says that

$$a^{(\log N)-1}[1] = \mathbf{M}_{i=1}^{N} a[i]$$

which is the desired result. But, how do we know that all phases of the calculation are flow-correct? We can use a similar argument on DEF to show that the ANTI predicate holds true throughout the iteration, because DEF(DEF(DEF(...))) is also DEF.

Intuitively, ANTI is TRUE as long as **mapin** and **mapout** occur within levels as shown in this example. That is, all parallel updates occur within the same level of the **tree**, and the phases do not advance up the **tree** until the current level has completed all parallel updates.

As a further argument for why the maximum example is a general proof of **tree** flow-correctness, we return to the problem of summation computed by a **fan** versus a **tree**. The **fan** solution produces a result in $O(N)$ steps, while the following **tree** produces a result in $O(\log_2 N)$ steps, assuming ideal conditions of no communication overhead, no delays due to task initialization, etc. But, is the **tree** version flow-correct?

Example 6.3

Consider the following **tree** for computing summation of the elements of vector $x[1..N]$ using N processes to compute the sum in $O(\log_2 N)$ steps instead of $O(N)$ steps as shown in Chapter 5. Here, $i := 1, 3, \dots, N$ means to generate $i = 1, 3, 5, \dots, N$ in steps of 2.

```
tree i := 1,3..N                          /* Odd enumeration   */
  mapin x[i] to First;
      if i < N then x[i + 1] to Last
              else 0 to Last
  {
      float First, Last,Sum;
      Sum := First + Last
  }
  mapout  Sum to x[(i + 1) div 2]
  endtree
```

This solution uses $top(N/2)$ processes to sum N elements of $x[1..N]$. Thus, for $N = 6$, the $k = 1$ phase uses 3 processes ($p = 1$, $p = 2$, $p = 3$) to sum $x[1] + x[2]$, $x[3] + x[4]$, and $x[5] + x[6]$ in parallel. Then, the $k = 2$ phase uses 2 processes ($p = 1$, $p = 2$) to sum $x[1] + x[2]$ and $x[3] + 0$. Finally, the $k = 3$ phase sums $x[1] + x[2]$ to obtain the total.

Once again, the proof of summation depends on the fact that the sum of sums is itself a sum. The **tree** invariant for this example is:

$$P_k = \bigcup_{i=1}^{N/2^k} \{x^k[i] = x^{k-1}[2i-1] + x^{k-1}[2i]\}$$

By induction, it can be shown that

$$P_{\log N} = \sum_{i=1}^{N} x[i]$$

Example 6.3 looks very much like the previous one. The proof by induction is based on the same assumptions. The only difference is the change in base function, from maximum to addition. In general, the proof will always depend on the recursive nature of the base function, i.e., $OP(OP(...))$.

6.1.2 Mapping an Array of Processes onto a Tree

To show how general the correspondence of Figure 6.3 is, we map a 2-D matrix onto N^2 processes by linearizing the two dimensions in the next example.

Example 6.4

To find the maximum of an array of error bounds $err[1..N,1..N]$, cut the y-dimension by half in each phase, and cut the sum of the x- and y-dimensions by half:

```
tree i := 1,2..N;
     j := 1,3..N
mapin err[i, j] to Left;
       if j < N then err[i, j + 1] to Right
                else err[i, j] to Right
{      float Left, Right ;
       if Left < Right then Left := Right
}
mapout Left to err[i, (j + 1) div 2]
endtree
```

The correspondence between the array of basic functions and the binary tree of processes is left as an exercise for the reader. This correspondence will look similar to that of Figure 6.2.

Also, note the **mapout** clause. After each phase, half of the input err elements are modified and used by the subsequent phase. The maximum value appears in $err[1, 1]$ after seven phases.

For example, when $N = 10$, top($\log_2 100$) is 7, and the halving at each phase goes like this:

Phase	Index i	Index j
$k = 1$	$i = 1, 2, ..., 10$	$j = 1, 3, ..., 10$
$k = 2$	$i = 1, 2, ..., 8$	$j = 1, 3, ..., 5$
$k = 3$	$i = 1, 2, ..., 7$	$j = 1, 3$
$k = 4$	$i = 1, 2, ..., 5$	$j = 1$
$k = 5$	$i = 1, 2, 3$	$j = 1$
$k = 6$	$i = 1, 2$	$j = 1$
$k = 7$	$i = 1$	$j = 1$

6.1.3 Performance of Tree

Given that the program graph of a **tree** is similar to the graph of a **fan**, we note that the time to execute the critical path of a **tree** is the same as the time to execute one iteration of the **tree** graph, see Figure 6.1. Keep in mind that we have assumed message-passing is sequential, and that the data distribution at the onset of each phase is performed sequentially:

$$T_k = (r_0 + r_1 + w_0 + w_1) + r_1 F(S) + (k - 1)(w_0 + w_1 S)$$

where $k = (N/2), (N/4), ..., (1)$. (This is a sum of $\log_2 N$ terms.) Thus, the total time to perform $\log_2 N$ iterations is:

$$T = \sum_{k = N/2}^{1} T_k = \sum_{k = N/2}^{1} (r_0 + r_1 + w_0 + w_1) + r_1 F(S) + (k - 1)(w_0 + w_1 S)$$

$$= (r_0 + r_1 + w_0 + w_1)\log_2 N + \sum_{k = N/2}^{1} \{r_1 F(S) + (k - 1)(w_0 + w_1 S)\}$$

In most cases, we can assume $F(S) = S \approx$ constant,

$$\sum_{k = N/2}^{1} r_1 F(S) \approx r_1 S$$

and furthermore, that

$$\sum_{k = N/2}^{1} (k - 1) \approx 1 - \log_2 N$$

Thus,

$$T = (r_0 + r_1 + w_0 + w_1)\log_2 N + r_1 S + (1 - \log_2 N)(w_0 + w_1 S)$$

$$= (r_0 + r_1 + (1 - S)w_1)\log_2 N + (w_0 + (r_1 + w_1)S)$$

Finally, if we use the same parameters as before (see Chapter 5):

$w_0 = 10$ ms
$w_1 = 0.001$ ms/character
$r_0 = 100$ ms
$r_1 = 10$ ms/operation

And, if we use $S \approx 1$, then

$$T \approx 20 + 110 \log_2 N$$

This is $O(\log_2 N)$, as expected. Furthermore, there is no optimization of k (number of processes), because the shape of a **tree** is totally dictated by its input data.

Under all of the assumptions made here, speedup is $O(N / \log_2 N)$ because

$$T_1 = r_0 + r_1 F(S) \approx r_0 + r_1 N \approx 100 + 10N$$

Thus, the **tree** converts an $O(N)$ sequential process into $N/2$ processes that execute in $O(\log_2 N)$ time. This happens because each phase is done in $O(1)$ time instead of $O(N)$ time. The sequential version of each phase would take $O(N)$ time, regardless of the phase.

6.2 APPLICATIONS OF TREES

There are many applications of reduction to the fundamental algorithms of parallel programming. We will study only a cross section in the remainder of this chapter. First, we will illustrate elementary algorithms such as sum, max, and min. Later, we will use these elementary algorithms as building blocks in other example applications.

6.2.1 Fundamental Algorithms

Trees are used to implement the most fundamental operations of maximum, minimum, and products. We will give **tree** algorithms for each of these, assuming the data are stored in a vector of simple integers as $x[1..N]$.

Sums

Summation can be expressed as a recursive function by noting that $a + b + c + d$ equals $(a + b) + (c + d)$, which means that $(a + b)$ can be computed at the same time as $(c + d)$, and then the intermediate sums added to obtain the grand total.

We want to compute

$$\sum_{i=1}^{N} x_i$$

The **tree** for this is

```
tree i := 1,2..top(N / 2)
mapin x[2*i – 1] to Left;
    if i < top(N / 2) then x[2*i] to Right          /* Padding */
                      else 0 to Right;
{    int Left, Right ;
    Left := Right + Left }
mapout  Left to x[i]
endtree;
```

For example, if $N = 4$, and $x = [1, 2, 3, 4]$, then $i = 1, 2$, and so 1 and 2 are added in process 1, and 3 and 4 are added in process 2. The subtotals, (3 and 7) replace $x[1]$ and $x[2]$, and the basic functions are performed again on $x[1..2]$. The grand total of 10 is stored in $x[1]$.

Note that the summation **tree** and the max/min **tree** are identical except for the base function. **Trees** that operate on vectors almost always differ only in their base functions. The same holds for 2-D and 3-D arrays.

Products

Consider the problem of computing the π-product of elements of vector x. We want to compute the product:

$$\prod_{i=1}^{N} x_i = x_1, x_2, ..., x_N$$

```
tree i := 1,2..top(N / 2)
mapin x[2*i – 1] to Left;
    if i < top(N / 2) then x[2*i] to Right          /* Padding */
                      else 1 to Right;
{    int Left, Right ;
    Left := Right * Left }
mapout Left to x[i]
endtree;
```

Once again, the code is identical to the max and sum **trees**, except for the base function, and padding in the **mapin** functions.

One variation on the monotonous **tree** construction occurs when we change the input data. Consider the problem of an inner product of vectors $x[1..N]$ and $y[1..N]$.

Inner Product

We want to compute

$$\sum_{i=1}^{N} x_i y_i$$

First, we use a **fan** to obtain the products, then we use a **tree** to compute the summation:

```
fan i := 1,2..N;
mapin  x[i] to Left;
        y[i] to Right
{ float Left, Right;
   Left := Left * Right}
mapout Left to z[i];
endfan;

tree i := 1,2..top(N / 2)
mapin z[2*i – 1] to Left;
      if i < top(N / 2) then z[2*i] to Right          /* Padding */
                        else 0 to Right;
{      int Left, Right ;
      Left := Right + Left }
mapout Left to z[i]
endtree;
```

Can the **fan** be eliminated? This is left as an exercise for the reader.

Sum of Squares

Can we compute a sum of squares using a **tree**?

$$\sum_{i=1}^{N} x_i^2$$

```
tree i := 1,2..top(N / 2)
mapin x[2*i – 1]^2 to Left;                    /* Square Inputs*/
      if i < top(N / 2) then x[2*i]^2 to Right
                        else 0 to Right;
{ int Left, Right ;
      Left := Right + Left}
mapout  Left to x[i]
endtree;
```

Explain what is wrong with this **tree**.

6.2.2 Parallel Statistics

In this section, we will use the fundamental algorithms to perform calculations frequently encountered in data reduction applications such as statistics. We will use the summation **tree** to compute averages and variances, and then show how a simple modification of the base function yields a geometric average.

Average and Variance

Consider the problem of computing the average and standard deviation of large sets of data, stored in the vector $x[1..N]$. The formulas we need are, respectively:

$$\mu = \frac{1}{N} \sum_{i=1}^{N} x_i$$

$$\sigma^2 = \frac{1}{N} \sum_{i=1}^{N} x_i^2 - \mu^2$$

The destructive nature of the **tree** construct dictates that we make copies of x:

```
fan i := 1,2..N                        /* Make copies of x   */
mapin x[i] to Copy
{ float Copy }                         /* Do nothing   */
mapout  Copy to y[i];
            Copy^2 to z[i]
endfan;
```

Then, the **tree** expressions for these computations are

```
tree i := 1,2..top(N / 2)              /* Average summation   */
mapin y[2*i – 1] to Left;
      if i < top(N / 2) then y[2*i] to Right   /* Padding */
                     else 0 to Right;
{     int Left, Right ;
      Left := Right + Left}
mapout Left to y[i]                    /* Destroy half of y[1..N/2]   */
endtree;
```

```
mu := y[1] / N;                        /* μ   */
```

```
tree i := 1,2..top(N / 2)              /* Sigma summation   */
mapin z[2*i – 1] to Left;
      if i < top(N / 2) then z[2*i] to Right   /* Padding */
                     else 0 to Right;
{     int Left, Right ;
      Left := Right + Left}
mapout Left to z[i]                    /* Destroy half of z[1..N/2]   */
endtree;
```

```
sigma := z[1] / N – mu^2;              /* σ²   */
```

This algorithm can be easily modified to compute the *geometric mean*.

Geometric Mean

Compute the geometric mean of data points $x[1..N]$, given a weighting function $w[1..N]$, as the Nth root of the π-product of the weighted points:

$$\text{gm} = \sqrt[N]{\prod_{i=1}^{N} x_i^{w_i}}$$

```
fan i := 1,2..N;                        /* Compute z[i] = x[i]^w[i]   */
mapin  x[i] to Left;
       w[i] to Right
{ float Left, Right;
  Left := Left ^ Right}
mapout Left to z[i];
endfan;


tree i := 1,2..top(N / 2)               /* Products */
mapin z[2*i − 1] to Left;
    if i < top(N / 2) then z[2*i] to Right   /* Padding */
                      else 1 to Right;
{      int Left, Right ;
     Left := Right * Left }
mapout Left to z[i]
endtree;


gm := root(z[1], N);                    /* Nth root of product   */
```

The following application to statistics is more interesting. It is related to the sorting algorithm implemented as a **fan** in Chapter 5.

Median

Compute the median of a vector $x[1..N]$. Recall that the median value, m, is the element of x such that m is greater than or equal to one-half of the other elements. Thus, the median of the list with duplicates x = [8, 3, 6, 5, 3, 3, 7, 2] is the third 3. To see this, we could sort the list into ascending order: [2, 3, 3, 3, 5, 6, 7, 8] and then pick the one nearest to $N/2 = 4$.

The sort idea is good, but may be overkill for this reduction operation. Rather, we can use a modification of the ranking **fan** of Chapter 5, followed by a **tree** to find the location of the element with the minimum difference between $N/2$ and the rank of each element.

The solution uses an array, Rank[1..N, 1..2], to hold the absolute value of $(N/2)$ in Rank[1..N, 1], and the index of the original element in Rank[1..N, 2]. We must find i such that Rank[i, 1] is minimal, and return Rank[i, 2] as the location of the original list element corresponding to Rank[i, 1].

The following algorithm uses a **fan** to compute the ranks in $O(N)$ time, and a **tree** to compute the minimum rank in $O(\log_2 N)$ time. Thus, this is an $O(N)$ time parallel algorithm that uses N processes.

```
fan j := 1,2..N                                /* Compute rank array    */
mapin x to List;                               /* Copy entire list   */
     x[j] to Key;                              /* Find the rank of this one    */
     j to Index                                /* Could also have used this    */
{    int List[1..N], Key, Index, R;
     R := 0;
     for(i := 1; i ≤ N; i++){
          if List[i] < key then R += 1;
          if (List[i] = Key) & (i ≤ Index) then R += 1}}
mapout abs(N div 2 - R) to Rank[j,1]        /* Find the mid point    */
endfan;

tree i := 1,2..top(N / 2)                       /* Find minimum    */
mapin Rank[2*i − 1, 1] to Left; 2*i − 1 to LeftLoc;
     if i < top(N / 2) then { Rank[2*i, 1] to Right;
                                   2*i to RightLoc}
                     else { Rank[2*i-1,1] to Right;
                                   2*i − 1 to RightLoc}
{    int Left, Right, LeftLoc, RightLoc ;
     if Right < Left then { Left := Right ; LeftLoc := RightLoc }
}
mapout Left to Rank[i, 1];                     /* Min value    */
     LeftLoc to Rank[i, 2]                      /* Location of min value    */
endtree;

median := x[Rank[1, 2]];                       /* The answer    */
```

For example, using the list with duplicates given earlier:

$N/2 = 4$
Original list   8, 3, 6, 5, 3, 3, 7, 2
Rank (before tree)   4, 2, 2, 1, 1, 0, 3, 3   = Rank[j, 1]
                       ?, ?, ?, ?, ?, ?, ?, ?   = Rank[j, 2]
Rank (after tree)   0, 0, 0, 3, 1, 0, 3, 3   = Rank[i, 1]
                       6, 6, 6, 7, 5, 6, 7, 8   = Rank[i, 2]
Median = $x[6]$ 3

6.2.3 String Searching with a Tree

As a final example of the power and diversity of **trees**, we consider a *string matching* problem. String matching has obvious applications in text retrieval and bibliographical searching. In addition, string matching is important in genome research because human DNA contains millions of patterns of amino acids, and to fully understand it, we must be able to match patterns. Such patterns are similar to strings of characters in text. Because of the millions of patterns, string matching appears to be a good application for parallel computers.

The string matching problem can be made more interesting and challenging by seeking the closest or *best match* between a long string and some smaller substring. The smaller substring is called the *key*, and the goal is to find the location within the longer string of the pattern nearest or most similar to the key.

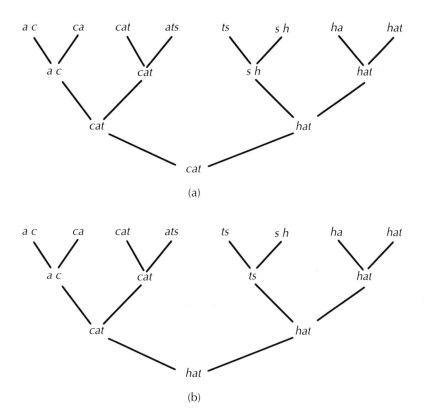

(a)

(b)

Figure 6.4   Binary search tree of string matching algorithm

Example 6.5

Find the best match between a key and the search string $s[1..10] = a\ cats\ hat$. The binary search tree of Figure 6.4 shows how the search string is partitioned into substrings, each of which must be compared with the key. In Figure 6.4a, we find an exact match for key = cat, but Figure 6.4b shows the result of a best match for key = mat.

The definition of *close* is left up to the reader. One metric might be to convert the substrings into a number by counting letter a as 1, b as 2, and so forth up to z as 26. Then a substring can be thought of as a radix 27 number (where a blank is 0). For example, cat is converted into a long integer: $3 \times 27^2 + 1 \times 27 + 20 = 2234$, $a\ c$ is $1 \times 27^2 + 0 \times 27 + 3 = 732$, and ca is 82. So, the closest match between cat and $a\ c$ versus ca is obtained by comparing 2234 against 732 and 82. The smallest difference is between 2234 and 732, so we take $a\ c$ as the best match (see Figure 6.4).

In the following algorithm, we use the function *distance* to compute a metric of closeness. This function must be provided by the programmer. We do not show its implementation, here. Clearly, a parallel **tree** is a most likely candidate for implementing the search illustrated in Figure 6.4.

The length of the key is assumed to be L; the search string is stored in vector $s[1..N]$, one character per element; and the distance function is provided outside of this algorithm. We use a working storage matrix $x[1..N, 1..L]$ to hold the substrings during the **tree** search.

First, we distribute the substrings to array $x[1..N, 1..L]$; see the top row of substrings in Figure 6.4 for an example. Each substring of length L is copied to a row of matrix x. The substrings overlap one another; hence there are $(N - L + 1)$ of them.

```
fan i :=1..(N – L + 1)
mapin s[i..i + L – 1] to Left;          /* Substrings    */
{ string Left[1..L]}                     /* Distribute, only   */
mapout Left to x[i, 1..L]                /* Vector of strings   */
endfan;
```

Now, we are ready to reduce the search to the best match according to a minimum distance metric:

```
k := (N – L + 1);
tree i := 1,2..top(k / 2)                /* Find minimum    */
mapin x[2*i – 1, 1..L] to Left;
    if i < top(k/2) then x[2*i, 1..L] to Right
                    else x[2*i – 1, 1..L] to Right;
    key to key;
{   int a,b;
    string key[1..L], Left[1..L], Right[1..L] ;
    distance(Left, key, a);              /* Send Left, key; return a   */
    distance(Right, key, b);             /* Send Right, key; return b   */
    if a > b then Left := Right
}
mapout Left to x[i, 1..L];               /* Min value    */
endtree;
```

The string matching algorithm uses a **fan** followed by a **tree**. What is its performance?

6.3 KEYWORDS AND CONCEPTS

In this chapter we have studied the flow-correctness and performance properties of the **tree** construct for performing the well-known reduction operations. The **tree** achieves data-parallel reduction by repeatedly invoking identical tasks over a binary tree of processes. The body of the **tree** construct is executed $\log_2 N$ times, each step repeatedly invoking the body of the **tree** with modified values obtained from the previous phase.

This construct has the following features:

- The reduction operation must be amenable to recursion.
- The input data is destroyed by the reduction.
- The tree of processes is binary.

The following keywords and concepts summarize the ideas in this chapter:

Addition reduction   The most common form of reduction is addition reduction, i.e., summation. The addition operator is distributed throughout a list of numbers, and when all additions are performed at once, a sum is obtained. When addition reduction is used in a **tree**, we must be very careful to distribute the data properly so as to include each number only once.

Base problem   The **tree** defines a distribution pattern, and a base procedure which solves some base problem. For example, in addition reduction, the base procedure is simple addition. This base procedure is repeated by each process, in parallel, and at every level in the **tree**. The final step in the reduction is to perform the base procedure at the single root process.

Best match   The best match problem has many applications. It is the problem of finding the best or closest match between a short string and a long string. The short string is compared with all possible substrings of the same length within the larger string. This problem seems to be inherently sequential, but a **tree** can be used to find the closest match by reduction.

Divide-and-conquer   Most reductions are essentially divide-and-conquer algorithms. Each level of the **tree** corresponds to the levels of divide-and-conquer. Yet, the **tree** is a regular data-parallel construct, which means it is limited to a restricted class of divide-and-conquer algorithms, i.e., pure recursive ones. A more general divide-and-conquer mechanism (the remote procedure call mechanism in the client-server model) is needed.

Tree invariant   To prove that a **tree** is flow-correct, we must find a **tree** invariant which remains TRUE as we pass from one level of the **tree** to another. Once we have found the invariant, the **tree** is flow-correct, because each level is flow-correct.

PROBLEMS

1   Draw the correspondence between processes in the **tree** for finding the maximum element of array err[1..N, 1..N] and the linear array of processes numbered 1..$N^2/2$. Your diagram should look similar to Figure 6.2.

2   Is it possible to compute

$$\sum_{i=1}^{N} x_i y_i$$

using a **tree**, only? If so, give your solution.

3   Write a parallel algorithm to compute the minimum element of vector $x[1..N]$.

4   What is the speedup of the algorithm for computing μ and σ^2?

5   Show that the string-matching algorithm is flow-correct. What dependencies need to be checked?

6   What is the performance of the string-matching algorithm?

7   Can the median value algorithm be improved? How so?

8   Design and write a parallel algorithm for computing the error value:

$$\text{error} = \sqrt{\frac{1}{N} \sum_{i=1}^{N} \frac{(x_i - \mu)^2}{x_i}}$$

9   Design and write a parallel algorithm for finding the best match between a misspelled last name and a list of last names. For example, *Smith* may be spelled *Smith*, *Smyth*, or *Smithe*. Give your assumptions concerning how the names are stored.

10   Give a **tree** expression for finding the largest element of a 3-D matrix, $e[1..N, 1..N, 1..N]$. What is the mapping of data for each phase?

11   For what class of recursive functions does a **tree** work? Does a **tree** work for doubly recursive functions such as SORT(SORT(), SORT())? Does it always work for singly recursive functions such as MAX(MAX())?

12   A parallel-computable function is one that runs N times faster on N processors. Is **tree** a parallel-computable function? Give an example.

13   Can you think of an application that would require early termination of a **tree**? What does it mean to **exit** from a **tree**?

CHAPTER 7

The Independent-Loop Par

The independent parallel loop is the best kind of loop as far as parallel execution is concerned, because it assumes there is no flow dependency among the statements of the loop. The **par** loop assumes independence of statements, but how do we guarantee this? How can a sequential loop be converted into a **par** loop? These are the questions answered in this chapter.

First, we will define four forms of the **par**: non iterative, which is useful as a fork/join construct when the peer processes must perform different tasks; while-loop, which tests a Boolean condition prior to entering the loop, and then iteratively executes the statements in parallel as long as the condition is true; repeat-until-loop, which iteratively executes all statements in parallel until a Boolean condition is found to be true at the end of the loop; and counting-loop, which repeats the loop, once for each value of the loop counter.

The noniterative **par** implements MIMD task parallelism; the two conditional versions implement the equivalent of conditional loops in sequential programming; and the counting loop implements the equivalent of a for-loop in sequential programming. Conversion from sequential to parallel form is intuitive; for each sequential loop, a corresponding **par** exists. The question is: Does the **par** loop increase performance over its sequential equivalent?

We will use iteration space diagrams to illustrate the fundamental result of this chapter, which is that **par** constructs can be used to convert sequential loops into parallel loops whenever there are flow dependencies among iterations (loop-carried dependencies), but not when there are dependencies among statements of

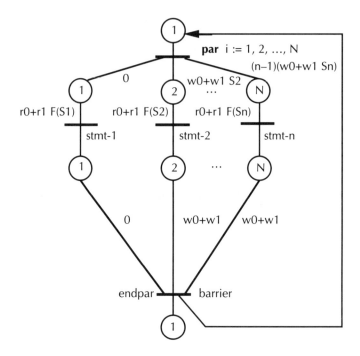

Figure 7.1   **Program graph definition of par loop parallelism**

the loop. We will give an algorithm for converting certain kinds of sequential loops into **par** equivalents.

Heuristic scheduling will be shown to be needed to increase the performance of noniterative **par** constructs. A simple greedy heuristic will be presented which optimizes the performance of such loops.

Finally, we will apply the **par** construct to the butterfly algorithm used in fast Fourier transforms (FFT), the LUD algorithm given in Chapter 5, and the quicker-sort routine. A comparison with the bitonic sort routine will illustrate an important lesson of parallel processing; good sequential algorithms often make poor parallel algorithms, and vice versa.

7.1 THE PAR

The **par** construct is used to repeatedly execute one or more statements, much like a serial loop (see Figure 7.1). However, the **par** construct permits parallel execution of independent statements, using more than one processor, thus parallelizing the loop as much as flow-correctness will permit. Note the visual similarity of the program graph in Figure 7.1 to a **fan** or **tree** as described in previous chapters. Semantically, there is little similarity, however. The **fan** has no loop-back to repeat. Even if it did, the **fan** processes execute identical code, whereas the **par** processes execute different code. The **tree** divides the number of processes in half, but the **par** does not.

The **par** performs one iteration of the clauses in its body in parallel, synchronizes the parallel executions with a *barrier* at the end of each iteration, and then repeats this pattern until the iterations cease. Because the parallel clauses contain different code, they most likely execute at different speeds. This means that one will finish after all the others. The barrier forces faster processes to wait for the slowest process.

The **par** statement is used to implement MIMD parallelism, independent loops, or a limited form of general loop parallelism. We will demonstrate each of these forms in the examples that follow.

In general, the **par** construct mimics three forms of looping, and one form of MIMD parallelism. This requires four forms for the **par**:

1 **par**
   <body>
   endpar

2 **par** <boolean-test>
   <body>
   endpar

3 **par**
   <body>
   until <boolean-test>

4 **par**<counter>
   <body>
   endpar

where <body> is defined as a list of labelled clauses:

<id1> : <mapin>{<routine1>}<mapout>;
<id2> : <mapin>{<routine2>}<mapout>;
  .
  .
  .
<idn> : <mapin>{<routinen>}<mapout>;

The <id$n$> clause is unique and merely numbers the statements. Each <id> clause is assigned to a process; thus, n processes are executed in parallel. Each <routine$n$> clause is a procedure containing declarations of local variables and one or more statements. The optional <mapin> and <mapout> directives work just as in the **fan** and **tree** constructs, causing messages to be passed into and out of the parallel processes of the **par** statement.

7.1.1 MIMD Par

The first form of the **par** construct defines n parallel processes that perform differ-ent things at the same time. Because the parallel processes execute different code, the **par** implements a restricted form of MIMD parallelism.

Example 7.1

Initialize variables TAX, RATE, and EMPL[1..N], using parallel MIMD clauses. Assum-ing we want TAX to be 1.0; RATE to be 0.33; and EMPL[i] = i; we can initialize every-thing at once as follows, using a **par** of the fourth type and a nested **fan**:

```
par
1: {float T; T := 1.0} mapout T to TAX;          /* No mapin. Mapout T    */
2: { float R; R := 0.33} mapout R to RATE;       /* No mapin. Mapout R    */
3: { int ID[1..N];                               /* Local to clause #3    */
      fan i := 1..N                              /* Nested parallelism    */
        { int IDENT;                             /* No mapin values. Mapout this    */
          IDENT := this }                        /* Set each element to itself    */
        mapout IDENT to ID[i]                    /* ID[i] = i   */
      endfan
    } mapout ID[1..N] to EMPL[1..N]              /* All at once    */
endpar
```

Clause 1 is carried out by a process that does nothing but set T to 1.0 and send the result back to TAX. We could have written this clause in much simpler terms as:

1: {} **mapout** 1.0 **to** TAX;

Clause 2 is similar, and in fact, we could have combined the two:

1: {} **mapout** 1.0 **to** TAX; 0.33 **to** RATE;

Clause 3 is more interesting due to the nested fan. We can simplify this clause too, but we cannot eliminate the intermediate storage ID[1..N]:

```
3: { int ID[1..N];                               /* Local to clause 3    */
      fan i := 1..N                              /* Nested parallelism    */
      {} mapout this to ID[i]                    /* ID[i] = i   */
      endfan
    } mapout ID[1..N] to EMPL[1..N]              /* All at once    */
```

7.1.2 The Conditional Par

Two forms of **par** depend on a Boolean test to determine their termination.This is the simplest form of an iterative **par**. But, unlike the iterative **tree**, the iterative **par** executes the same number of different routines each time the loop is repeated.

Both forms of iterative **par** statements have analogs in the sequential program-ming world. The *while-loop* and *repeat-until loop* of Pascal carry out similar itera-tions, but not in parallel. Hence, wherever we see a while-loop, we try to replace it with a **par** Boolean test equivalent. Similarly, wherever we see a repeat-until loop we attempt to speed it up by substituting a **par-until** Boolean test loop.

Example 7.2

Consider the following sequential code in Pascal for computing the square root of A, using the *Newton–Raphson* technique for solving $x^2 - A = 0$:

```
oldx := 0.0; x := 1;                    /* Initial guesses   */
while abs(x – oldx) > eps do            /* Eps is the error limit */
    begin
        oldx := x;                      /* Save x for later   */
        x := 0.5*(x + A / x);           /* Iterate x   */
    end;                                /* New approximation   */
```

Now, using **par**, we can gain a small speedup by doing the two statements in the loop in parallel. Recall that the **par** synchronizes at the end of each iteration, so there are no flow-dependency problems:

```
oldx := 0; x := 1.0;                    /* Could have done these in par   */
par fabs(x – oldx) > eps                /* convert (x-oldx) to floating abs   */
1: mapin x to RHS
      { float RHS }
      mapout RHS to oldx;
2: mapin x to RHS; A to A
      { float LHS, RHS, A;
        LHS := 0.5*(RHS + A / RHS) }
      mapout LHS to x
endpar
```

This version is an improvement only if there is no penalty for communication. The value of x is mapped into both parallel clauses at the same time, and then the resulting value of oldx and x are mapped out at the same time. What is the output dependency of this **par**?

As an illustration, let $A = 4$, and observe the successive values of x as the **par** is repeated. Assuming eps = .001, we get:

iteration	oldx	x
0	0.00	1.00
1	1.00	2.50
2	2.50	2.05
3	2.05	2.00

7.1.3 The Counting Par

In the fourth form of **par**, the counter enumerates iterations much like a serial loop index. Given n clauses in the body, we map one clause to each process. If there are more clauses than processors, $P < k$, so as many as (k **div** P) clauses are mapped onto each process. In either case, all clauses wait at the **endpar** barrier before repeating.

Example 7.3

Consider the following sequential loop with the dependencies shown in Figure 7.2. We want to convert it to a **par**.

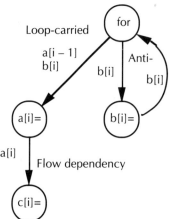

Figure 7.2   Dependencies in a parallel loop body

```
for(i := 1; i ≤ N; i++){          /* Repeat N times    */
    a[i] := a[i – 1] + b[i];      /* Loop-carried dependency   */
    b[i] := 2 * b[i];             /* Antidependency   */
    c[i] := a[i] – 1              /* Dataflow-dependency   */
}
```

We can use the general program graph model of a **par** to construct a computational model of this example (see Figure 7.3). The antidependency and flow dependency places must be inserted to force proper synchronization of clauses, however.

In Figure 7.2, a token is put in the initial place to signify the start of the **par**. Multiple tokens flow from the first transition, signifying a *fork* in the control flow. Similarly, multiple tokens are required to fire the final transition, signifying a *join* in the control flow. The **barrier** transition construct performs the barrier synchronization, tests the counter, and determines if the token should return to the beginning state, or if the **par** construct should terminate. Additional iterations occur when a token is returned to the starting place.

The **par** solution must be carefully designed to avoid antidependency and flow dependency as well as the loop-carried dependency (see the iteration space of Figure 7.4a). From Figure 7.4, it is clear that we need to remove all dependency arcs to write a correct **par** statement. The derivation can be done in steps. First, we note that the loop-carried dependency is removed by the barrier at the end of each iteration, see Figure 7.4b.

Second, we remove the flow dependency by combining clauses. Thus, if clause 3 is combined with clause 1, the flow dependency is honored by the sequential nature of the clause. That is, we pack the two clauses into one, with the two sequential actions:

a[i] := a[i – 1] + b[i];
c[i] := a[i] – 1;

This forces correct flow according to the FLOW predicate:

FLOW(a[i], t) :-
$\quad$ ($\exists \Delta t > 0 \mid$ DEF(a[i], t – Δt)),
$\quad$ USE(a[i], t + Δt).

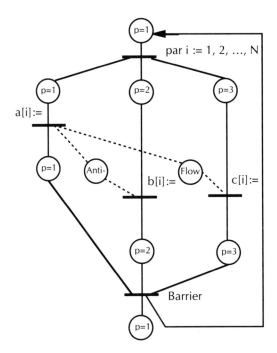

Figure 7.3 **Program graph semantics of the par loop calculation of Figure 7.2**

Finally, note that each clause of the **par** copies values to separate processes, so the $b[i]$ on the right-hand sides of two statements are simultaneously copied to the two remaining clauses. This avoids the antidependency, because the copies are made at time t, and the new value of $b[i]$ is set at time $t + \Delta t$, with $\Delta t > 0$:

ANTI($b[i]$, t) :-
    ($\exists \Delta t > 0$ | USE($b[i]$, t),
    DEF($b[i]$, t + Δt).

Now we can write a flow-correct **par** for this sequential code:

```
par i := 1..N                        /* Repeat N times */
1: mapin a[i − 1] to a1; b[i] to b;
    { float a, b, a1, c;
      a := a1 + b;                    /* Combine 1 and 3 to serialize */
      c := a − 1
    }
  mapout a to a[i]; c to c[i];
2: mapin b[i] to b;
    { float b;
      b := 2 * b;                     /* Only 2 processes in parallel */
    }
  mapout b to b[i]
endpar
```

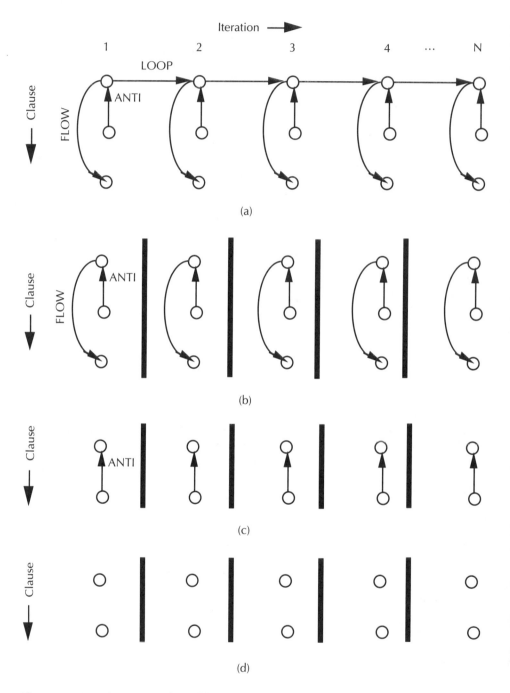

Figure 7.4   **Iteration space analysis of Figure 7.3 par: (a) dependencies in iteration space, (b) barrier removes loop-carried dependency, (c) combining clauses 1 and 3 removes flow dependency, and (d) copying _b[i]_ removes antidependency.**

The preconditions and postconditions for this solution give USE–DEF patterns that match the flow-correctness predicates ANTI and FLOW noted above. The **mapin** constructs yield USE(a[i – 1], b[i], t) and the **mapout** constructs yield DEF(a[i], c[i], b[i], t + Δt). The ANTI and FLOW predicates verify that these patterns are flow-correct.

7.2 PERFORMANCE ANALYSIS

The graph of Figure 7.1 contains all the information needed to analyze the performance of a **par**. The number of iterations through the **par**, multiplied by the elapsed time for a single iteration, yields the total elapsed time. But we cannot change the number of iterations, N, and the number of parallel processes, n, is decided by the dependencies among the processes. That is, data-dependency is the main constraint on the number of processes in a **par**, which in turn determines its performance.

Let the S characters of input data to a **par** be distributed in sizes given by S_i. This will be determined by the problem. The amount of computation in each clause is $F(S_i)$. For each iteration, the elapsed time of a serial **par** (single process) is:

$$T_1 = r_0 + r_1 \left(\sum_{i=1}^{n} F(S_i) \right)$$

and the elapsed time for a parallel **par** (n processes) is:

$$T_n = \underset{i=2}{\overset{n}{M}} \{ [r_0 + r_1 F(S_1)]; [(i-1)(w_0 + w_1 S_i) + r_0 + r_1 F(S_i) + w_0 + w_1] \}$$

The maximum function selects the *critical path* which is $[r_0 + r_1 F(S_1)]$, or one of the other n paths of length $[(i-1)(w_0 + w_1 S_i) + r_0 + r_1 F(S_i) + w_0 + w_1]$. The critical path may *not* be through the nth clause if $F(S_n) \ll F(S_i)$ for some $i \neq n$.

In many cases, it is reasonable to assume that all processes are approximately the same in terms of data length and execution time. That is, $S_i = S_0$ and $F(S_i) = F_0$, where S_0 and F_0 are relatively small constants. Under these conditions, the critical path is through clause $i = n$, so the speedup for a single iteration is

$$\text{Speedup} = \frac{r_0 + n r_1 F_0}{(n-1)(w_0 + w_1 S_0) + r_0 + r_1 F_0 + w_0 + w_1} = O(1)$$

This is counterintuitive. But if we ignore communication delays, the intuitive result is obtained, i.e., $w_0 = w_1 = r_0 = 0$:

$$\text{Speedup} \;=\; \frac{nr_1F_0}{r_1F_0} \;=\; \frac{n}{1} \;=\; O(n)$$

Example 7.4

Assuming target machine parameters as follows:

$w_0 = 10$
$w_1 = 0.001$
$r_0 = 100$
$r_1 = 10$

and $F_0 = S_0 = 1$, what is the speedup of an $n = 3$ process **par**? Substituting into the equation above gives:

$$\text{Speedup} \;=\; \frac{100 + 3\,(10)\,(1)}{2\,(10 + 0.001) + 100 + 10 + 10 + 0.001} \;=\; 0.93$$

This **par** runs *slower* on 3 processes than on a single process, because the processes are too fine-grained for the particular target machine. But, if we increase the *grain size* of each process, then we begin to see the effects of parallelism, instead of communication and initiation delays.

Suppose $F_0 = S_0 = 10$, what is the speedup of an $n = 3$ process **par**?

$$\text{Speedup} \;=\; \frac{100 + 3\,(10)\,(100)}{2\,(10 + 0.001) + 100 + 1000 + 10.001} \;=\; 2.74$$

This shows the dramatic effect of grain size on performance. It is an illustration of the *min–max problem*.

The performance of a **par** is governed by the size and number of its clauses. These are in turn governed by data dependencies and the way in which we combine statements to form the clauses. Finally, data dependencies must be honored to achieve flow-correctness.

7.3 HEURISTIC SCHEDULING

The performance of a **par** is determined by the placement of processes (tasks) on processors, as well as by the degree of parallelism and the extent of communication costs. Figure 7.5 illustrates this effect. Gray areas indicate communication delays, black areas indicate task processing, and white areas indicate process idling. The tasks have been labelled $t1$, $t2$, ..., $t7$ for convenience. In this example, all communication times are 10 units. (Recall that a communication time delay is assumed to be zero if the message is passed between processes on the same processor.)

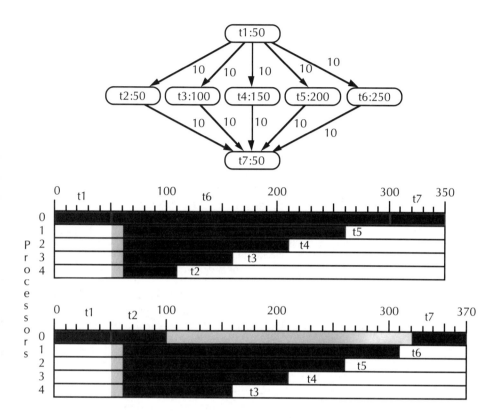

Figure 7.5 Two schedules for the same par, showing different elapsed times

The **par** in Figure 7.5 is given as a task graph: the **par** forks 5 parallel processes with execution times of $t2 = 50$, $t3 = 100$, $t4 = 150$, $t5 = 200$, and t6 = 250 units, respectively. Note the difference in elapsed time in the Gantt charts for the two schedules: 350 versus 370 time units. This difference is due to the placement pattern alone, and has nothing to do with the **par**. Depending on how we allocate tasks to processors, we will obtain either poor or good results. If we start the shortest process first, the elapsed time is 370 units. Allocating the longest process first, to processor 0, leads to the shorter elapsed time of 350 units.

The optimum schedule is not always clear cut. In fact, it has been shown that the scheduling problem is *NP-complete*, meaning it is nearly intractable if we insist on an exact optimum all the time. Therefore, heuristics are used to find near-optimal solutions. When communication delays are taken into consideration, the optimum placement of processes onto processors is not easy to determine.

A simple heuristic works as follows: find the *critical path* through the **par**, including communication delay times, and then allocate all processes along this path to the same processor. All other processes are allocated to successive processors.

Applying this heuristic to the example in Figure 7.5 we see that the critical path is through the largest clause, t6:250. Thus, it is placed on the same processor as the **par**, and leads to a shorter elapsed time.

Example 7.5

What is the critical path through a **par** containing the following communication and execution time estimates?

Clause	Communication time	Execution time	Sums
1	**mapin** = 100, **mapout** = 100	250	450
2	**mapin** = 150, **mapout** = 50	100	300
3	**mapin** = 225, **mapout** = 200	175	600
4	**mapin** = 50, **mapout** = 150	310	510
5	**mapin** = 125, **mapout** = 100	300	525

The largest sum is 600, which corresponds to clause 3. Thus, we place clause 3 on the same processor as the **par**. The remaining clauses are placed, one each, on other processors.

The scheduling heuristic suggested above does not always produce the best schedule, because communication delays drop to 0 when adjacent processes are placed on the same processor. Thus, the critical path of 600 units in Example 7.5 drops to an execution time of 175 units when placed on the same processor as the **par**.

Figure 7.6 illustrates a counterexample where the simple heuristic does not give the best schedule. Instead of placing clause 3 on process 0 as suggested by the heuristic, we must place it on process 2 to obtain the best schedule for the **par**. The optimal schedule is shown in Figure 7.6, and listed below.

Clause	Processor
1	3
2	4
3	2
4	0
5	1

7.4 FLOW-CORRECTNESS ANALYSIS

To assure flow-correctness within the **par**, we must assert the three predicates FLOW, ANTI, and OUT within a single iteration of the **par**. Loop-carried dependencies are avoided by the barrier at the end of each iteration.

OUT is clearly satisfied if the **par** follows *single-assignment*, meaning that all output variables appear on the left-hand side of an assignment (or input statement) at most once. However, should a variable be defined in more than one process, OUT fails. Thus, **par** processes must obey the single assignment rule across

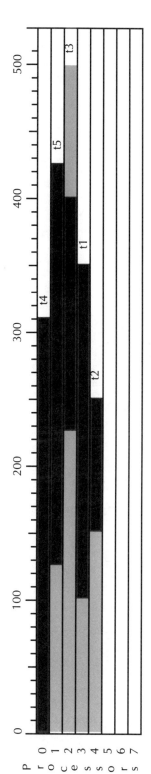

Figure 7.6   Optimal schedule for a par that does not
follow the scheduling heuristic

all processes of the **par**. Multiple assignment is allowed in the serial code of an individual process, but not within two or more separate processes.

The FLOW and ANTI predicates obey similar rules across the processes of a **par**. First, we must identify the input and output sets of all processes. These are the USE and DEF variables in FLOW and ANTI.

Next, we apply the rules of FLOW and ANTI to each variable in the input/output sets.

Example 7.6

Consider Example 7.3, given earlier:

```
par i := 1,4..N
{
   p1 : a[i] := a[i − 1] + b[i];
   p2 : b[i] := 2 * b[i];
   p3 : c[i] := a[i] − 1
}
```

The input/output sets are

p1: Input = [a[i − 1], b[i]]	Output = [a[i]]
p2: Input = [b[i]]	Output = [b[i]]
p3: Input = [a[i]]	Output = [c[i]]

These are used to obtain the preconditions and postconditions on each process:

{ i **in** [1..N] } [p1] {DEF(a[i]) **and** USE(a[i − 1]) **and** USE(b[i]) }
{ i **in** [1..N] } [p2] {DEF(b[i]) **and** USE(b[i]) }
{ i **in** [1..N] } [p3] {DEF(c[i]) **and** USE(a[i]) }

Recall that these three preconditions and postconditions are asserted simultaneously, say at time t. That is, all three processes are executed at once, within an iteration of the **par**.

We then test FLOW on all variables in the input/output sets at time t. For $a[i]$, we have

FLOW(a[i], t) :-
    ($\exists \Delta t > 0$ | DEF(a[i], $t − \Delta t$)),
    USE(a[i], t).

This fails as it is true for $\Delta t = 0$, because $p1$ defines $a[i]$ at the same time that $p3$ uses $a[i]$. This can only be fixed by serializing the DEF and USE.

For $b[i]$, we have

FLOW(b[i], t) :-
    ($\exists \Delta t > 0$ | DEF(b[i], $t − \Delta t$)),
    USE(b[i], t).

This is true for $\Delta t > 0$, noting that $b[i]$ is both defined and used within $p2$, which is self-serializing. Thus, there are no FLOW failures on $b[i]$.

For $c[i]$, we have

FLOW(c[i], t) :-
    ($\exists \Delta t > 0$ | DEF(c[i], t − Δt)),
    USE(c[i], t).

No DEF–USE patterns exist for $c[i]$; hence this need not be tested.
    For $a[i − 1]$, we have

FLOW(a[i − 1], t) :-
    ($\exists \Delta t > 0$ | DEF(a[i − 1], t − Δt)),
    USE(a[i − 1], t).

No DEF–USE patterns exist for $a[i − 1]$; hence this need not be tested.
    ANTI is tested in much the same manner. For $a[i]$, we have

ANTI(a[i], t) :-
    ($\exists \Delta t > 0$ | USE(a[i], t − Δt)),
    DEF(a[i], t).

No such USE–DEF pattern exists for $a[i]$.
    For $b[i]$, we have

ANTI(b[i], t) :-
    ($\exists \Delta t > 0$ | USE(b[i], t − Δt)),
    DEF(b[i], t).

A USE–DEF pattern exists between $p1$ and $p2$; hence $\Delta t = 0$. The correction is made by serializing $p1$ and $p4$.
    For $c[i]$, we have

ANTI(c[i], t) :-
    ($\exists \Delta t > 0$ | USE(c[i], t − Δt)),
    DEF(c[i], t).

No USE–DEF pattern exists.
    Finally, for $a[i − 1]$, we have

ANTI(a[i − 1], t) :-
    ($\exists \Delta t > 0$ | USE(a[i − 1], t − Δt)),
    DEF(a[i − 1], t).

No USE–DEF pattern exists. However, if it were not for the barrier at the end of each iteration, this dependency could span two successive iterations. That is, $a[1]$ is used in iteration $i = 2$, and defined in iteration $i = 1$. This would establish a DEF–USE pattern across two iterations, but the barrier prevents the pattern.

7.5 CONDITIONS FOR FLOW-CORRECTNESS

The results of the foregoing analysis can be summarized in two rules for when to apply **par** parallelism to loops. These rules are especially valuable for converting a serial loop into a **par** loop, as we will see in later examples.

We assume that the serial loop to be analyzed has been expressed in the form of an iteration statement diagram as illustrated earlier, in Figure 7.4. Then, the dependencies are shown as arcs in the diagram:

Rule 1   Loop-carried dependencies shown as horizontal arcs in the iteration-statement diagram can be ignored because of the barrier at the end of each iteration of the **par** loop.

Rule 2   All other dependencies, output, flow, and anti- (represented by vertical arcs) must be eliminated; otherwise, the **par** loop is incorrect.

These rules can be turned into a prescription for how to convert a serial loop into an equivalent **par** loop:

1   Draw the *iteration statement diagram* of the serial loop.

2   Project dependency arcs onto the vertical axis (statements), ignoring the horizontal axis.

3   Convert into independent statements as follows: use forward substitution to remove flow dependencies, and combine statements containing antidependencies and output dependencies.

The resulting iteration statement diagram will consist of independent statements. That is, all arcs will be removed, leaving only nodes. The nodes represent the parallel processes of the **par** loop. These can then be written as clauses of the **par**.

It is highly likely that this procedure will result in a single node, in which case, the serial loop is not parallelizable using a **par**. In the next chapter we will give other methods of converting serial loops into parallel loops. Note that it is not always possible to convert a serial loop into an equivalent parallel loop.

7.6 APPLICATIONS OF PAR

We will apply the theory of the preceding sections to two real applications known to involve computationally intense calculations, and to another sort algorithm. In the first example, we will show how to convert the core of the FFT summation used in *spectral analysis* into a **par** loop. In the second example, we will make a slight performance improvement in the LUD algorithm introduced in Chapter 5. Finally, the third example is yet another sort algorithm that can be slightly improved using **par**. For a comparison with another (faster) sort, see Chapter 5.

d[1]   d[2]

d[3]   d[4]   **Figure 7.7   Butterfly algorithm at the core of the Cooley–Tukey FFT algorithm**

7.6.1 Spectral Analysis

The fast Fourier transform (*FFT*) is a well-known algorithm for converting time-sampled data into a frequency domain. The famous *Danielson–Lanczos algorithm* invented in 1942 and refined by Cooley and Tukey in the 1960s, is known to be $O(N\log_2 N)$ time complex. For details of the algorithm, see Press et al (see References at chapter end).

Might it be possible to perform the FFT even faster using parallel processors? The answer is affirmative, but the method is not easy to derive.

Suppose that time-domain data are stored in an array $d[1..2^n]$, and that the real/imaginary parts of the calculation are stored in variables ending in r and i, respectively. For example, the weighting factor W is stored in wr and wi. The core of the FFT algorithm is a serial loop that computes the *butterfly* shown in Figure 7.7. The butterfly is at the heart of the *Cooley–Tukey algorithm*, and expresses the data dependencies of the serial loop:

```
for k := 0 to (n – m) div 4 do
    begin
    i := m + 4 * k;
    j := i + 2;
    tempr := wr * d[j] – wi * d[j + 1];
    tempi := wr * d[j + 1] + wi * d[j];
    d[j] := d[i] – tempr;
    d[j + 1] := d[i + 1] – tempi;
    d[i] := d[i] + tempr;
    d[i + 1] := d[i + 1] + tempi;
    end;
```

The dependencies of Figure 7.8 appear to be so dense that there is little hope of converting this serial loop into a parallel **par** loop. But, application of the algorithm for conversion reveals that, indeed, parallelism exists within this seemingly serial loop:

Step 1   Draw the iteration-statement diagram of the serial loop. The iteration-statement diagram is shown in Figure 7.8. It shows all dependencies, but of course, we want to remove these.

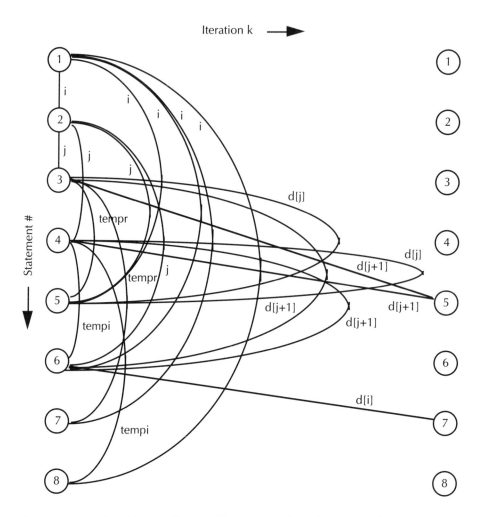

Figure 7.8   Iteration statement diagram of butterfly calculation in Cooley–Tukey loop

Step 2   Project dependency arcs onto the vertical axis (statements), ignoring the horizontal axis. This gives the dependencies of the first column of nodes in Figure 7.8. We can effectively ignore the second column of the diagram. Many dependencies remain.

Step 3   Convert into independent statements as follows: use forward substitution to remove flow dependencies, and combine statements containing antidependencies and output dependencies.

Removing the dependencies on i, j, tempr, and tempi greatly reduces the number of dependency arcs in Figure 7.8, leaving a dependency diagram containing only antidependencies, as contained in the serial loop below. Forward substitution of i, j, tempr, and tempi into the statements that use them, results in:

```
for k := 0 to (n – m) div 4 do
    begin
    d[m + 4*k + 2] := d[m + 4*k] – (wr * d[m + 4*k + 2] – wi * d[m + 4*k + 3]);
    d[m + 4*k + 3] := d[m + 4*k + 1] – (wr * d[m + 4*k + 3] + wi * d[m + 4*k + 2]);
    d[m + 4*k] := d[m + 4*k] + (wr * d[m + 4*k + 2] – wi * d[m + 4*k + 3]);
    d[m + 4*k + 1] := d[m + 4*k + 1] + (wr * d[m + 4*k + 3] + wi * d[m + 4*k + 2]);
    end;
```

The serial loop contains only antidependencies on the subscripted elements of array $d[]$. But, these antidependencies are acceptable to the **par**, because of the delay $\Delta t > 0$ that occurs in its USE–DEF precondition/postcondition:

ANTI(d[m + 4*k], t) :-
    ($\exists \Delta t > 0$ | USE(d[m + 4*k], t – Δt)),
    DEF(d[m + 4*k], t).

ANTI(d[m + 4*k + 1], t) :-
    ($\exists \Delta t > 0$ | USE(d[m + 4*k + 1], t – Δt)),
    DEF(d[m + 4*k + 1], t).

ANTI(d[m + 4*k + 2], t) :-
    ($\exists \Delta t > 0$ | USE(d[m + 4*k + 2], t – Δt)),
    DEF(d[m + 4*k + 2], t).

ANTI(d[m + 4*k + 3], t) :-
    ($\exists \Delta t > 0$ | USE(d[m + 4*k + 3], t – Δt)),
    DEF(d[m + 4*k + 3], t).

The order of execution of the clauses of a **par** does not matter, because all clauses are independent. Hence, the **par** can be written directly from the forward-substitution version of the loop as follows, noting the new order of the statements:

```
par k := 0..(n – m) div 4
1:    mapin                          /* Do 4 clauses in parallel   */
      d[m + 4*k] to d;
      d[m + 4*k + 2] to d2;
      d[m + 4*k + 3] to d3;
      wi to wi; wr to wr;
      { float d, d2, d3, wr, wi;
      d2 := d – (wr * d2 - wi * d3)}
      mapout d2 to d[m + 4*k + 2];
2:    mapin
      d[m + 4*k + 1] to d1;
      d[m + 4*k + 2] to d2;
      d[m + 4*k + 3] to d3;
      wi to wi; wr to wr;
      { float d1, d2, d3, wr, wi;
      d3 := d1 – (wr * d3 + wi * d2)}
      mapout d3 to d[m + 4*k + 3];
```

```
3:   mapin
     d[m + 4*k] to d;
     d[m + 4*k + 2] to d2;
     d[m + 4*k + 3] to d3;
     wi to wi; wr to wr;
     { float d, d2, d3, wr, wi;
     d := d + (wr * d2 – wi * d3);
     mapout d to d[m + 4*k];
4:   mapin
     d[m + 4*k + 1] to d1;
     d[m + 4*k + 2] to d2;
     d[m + 4*k + 3] to d3;
     wi to wi; wr to wr;
     { float d1, d2, d3, wr, wi;
     d1 := d1 + (wr * d3 + wi * d2);
     mapout d1 to d[m + 4*k + 1];
endpar;
```

In fact, this solution is easier to comprehend than the serial version. The butterfly pattern is easily revealed by looking only at the **mapin/mapout** patterns of clauses 3 and 4, which compute results for $d[m + 4*k]$ and $d[m + 4*k + 1]$.

The proof of flow-correctness is also based on the **mapin/mapout** patterns because they perform the USE–DEF operations on the data. That is, **mapin** performs USE, and **mapout** performs DEF operations. Hence, looking once again to the **par**:

Precondition = USE($d[m + 4*k]$, $d[m + 4*k + 1]$, $d[m + 4*k + 2]$, $d[m + 4*k +3]$)
Postcondition = DEF($d[m + 4*k]$, $d[m + 4*k + 1]$, $d[m + 4*k + 2]$, $d[m + 4*k +3]$)

And, because $\Delta t > 0$, this is a flow-correct calculation.

7.6.2 A Faster Solution to $Ax = b$

The LUD solution to $Ax = b$ was given in serial and parallel forms in Chapter 5. This solution used a serial loop to iterate over all n rows of matrix A, and in the process, to compute an upper A, and lower matrix m. The algorithm, repeated here for convenience, contains three fans; $f1$, $f2$, and $f3$. The iteration statement diagram for the serial loop is shown in Figure 7.9, where the three statements correspond to the three fans:

```
for(t := 1; t < n; t++)                 /* Flow-dependencies exist in loop   */
{/*f1*/ fan i := (t + 1)..n             /* Calculate multipliers    */
    mapin A[t, t] to pivot;             /* Replace O(n) loop with O(1) fan    */
        A[i, t] to ColElem;
    {float pivot, ColElem;
        ColElem := ColElem / pivot}
    mapout ColElem to m[i, t]
    endfan;
```

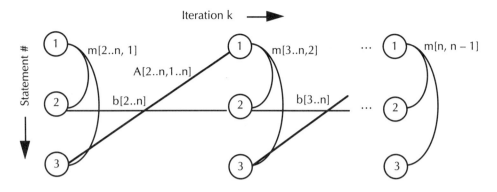

Figure 7.9   Iteration statement diagram of fans in the LUD loop

```
/*f2*/ fan i := (t + 1)..n            /* Calculate modified b[i]   */
     mapin m[i, t] to mpy;            /* Distribute to (n − t) processes   */
          b[i] to rhs;
          b[t] to bt
     { float  mpy, rhs, bt;           /* Local variables at each process   */
          rhs −= mpy * bt }           /* SIMD decrement   */
     mapout rhs to b[i]               /* Aggregate solution   */
     endfan;                          /* (n − t) processes take 1 time unit   */

/*f3*/ fan i := (t + 1)..n;           /* O(n**2) processes take 1 time step   */
          j := t..n                   /* One process for each (i, j)   */
     mapin m[i, t] to mpy;
          [i, j] to RowElem;
          A[t, j] to ColElem;
     {float  mpy, ColElem, RowElem;
          RowElem −= mpy * ColElem }  /* SIMD decrement   */
     mapout RowElem to A[i, j]
     endfan;                          /* Mesh of procs compute upper A[i, j]   */
}
```

The iteration-statement diagram cannot be reduced using projection followed by combining dependent statements. Combining dependent statements results in no parallelism. However, a small amount of parallelism is possible if we partition the body of the serial loop into two parts: one part consists of fan *f*1, while the other consists of fans *f*2 and *f*3. The second part can be expressed as a **par** containing two parallel **fans** operating adjacent to one another.

```
for(t := 1; t < n; t++)
{/*f1*/ fan i := (t + 1)..n
          mapin  A[t,t] to pivot;
                 A[i,t] to ColElem;
```

```
{float pivot, ColElem;
      ColElem := ColElem / pivot}
mapout ColElem to m[i,t]
endfan;

par                                          /* Non iterative par    */
1: mapin    b[t + 1..n] to Temp[t + 1..n];
            m[t + 1..n, t] to Lower[t + 1..n]
   {float  Temp[1..n], Lower[1..n];
   /*f2*/ fan i := (t + 1)..n
            mapin Lower[i] to mpy;           /* b[i,t] to mpy    */
            Temp[i] to rhs;                  /* m[i,t] to rhs    */
            Temp[t] to bt                    /* b[t] to bt       */
            { float  mpy, rhs, bt;
                   rhs -= mpy * bt }
            mapout rhs to Lower[i]           /* rhs to b[i]      */
            endfan
   }
   mapout Lower[t + 1..n] to  b[t + 1..n];

2: mapin    m[t + 1..n, t] to Lower[t + 1..n];
            A[t + 1..n, t..n] to Upper[t + 1..n, t..n]
   { float Lower[1..n], Upper[1..n, 1..n];
   /*f3*/ fan i := (t + 1)..n;
              j := t..n
            mapin Lower[i,t] to mpy;         /* m[i,t] to mpy    */
            Upper[i,j] to RowElem;           /* A[i,j] to RowElem */
            Upper[t,j] to ColElem            /* A[t,j] to ColElem    */
            {float  mpy, ColElem, RowElem;
             RowElem -= mpy * ColElem }
            mapout RowElem to Upper[i,j]     /* RowElem to A[i,j] */
            endfan
   }
   mapout Upper[t + 1..n, t..n] to A[t + 1..n, t..n];
}
```

This increase of parallelism may not be worthwhile, because of the added storage and message passing, not to mention the added processes required by the parallel fans in clause 2 of the inner **par**. However, the structured control imposed by the **par** and **fan** constructs makes this a flow-correct algorithm for solving $Ax = b$ using LUD.

7.6.3 Another Way to Sort

In this section, we adapt the famous sequential *quicksort algorithm* to parallel execution. Because this algorithm runs very quickly on serial machines, we might be misled into believing that it is faster on a parallel machine. However, parallel

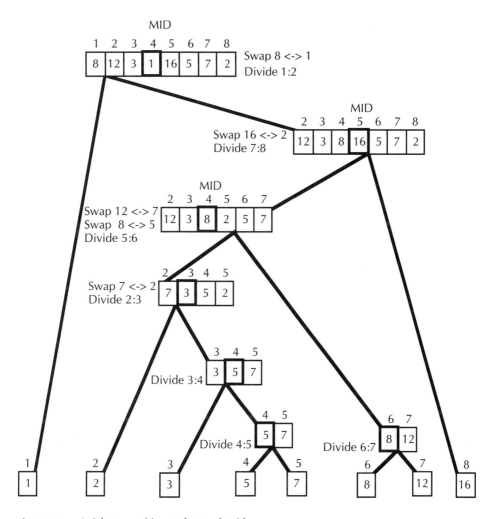

Figure 7.10   Quicksort partition-exchange algorithm

quicksort is slower than parallel bitonic sort or parallel rank sort. The solution given below is still $O(N\log_2 N)$, rather than $O(N)$ or $O(\log_2^2 N)$. This illustrates why sequential algorithms are often poor parallel algorithms. In Chapter 5 we showed that rank sort runs in time $O(N)$ and bitonic sort runs in $O(\log_2^2 N)$ time.

We want to sort a list into ascending order (see Figure 7.10). The fundamental idea of quicksort is to divide the list into two (uneven) sublists, and then exchange all elements of one sublist with elements of the other sublist, such that all elements less than a certain size are in one sublist, and all elements greater than or equal to a certain size are in the other sublist. The two sublists are then treated as original lists, and the partition–exchange repeated on each. This process is repeated until all sublists are sorted. The concatenated sublists form an ordered list.

We use a pushdown stack to hold the sublist indexes. While we are partitioning the list into sublists, the stack is pushed with start and stop indexes, marking the start and stop of each sublist. As we perform exchanges we pop the start/stop indexes to recall the sublists. This corresponds to a depth-first traversal of the tree shown in Figure 7.10.

The sequential version of quicksort is shown below:

```
procedure Quicksort( var LIST: Lists );
var L, R, NewL, NewR : indexes;
begin                              /* Depth-first traversal via stack   */
    INITSTACK;                     /* Initialize push down stack   */
    PUSH(1, N);                    /* Remember bound of original list   */
    repeat                         /* Process a sublist   */
        POP(L, R);                 /* Recall indexes   */
        repeat                     /* Exchanges   */
            SWAP(L, R, NewL, NewR);                    /* Exchange   */
            if NewL < R then PUSH(NewL, R);            /* Partition */
            R := NewR;
        until L ≥ R;
    until STACKSIZE = 0;
end;
```

The SWAP routine performs an exchange that forces all "small" elements into the left sublist, and all "large" elements into the right sublist (see Figure 7.10). How do we select lists of small and large elements? The mid element (MID) of a sublist is selected as a pivot element. All elements are judged against MID; elements in the left sublist that are greater than MID are exchanged with elements in the right sublist that are smaller than MID. The routine below uses an EXCHANGE procedure to swap individual elements:

```
procedure SWAP(L, R : indexes; var NewL, NewR : indexes);
var MID : ListElement;
begin
    NewL := L; NewR := R; MID := LIST[(L + R) div 2];
    repeat
        while LIST[NewL] < MID do NewL := NewL + 1;
        while LIST[NewR] > MID do NewR := NewR - 1;
        if NewL ≤ NewR then begin
            EXCHANGE (LIST[NewL], LIST[NewR]);
            NewL := NewL + 1; NewR := NewR - 1;
        end;
    until NewL > NewR;
end;
```

Now, when we attempt to speed up this algorithm by parallelizing one or more of the loops, we note that the repeat-loops of the quicksort procedure are highly data dependent. But, the two inner while-loops of the SWAP procedure are relatively independent. Furthermore, the EXCHANGE procedure can be done in one **par**. Here is the parallel version of SWAP:

```
NewL := L; NewR := R; MID := LIST[(L + R) div 2];
repeat
    par
    1 : mapin LIST[NewL..NewR] to L[NewL..NewR];
             MID to MID; NewL to NL;
    { ListElement  L[NewL..NewR];
    while L[NL] < MID do NL := NL + 1}
    mapout NL to NewL;

    2 : mapin LIST[NewL..NewR] to L[NewL..NewR];
             MID to MID; NewR to NR;
    { ListElement  L[NewL..NewR];
    while LIST[NR] > MID do NR := NR – 1}
    mapout NR to NewR;
    endpar;

    if NewL ≤ NewR then begin
        par
        1 : mapin LIST[NewL] to L;
        { ListElement L}
        mapout L to LIST[NewR];          /* LIST[NewL] → LIST[NewR] */

        2 : mapin LIST[NewR] to L;
        { ListElement  L}
        mapout L to LIST[NewL];          /* LIST[NewR] → LIST[NewL] */
        endpar;

        NewL := NewL + 1; NewR := NewR – 1;
        end;                             /* endif */
    until NewL > NewR;
end;
```

How much of an improvement is this version of SWAP? The two **while** loops are done in parallel, but the clauses of the **par** still take $O(N)$ time. Similarly, the EXCHANGE takes constant time, as does the **par** version. Thus, this algorithm runs faster, but is still $O(N\log_2 N)$.

The flow-correctness of this version of quicksort is left as an exercise for the reader.

7.7 KEYWORDS AND CONCEPTS

We have used iteration space diagrams to illustrate the fundamental result of this chapter, which is that the **par** can be used to convert sequential loops into parallel loops whenever there are loop-carried dependencies, but that it cannot be used when there are dependencies among statements of the loop. We have given an algorithm for converting certain kinds of sequential loops into **par** equivalents.

We have shown that heuristic scheduling increases the performance of non iterative **par** constructs. We presented a simple greedy heuristic which often optimizes the performance of such loops.

The following keywords and concepts summarize the ideas of this chapter:

Cooley–Tukey algorithm   The Danielson–Lanczos algorithm (*aka* butterfly algorithm, and FFT), which was re-discovered by Cooley and Tukey, can be implemented as a parallel **par**, as shown in this chapter. This algorithm was shown to be flow-correct by data dependency analysis, i.e., by an iteration space diagram.

Iteration statement diagram   An iteration-statement diagram is a modification of the iteration space diagram, whereby a non nested loop can be analyzed and shown to be flow-correct. In place of the iterations of an inner nested loop, we list the statements of a single loop, versus the loop counter. This reveals loop-carried flow dependencies, which can be visually inspected to show that the equivalent **par** is flow-correct.

NP-complete   The scheduling problem is NP-complete, because of combinatorial increases in the number of trial schedules that would have to be checked to find the shortest schedule. Thus, we are driven to find heuristics which work most of the time, but not always. The statements of a **par** construct cannot be scheduled without facing the scheduling problem.

Scheduling problem   The scheduling problem is to find the shortest elapsed-time schedule for a given set of processes, and a fixed number of processors. This problem is known to be NP-complete in even its simplest forms. However, it becomes even more difficult when we consider communication delays, processor overhead, and network contention.

Single-assignment   One way to avoid the possibility of output dependency is to eliminate it. This is done by requiring that each variable of a program be assigned a value at most once! The single-assignment rule dictates that every variable be given one, and only one, value throughout its life. While rather restrictive, it is possible to write a single-assignment program, by using many variables.

PROBLEMS

1   Write a parallel program to evaluate the quadratic equation that solves for all solutions to

$$Ax^2 + Bx + C = 0$$

Consider all cases, i.e., real and imaginary roots.

2 Can the following sequential sort routine be converted into a parallel form using **par** and **fan** constructs? Show the solution, if one is possible.

```
procedure SELECT(var LIST: ListArray);
var I, J, K : integer;
    MIN : ListElement;
begin
    for I := 1 to N – 1 do
        begin
            K := I; MIN := LIST[I];
            for J := I + 1 to N do
                if LIST[J] > MIN then
                    begin
                        K := J;
                        MIN := LIST[K]
                    end;
            EXCHANGE( LIST[I], LIST[K]);
        end
end
```

3 Give a parallel algorithm for finding the cube root of A, using Newton–Raphson iteration. That is, find the value of x, where $F(x) = x^3 – A = 0$. Recall the iteration is based on $x_i = x_{i-1} – F(x_i)/F'(x_i)$.

4 Draw a program graph similar to Figure 7.3 for the following loop. Be sure to insert the synchronization places that would be necessary to force flow-correctness on this loop if it were written as a **par** loop.

```
for(i := 1; i ≤ N; i++){
    a[i] := a[i – 2] + b[i];
    b[i] := c[i] – b[i];
    c[i] := a[i] – 1;
    a[i] := a[i] / d[i]
}
```

5 Write a flow-correct **par** loop for the example in Problem 4. Using FLOW and ANTI predicates, show that your solution is flow-correct.

6 Draw the iteration space diagram for the code in Problem 4.

7 Assuming target machine parameters $w_0 = 10$, $w_1 = 0.001$, $r_0 = 100$, and $r_1 = 10$, for what value of n (number of **par** clauses) does speedup of a **par** equal 1.0? What does this say about the cost of overhead in a **par**?

8 Show that the parallel algorithm for Newton–Raphson square root is output dependency correct.

9 Can the bitonic sort of Chapter 5 be rewritten using **par** instead of **fan**?

10 Show that the parallel version of quicksort is flow-correct.

11   Can you find a better (shorter elapsed time) Gantt chart schedule for the problem of Figure 7.5? If so, show it.

12   What is forward-substitution? Give an example.

13   Show that the butterfly algorithm of the FFT program is flow-correct.

14   Is it possible to write a parallel sort algorithm that runs in $O(\log_2 N)$ time? Why is parallel quicksort a poor algorithm for parallel machines?

15   Show that the parallel quicksort algorithm is flow-correct.

REFERENCES

W. H. Press, B. P. Flannery, S. A. Teukolsky, W. T. Vetterling, *Numerical Recipes*, Cambridge University Press, Cambridge England, 1989.

CHAPTER 8

The Dependent-Loop
Pipe

The **pipe** construct implements a loop containing flow-dependent
statements. Specifically, any sequential loop containing flow dependencies caused by serial OUT, ANTI, and FLOW patterns, as well as loop-carried
dependencies, can be converted into an iterative **pipe**. Therefore, the **pipe** is the
most general form of parallel loop, but as we shall see, it is also the most limited in
terms of potential for performance speedup.

A **pipe** achieves loop parallelism at the statement level, much like the **fan** and
par. But, **pipes** are not synchronized after each iteration. Instead, the statements
in the body of a **pipe** are executed asynchronously, staggered in time, so that
statements from earlier iterations overlap with the same statements from later
iterations. Statement 1 of iteration 1 is started first, followed by statement 1 of
iteration 2. After executing two statements of iteration 2, the third iteration is
started, and executes statements in parallel with iterations 1 and 2. The different
iterations of the loop are run in parallel, but staggered in time, due to their different starting times. Statements from different iterations execute at the same time.

Given a **pipe** body containing k statements, the **pipe** uses k processes to speed
up the loop by a factor of k. The first process executes the first, $(k + 1)$, $(2k + 1)$,
$(3k + 1)$, ..., iterations. The second process executes the second, $(k + 2)$, $(2k + 2)$,
$(3k + 2)$, ..., iterations. Finally, process k executes the kth, $(k + k)$, $(2k + k)$,
$(3k + k)$, ..., iterations. This pattern stops as soon as the Nth iteration completes.
Thus, regardless of the number of iterations, N, the speedup of a pipe is limited to k.

171

We will define the conditions under which highly dependent sequential loops can be rewritten as parallel **pipe** loops. They are used when it is not possible to use a **fan** or a **par** due to dependencies. But in general, **pipe**s return limited speedup, so they should be used only after **fan** and **par** constructs have been considered.

A **pipe** implements a form of *systolic parallelism* with the following features:

- Statements are numbered and executed in order.

- Iterations are not tightly synchronized, but statement $j < k$ is always executed before statement k, in each iteration. Statements from different iterations execute at the same time.

- Backward loop-carried dependencies are safe, but *forward loop-carried* dependencies can lead to flow errors. A **pipe** must be carefully designed to remove forward dependencies.

- Parallel execution is achieved by overlapping iterations of the loop body, achieving at most a k-fold increase in performance for a loop of $N \geq k$ iterations.

The concepts of *grain packing* and *skew* will be introduced to handle forward loop-carried dependency. These reduce parallelism, but allow limited parallelism to be mined from highly dependent loops. We will illustrate these concepts with three examples: a matrix algorithm, a merge algorithm, and a hashing function optimization algorithm.

In this chapter we will show how to use **pipe**s to parallelize loop-carried dependent, as well as flow dependent loops. We will generalize our results to show that a **par** should be used when there are only loop-carried dependencies, and a **fan** should be used when there are only flow-dependencies within an iteration.

8.1 PIPE PARALLELISM

The major difference between a **par** and a **pipe** is that a **pipe** does not synchronize at the end of each iteration. That is, a **pipe** lacks the barrier at the end of the loop. In Figure 8.1 we see that k processes are needed to execute k **pipe** statements in parallel. Each process copies all k statements, and executes them in sequence. However, the k processes are staggered in time.

The **pipe** construct overlaps statements as if they were processes in a vector processor, see Figure 8.1. Thus, as soon as process 1 completes statement 1, it signals process 2 to begin iteration 2. Once statement 2 is completed by process 2, it signals process 3 to begin iteration 3, and so on. In general, when statement i of iteration i is completed by process i, iteration $(i + 1)$ is started in process $(i + 1)$. This wraps around to the first process, assuming there are more iterations to be performed: the last process begins iteration $(k + 1)$ on the first process as soon as its first statement is finished.

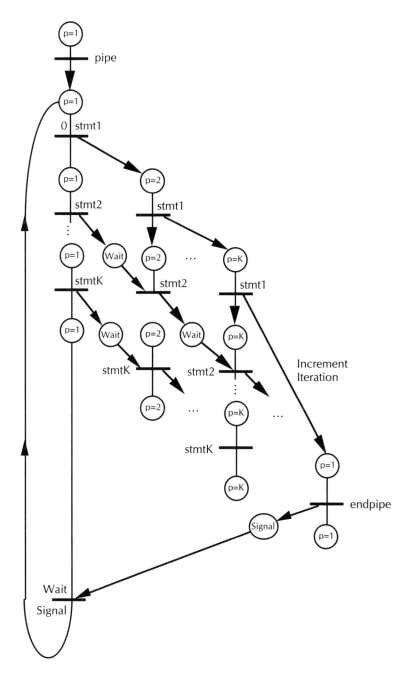

Figure 8.1   **Program graph for pipe parallelism**

A **pipe** is executed much like a **fan** where each process is synchronized at the statement level, as shown by the equivalent code below. The *signal* and *wait* functions perform synchronization. A signal message is sent to a corresponding wait to force delays.

```
for i := 1 to n {
    if i > 1 then wait(1, i);
    stmt 1, i;                          /* stmt 1, i means do statement 1, iteration i */
    if i < n then signal(1, i + 1);
    if i > 1 then wait(2, i);
    stmt 2,i;
    if i < n then signal(2, i + 1);
    .
    .
    .
    if i > 1 then wait(k, i);
    stmt k, i;
    if i < n then signal(k, i + 1)
}
```

If the loop repeats more than k times, the process described above is repeated with process 1 running iteration $(k + 1)$, process 2 running iteration $(k + 2)$, and so forth, until all iterations are finished. Each process executes all statements of the loop, in sequence, but overlapped with parallel iterations staggered in time.

If there are fewer than k iterations of the loop, this cascading sequence is stopped as soon as the Nth iteration is completed by processes $N < k$. In this case, the program graph of Figure 8.1 is shortened to $p = N$ processes, with no loop back.

The k statements of a **pipe** are mapped onto each of k processes. If the body is iterated $N > k$ times, the **pipe** still takes k processes to run all iterations, but each process runs approximately $(N \text{ div } k)$ iterations. Hence, an $O(k * N)$ complex sequential loop can be run in $O(N)$ time, if communication and process creation overhead are ignored. This k-fold speedup is far from the desirable N-fold speedup, resulting in only modest improvement in speed.

Example 8.1

Compare the way the statements of the following sequential loop are executed to show the way they are executed in a **pipe**. This loop was introduced in Chapter 5. In this example, assume $N = 5$ and $k = 3$.

```
for(i := 1; i ≤ N; i++){          /* Repeat N times    */
    a[i] := a[i – 1] + b[i];      /* Loop-carried dependency   */
    b[i] := 2 * b[i];             /* Antidependency   */
    c[i] := a[i] – 1              /* Dataflow dependency   */
}
```

The **pipe** version of this loop overlaps the execution of statements as follows:

Time, t	$p = 1$	$p = 2$	$p = k = 3$
1	a[1] := a[0] + b[1]	Idle	Idle
2	b[1] := 2 * b[1]	a[2] := a[1] + b[2]	Idle
3	c[1] := a[1] − 1	b[2] := 2 * b[2]	a[3] := a[2] + b[3]
4	a[4] := a[3] + b[4]	c[2] := a[2] − 1	b[3] := 2 * b[3]
5	b[4] := 2 * b[4]	a[5] := a[4] + b[5]	c[3] := a[3] − 1
6	c[4] := a[4] − 1	b[5] := 2 * b[5]	
7	c[5] := a[5] − 1		

At time $t = 1$, only the first statement is performed by a process labelled in Figure 8.1 as $p = 1$. Nothing happens in any other process until process 1 signals the second process to start.

At time $t = 2$, processes $p = 1$ and $p = 2$ execute stmt1 = {b[1] := 2 * b[1]}, stmt2 = {a[2] := a[1] + b[2]}, respectively, as per Figure 8.1. Then, at time $t = 3$, process $p = 3$ executes stmt3 = { a[3] := a[2] + b[3]} while the other two processes execute their next statements. Continuing in this fashion, all processes execute statements at the same time, but with corresponding statements staggered in time.

Note that the loop-carried dependencies on $b[i]$ and $a[i]$ do not cause data flow anomalies because of the staggering. The value of $b[i]$ used in an earlier process can be changed by a later process without output dependency, antidependency, or flow dependency. However, this is not a general rule, as we will see later.

8.2 THREE KINDS OF PIPES

The **pipe** statement is used to implement systolic parallelism, dependent loops, or a restricted form of general loop parallelism. Specifically, the **pipe** mimics three forms of looping, as follows:

1 **pipe** <boolean-test>
   mapin <mapin-list>
   {<body>}
   mapout <mapout-list>
   endpipe

2 **pipe**
   mapin <mapin-list>
   {<body>}
   mapout <mapout-list>
   until <boolean-test>

3 **pipe** <counter>
   mapin <mapin-list>
   {<body>}
   mapout <mapout-list>
   endpipe

The optional **mapin** and **mapout** directives work much like they do in a **fan**, sending or receiving messages from the parallel processes. The <body> consists of k labelled statements, each statement overlapped in execution time with the others. This overlap is the source of the speedup, but it is also the source of potential flow-dependency errors if we improperly group actions into statements.

The number k determines how many parallel processes are created to perform the **pipe**. One parallel process is created for each of the k statements. Thus, the speedup is determined by the number of statements rather than by the number of iterations of the **pipe**.

```
1 : <stmt1>;
2 : <stmt2>;
 .
 .
 .
k : <stmtk>;
```

The statement number is unique and serves to number the statements in <body>. All statements of the **pipe** <body> are assigned to k identical processes that are staggered in time. Therefore, on each iteration through the **pipe**, the statements are skewed in starting times, as shown below:

Time t	$p = 1$	$p = 2$	...	$p = k$
1	1 : <stmt1>;			
2		2 : <stmt2>;		
.				
.				
.				
k				k : <stmtk>;

The **pipe** is interpreted as follows. First, k processes containing a copy of the code for <body> are forked from the parent process. Then, the first process executes statement 1, and signals the second process to execute statement 1 of the second iteration. After each statement is executed, the next iteration is signalled to execute in the next process. Each statement waits to be signalled by the previous iteration. Each iteration is executed by a process.

If process 1 reaches the end of the current iteration before all other processes, it waits until *signalled* to begin a subsequent iteration. When the last process ($p = k$) completes its first statement, it signals process 1 to begin iteration ($k + 1$), which in turn causes processes ($k + 2$), ($k + 3$), ..., ($2k$) to begin staggered executions of iterations ($k + 2$), ($k + 3$), ..., ($2k$) of the loop.

Once all staggered processes are started, they run in parallel. But since it is possible for a statement in one process to change a variable used by another process, **mapin/mapout** messages are sent to adjacent processes when updates are needed. This is a source of great overhead in the **pipe**, limiting the practical speedup achieved to cases where the time to execute each statement is relatively significant.

As each process completes its final iteration, the number of active processes declines, one-by-one, until all cease due to a lack of statements and iterations to execute.

Example 8.2

Example 8.1 can be rewritten as a **pipe** with $k = 3$ statements. The right-hand side variables are mapped into the **pipe**, and the left-hand side variables are mapped out of the **pipe**. Parallelism speeds up the loop by forking $k = 3$ processes to perform staggered iterations in parallel.

The construct <body>, which contains the $k = 3$ statements, is copied to each of the $k = 3$ processes. They execute the same three statements asynchronously, much like a **fan**. However, unlike a **fan**, they are started at different times. Each process is forced to wait until its predecessor signals it to begin. This chain reaction of signals propagates through the processes, wave after wave, until all N iterations have ceased.

First, we show the **pipe** code for parallel execution of the sequential code:

```
for(i := 1; i ≤ N; i++){          /* Repeat N times    */
    a[i] := a[i – 1] + b[i];      /* Loop-carried dependency   */
    b[i] := 2 * b[i];             /* Antidependency   */
    c[i] := a[i] – 1              /* Dataflow dependency    */
}
```

Then, we show the synchronization code along with message-passing needed to implement the **pipe**. First, the parallel **pipe** version:

```
pipe i := 1,2..N;                 /* Fork k = 3 parallel processes, but stagger them */
mapin a[i – 1] to am1;
      b[i] to bi;
{ float am1, bi, ci, a;
      1: a := am1 + bi
      2: bi := 2 * bi
      3: ci := a – 1 }
mapout a to a[i];
       bi to b[i];
       ci to c[i]
endpipe
```

The iteration space diagram for this loop ($k = 3$, $N = 3$) is shown as both a diagram and a table (see Figure 8.2). Note that at time step 3, iteration 1 of statement 3, iteration 2 of statement 2, and iteration 3 of statement 1 execute.

The reader should further observe in Figure 8.2 that dependencies are honored between statements 1 and 2, and 1 and 3. Statement 1 always executes before statement 2 within the same iteration, corresponding to the vertical dependency arc from 1 to 2 in Figure 8.2. This dependency also corresponds to a column in the table.

Similarly, the loop-carried dependency shown as a horizontal arc between iterations is honored. Why?

Now, we show how this **pipe** is implemented:

```
for i := 1 to n {
    if i > 1 then wait(1, i);      /* Statement 1    */
    mapin a[i – 1] to am1;
          b[i] to bi;
```

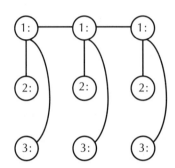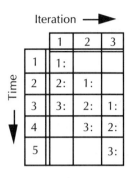

Figure 8.2   Iteration space diagram and table for the pipe of Example 8.2

```
{ float am1, bi, a;
    a := am1 + bi }
mapout a to a[i];
if i < n then signal(1, i + 1);

if i > 1 then wait(2, i);                /* Statement 2   */
mapinb[i] to bi;
{ float bi;
    bi := 2 * bi
mapout bi to b[i];
if i < n then signal(2, i + 1);
  .
  .
  .
if i > 1 then wait(k, i);                /* Statement k   */
mapin  a[i] to a;
{ float  ci, a;
    ci := a – 1 }
mapout ci to c[i];
if i < n then signal(k, i + 1)
}
```

8.2.1 Conditional Pipe

There are two general forms of a **pipe**: the *conditional loop*, and the *counting loop*. These correspond to the sequential programming constructs **while, repeat-until**, and **for**. The two conditional forms iterate when the Boolean test is satisfied, and correspond to **while** and **repeat-until**.

The two forms of *conditional **pipe*** are the following:

1   **pipe** <boolean-test>
    mapin <mapin-list>
    {<body>}
    mapout <mapout-list>
    endpipe

```
2   pipe
      mapin <mapin-list>
      {<body>}
      mapout <mapout-list>
      until <boolean-test>
```

These two forms can sometimes be used to convert a **while** or **repeat-until** into a **pipe**. Example 8.3 illustrates an application of this principle, while Example 8.4 illustrates an application for which this principle fails.

Example 8.3

Consider the sequential loop for computing pairwise averages up to some maximum number, max. The averages are obtained by adding the two numbers from an array to obtain another array, avg[], which stores the averages. (This can also be done with a **par**. Would a **par** be faster?)

```
i := 1; avg[i] := 0;
while f[i] < max do                     /* Stop when we reach max   */
   begin
      i := i + 1;                        /* Next number, please   */
      avg[i] := (f[i] + f[i – 1]) / 2.0  /* Average pairs   */
   end
```

Simply replacing **while** with **pipe**, and mapping the data, yields:

```
i := 1; avg[i] := 0;                    /* Initial Fibonacci numbers   */
pipe f[i] < max                         /* Quit when max is reached   */
mapin i to i; f[i] to f; f[i – 1] to f1;
{float a, f, f1;
 int i;
      1: i := i + 1;                     /* Increment, while   */
      2: a := (f + f1) / 2.0}            /* Averaging   */
mapout i to i; a to avg[i]
endpipe
```

The iteration space showing a *wavefront* for this loop is shown in Figure 8.3. Clearly, any dependency lagging the wavefront is of no concern as far as flow-correctness goes. Any dependency in front of the wavefront leads to a flow error. So to be sure, we check the FLOW predicate as follows:

FLOW(i, t) :-
    $(\exists \Delta t > 0 \mid \text{DEF}(i, t - \Delta t))$,   e.g., $i := 1$; at $t = 0$
    USE(i, t). $i := 2$; at $t = 1$

This predicate is TRUE along the vertical dependency arc in Figure 8.3, but $\Delta t = 0$ along the horizontal arc. So, is this **pipe** flow-correct? The control shown in Figure 8.1 shows that stmt1 of the second process is started after stmt1 of the first process. The value mapped from the first $\{i := i + 1\}$ is used by the second $\{i := 1 + 1\}$ in process 2. Thus, i is mapped in as 1 in the first process, and i is mapped in as 2 in the second process, and so forth. The first process uses $1 + 1$ to compute avg[2], the second process uses $2 + 1$ to compute avg[3], and so forth. This assures us that the antidependency is preserved by the mapping functions.

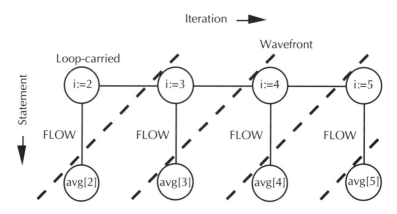

Figure 8.3   Iteration diagram for calculation of average

The previous example illustrates a general principle of **pipes**: *Dependencies which lag the diagonal wavefront are permitted; dependencies which lie on or ahead of the wavefront are flow errors.*

Violation of this rule means we must either pack statements into *grains* to remove the forward dependencies, or else avoid the **pipe**. The next example illustrates this limitation.

Example 8.4

Consider the example presented in Chapter 5 where we used Newton–Raphson approximation to compute the square root of a number as follows:

```
oldx := 0.0; x := 1;               /* Initial guesses   */
while abs(x – oldx) > eps do        /* eps is the error limit   */
    begin
    oldx := x;                      /* Save x for later   */
    x := 0.5 * (x + A / x);         /* Iterate x   */
    end;                            /* New approximation   */
```

Replacing **while** with **pipe**, and adding the necessary mapping functions, leads to the following:

```
oldx := 0.0; x := 1;               /* Initial guesses   */
pipe abs(x – oldx) > eps           /* eps is the error limit   */
mapin A to a; x to x;              /* Create two staggered procs   */
{ float x, oldx, a;
    1: oldx := x;                  /* Save x for later   */
    2: x := 0.5 * (x + A / x)}     /* Iterate x   */
mapout oldx to oldx; x to x        /* Output the results   */
endpipe
```

The problem with this pipe is that the forward loop-carried dependency represented by the diagonal arc leads to a flow dependency error. The next value of oldx is computed before the new value of *x* is mapped back out of the previous process. Thus, {oldx := x} leads to the wrong value for oldx (see Figure 8.4).

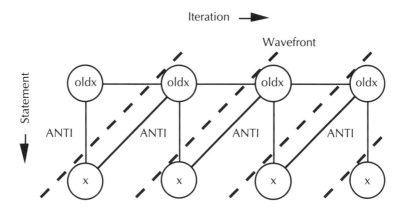

Figure 8.4   Iteration diagram for failed pipe in Example 8.4

8.2.2 Counting Pipe

We have already seen several examples of correct and incorrect applications of **pipe** iterations. The counting pipe must obey the same rules of dependency, but because it is controlled by a counter, we can predict its performance. The general form of the *counting pipe* is:

pipe <counter>
mapin <mapin-list>
{<body>}
mapout <mapout-list>
endpipe

In addition, we introduce an extension to the <counter> syntax which allows us to control the degree of *skew*. Skew is the amount of staggering between processes. Increasing the skew changes the wave-front angle so that forward dependencies do not cause errors. Increasing the skew may be useful for removing the kind of dependency errors shown in Figure 8.4 without packing statements into larger grains.

Example 8.5

Can the following serial loop be parallelized using a **pipe**? Pay particular attention to the last statement, which contains a forward loop-carried dependency:

```
for(i := 1; i ≤ N; i++){        /* Repeat N times   */
    a[i] := a[i − 1] + b[i];     /* Loop-carried dependency   */
    b[i] := 2 * b[i];            /* Antidependency   */
    c[i] := a[i + 1] − 1         /* Forward loop-carried dependency    */
}
```

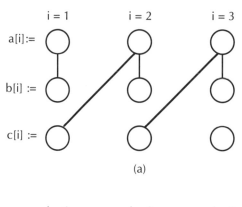

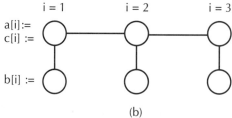

(b)

Figure 8.5   **Conversion of forward dependency into backward dependency by group-ing: (a) dependencies in original loop, and (b) dependencies in pipe loop**

The meaning of this sequential loop is shown below and in Figure 8.5a, for the first 3 iterations:

Time, t	$i = 1$	
1	a[1] := a[0] + b[1];	
2	b[1] := 2 * b[1];	
3	c[1] := a[2] – 1;	/* Use $a[2]$ before it is changed */

Time, t	$i = 2$	
4	a[2] := a[1] + b[2];	/* Change $a[2]$ after it is used */
5	b[2] := 2 * b[2];	
6	c[2] := a[3] – 1;	/* Use $a[3]$ before it is changed */

Time, t	$i = 3$	
7	a[3] := a[2] + b[3];	/* Change $a[3]$ after it is used */
8	b[3] := 2 * b[3];	
9	c[3] := a[4] – 1;	

For example, the precondition and postcondition on $a[i + 1]$ is clearly

$$\text{USE}(a[i + 1]) \ \{i \ \textbf{is} \ i + 1\} \ \text{DEF}(a[i]) \Rightarrow \text{USE}(a[i + 1]) \ \text{DEF}(a[i + 1])$$

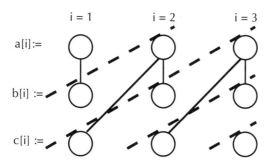

Figure 8.6   **Wavefront of diagram in Figure 8.5a**

When applied to the ANTI predicate we get the following, which is TRUE for $\Delta t = 1$:

ANTI(a[i + 1], t) :-
     ($\exists \Delta t > 0$ | USE(a[i + 1], t − Δt)),
     DEF(a[i + 1], t).

What is the meaning of an equivalent **pipe**? Arranging the statements in an iteration space diagram as before, shows that the forward loop-carried dependency *can lead* to a race condition:

Time, t	$p = 1$	$p = 2$	$p = 3$
1	a[1] := a[0] + b[1];		
2	b[1] := 2 * b[1];	a[2] := a[1] + b[2];	
3	c[1] := a[2] − 1;	b[2] := 2 * b[2];	a[3] := a[2] + b[3];
4		c[2] := a[3] − 1;	b[3] := 2 * b[3];
5			c[3] := a[4] − 1;

The forward dependency on $a[2]$ leads to an incorrect result, because the value of $a[2]$ is changed at $t = 2$ in $p = 2$ and used at $t = 3$ in $p = 1$. A similar error occurs between $t = 3$ in $p = 3$ and $t = 4$ in $p = 2$. This forward loop-carried dependency leads to an antidependency error:

ANTI(a[2], t) :-
     ($\exists \Delta t > 0$ | USE(a[2], t − Δt)),
     DEF(a[2], t).

By inspection, we see that this predicate is TRUE only if $\Delta t < 0$, which reveals the error. For example, from the table above:

ANTI(a[2], 2) :-
     ($\exists \Delta t = -1$ | USE(a[2], 2 + 1)),
     DEF(a[2], 2).

If we draw a wavefront in Figure 8.5a, the forward dependency clearly leads the wavefront (see Figure 8.6). The solution to this problem is to either remove the forward dependency or force it to lag the wavefront. First, we will show in an example how to remove it.

From Example 8.5, it is clear that we must check **pipe** statements for *forward loop-carried dependencies*. One remedy is to pack such dependent statements together to guarantee flow-correctness. Grain packing is one solution. A corrected **pipe** for this example is given in the next example.

Example 8.6

Correct the previous example by combining forward loop-carried dependent statements into one statement. The modified dependencies are shown in Figure 8.5b. A **pipe** based on Figure 8.5b is given below. We have used grain packing to remove the forward dependencies:

pipe i := 1,2..N;	/* Fork N parallel processes, but stagger them */
mapin a[i – 1] **to** a1;	/* := a[i – 1] + b[i] */
b[i] **to** bi;	/* := a[i + 1] – 1 */
a[i + 1] **to** ap1;	
b[i] **to** bi	/* := 2 * b[i] */
{ **float** a, a1, ap1, bi;	
1: { a := a1 + bi;	/* Packed grain */
a1 := ap1 – 1};	
2: bi := 2 * bi ;	
}	
mapout a **to** a[i];	/* a[i] := */
a1 **to** c[i];	/* c[i] := */
bi to b[i];	/* b[i] := */
endpipe	

This solution gives the iteration diagram shown in Figure 8.5b, leading to a sequence of calculations as shown below, for $k = 2$, $N = 3$:

Time, t	$p = 1$	$p = 2$
1	a[1] := a[0] + b[1]; c[1] := a[2] – 1;	
2	b[1] := 2 * b[1];	a[2] := a[1] + b[2]; c[2] := a[3] – 1;
3	a[3] := a[2] + b[3]; c[3] := a[4] – 1;	b[2] := 2 * b[2];
4	b[3] := 2 * b[3];	

Compare this with the sequential version. Testing for antidependency, we see that the flow-correctness error has been removed. However, this loop runs slower, because 2 processes are used instead of 3 processes.

$$ANTI(a[i + 1], t) :- $$
$$(\exists \Delta t > 0 \mid USE(a[i + 1], t - \Delta t)),$$
$$DEF(a[i + 1], t).$$

This predicate is TRUE when $\Delta t = 1 > 0$. The dependencies shown in Figure 8.5b are acceptable to the **pipe** construct. But, the forward loop-carried dependency shown in Figure 8.5a is not. What are the limitations of the **pipe**?

We can cope with the forward dependencies in another way. Suppose a skew is added to the staggered processes. A skew is a form of delay, as illustrated in the next example.

Example 8.7

The previous example might be corrected by exchanging statements, so that the $c[i]$ calculation is performed before the $b[i]$ calculation. For example, the body of the loop can be rearranged as follows:

a[i] := a[i − 1] + b[i];	/* Loop-carried dependency */
c[i] := a[i + 1] − 1	/* Forward loop-carried dependency */
b[i] := 2 * b[i];	/* Antidependency */

Does this remove the problem? Not quite, but if we add a skew to each subsequent process, delaying it for one additional time step, then the iteration diagram of the skewed **pipe** with $k = 3$ and $N = 5$ becomes

Time, t	p = 1	p = 2	p = 3
1	a[1] := a[0] + b[1];	Skew = 1	Skew = 1
2	c[1] := a[2] − 1;	Skew = 2	Skew = 2
3	b[1] := 2 * b[1];	a[2] := a[1] + b[2]	Skew = 3
4		c[2] := a[3] − 1;	Skew = 4
5		b[2] := 2 * b[2];	a[3] := a[2] + b[3];
6			c[3] := a[4] − 1;
7	a[4] := a[3] + b[4];		b[3] := 2 * b[3];
8	c[4] := a[5] − 1;		
9	b[4] := 2 * b[4];	a[5] := a[4] + b[5];	
10		c[5] := a[6] − 1;	
11		b[5] := 2 * b[5];	

The loop-carried antidependency is resolved, but the loop takes longer to execute all $N = 5$ iterations. Checking the ANTI predicate, we see that $\Delta t > 0$, as it should be.

ANTI(a[i + 1], t) :-
    ($\exists\, \Delta t > 0$ | USE(a[i + 1], t − 1)),
    DEF(a[i + 1], t).

For example, when $t = 3$:

ANTI(a[i + 1], 3) :-
    ($\exists\, \Delta t = 1$ | USE(a[i + 1], 2)),
    DEF(a[i + 1], 3).

The **pipe** for this solution is shown below:

pipe i := 1,2..N **by** 2	/* Skew by 2 */
mapin a[i − 1] **to** a1;	/* := a[i − 1] + b[i] */
b[i] **to** bi;	/* := a[i + 1] − 1 */
a[i + 1] **to** ap1;	
b[i] **to** bi	/* := 2 * b[i] */

```
{ float a, a1, ap1, bi;
      1: a := a1 + bi;                    /* Packed grain   */
      2: a1 := ap1 – 1;
      3: bi := 2 * bi ;
}
mapout a to a[i];                         /* a[i] :=   */
       a1 to c[i];                        /* c[i] :=   */
       bi to b[i];                        /* b[i] :=   */
endpipe
```

Note that the skew is indicated in the counter using the keyword **by**. When absent, **by** is assumed to be 1.

The skewed **pipe** illustrated above runs slower than a nonskewed **pipe**. This is due to the reduced *degree of parallelism*. Skewing is limited to $1 \leq skew \leq k$. When skew = k, the loop runs exactly like a sequential loop. When skew = 1, we get the maximal parallelism. Later, we will show that speedup is asymptotic to k / skew, when overhead is ignored. The degree of parallelism, assuming no loss due to overhead, is $d = k - skew$. Skewing removes the forward dependencies, but it also reduces performance.

All **pipe**s are skewed. If the skew is 1, we simply drop the **by** clause. If the skew is greater than 1, we must specify an integer constant or expression which evaluates to an integer constant. The range of values of this constant must be $1 \leq skew \leq k$. Forward dependencies that extend beyond $(k - 1)$ pose no risk. Why? What is the relationship between the statement number and the amount of skewing needed to guarantee flow-correctness?

8.3 FLOW CORRECTNESS OF PIPE

From Figure 8.1 and the foregoing examples, we can assert some general properties of **pipe**s. In particular:

1   For a given iteration, all statements are executed in exactly the same order as they would be executed by a sequential loop. Thus, within an iteration, dependencies such as anti-, output, and flow obey the same rules as sequential code. This means that a **pipe** can be used to increase the parallelism of loops containing simple dependencies.

2   Across iterations, there may exist loop-carried dependencies. Forward loop-carried dependencies cause no errors if they lag the wavefront established by a skew. Backward loop-carried dependencies cause no problems at all.

3   Forward loop-carried dependencies may be reduced or removed by two techniques: grain packing, or skewing. Both techniques reduce performance, but assert flow-correctness.

From these assertions, we can guarantee that the order of execution of statements in a properly formed **pipe** is flow-correct. However, we must check for

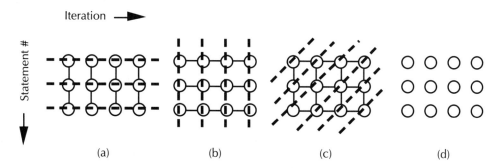

Iteration ──▶

Statement #

Figure 8.7 Iteration spaces and their corresponding programming constructs: (a) fan, (b) par, (c) pipe, (d) fan + par. Dotted lines indicate flow-correct wave fronts.

adherence to these rules. The danger in using a **pipe** stems from the fact that iterations overlap, so it is possible that statements from different iterations execute at the same time. Therefore, all **pipe**s must be checked for forward loop-carried dependencies. When they are found, one must apply rule 3 to guarantee flow-correctness.

The general method for converting sequential loops into pipes is as follows:

- Draw the iteration diagram for the body of the loop.
- Divide the diagram into two parts by drawing a diagonal wavefront such that all forward loop-carried dependencies lag the wavefront.
- Apply grain packing or skewing to implement the pipe.

8.4 CLASSIFICATION OF LOOPS

Loops can be classified according to their dependencies. The appropriate construct to use is dictated by these dependencies, which are graphically depicted as iteration diagrams (see Figure 8.7).

A **fan** can be used whenever statements within an iteration of a loop depend on one another. This is shown as a vertical arc in the iteration diagram. Because each process of a fan sequentially executes all statements of the body, all forms of statement dependencies are permitted.

A **par** can be used whenever the loop body contains loop-carried dependencies. This is shown as a horizontal arc connecting statements in different iterations. Because each process of a **par** synchronizes at the **endpar** barrier, the loop-carried dependencies are obeyed.

A **pipe** is useful for executing statements that contain both loop-carried and statement dependencies. But, we must be careful to prevent forward loop-carried dependencies from leading to flow errors.

Finally, a nested **par** within a **fan** is useful for parallel execution of statements that are totally independent of one another.

In each case, except the last one, a wavefront is shown as a dotted line. The wavefront establishes a safety zone. Dependencies behind the wave cause no problems. Dependencies ahead of the wave need to be checked, as they lead to flow errors.

The **fan** is flow-correct for vertical dependencies, the **par** is appropriate for horizontal dependencies, and the **pipe** is flow-correct when either vertical or horizontal dependencies occur.

The iteration space examples in Figure 8.7 are two-dimensional. A similar result can be shown for three-dimensional iteration spaces corresponding to nested loops. Also, these examples assume a unit step size in the loop counter.

8.5 PERFORMANCE OF PIPE

How much speedup can we expect from a **pipe** if communication and process overhead is included? Intuitively, we know that the **pipe** implements k-fold parallelism, but how much of this potential is realized for a real-world implementation?

We know that the execution time of a sequential loop of k statements, where statement i takes t_i time units to execute, and there are N iterations, is given by

$$T_1 = r_0 + r_1 N \sum_{i=1}^{k} t_i$$

where r_0 is the process startup time, and r_1 is the processing time per operation.

Then, using Figure 8.8 as our guide, we can compute the delay time for a skewed **pipe** as follows. The first round of k statements takes time

$$\sum_{i=1}^{k} t_i$$

The remaining $(N-1)$ rounds are staggered by an amount that depends on the skew. Each skew delay equals the time of a corresponding statement, so a skew of 1 adds a delay of t_1; a skew of 2 adds a delay of $t_1 + t_2$, and so forth. Thus, the total amount of skewing for the entire **pipe** is

$$(N-1) \sum_{i=1}^{skew} t_i$$

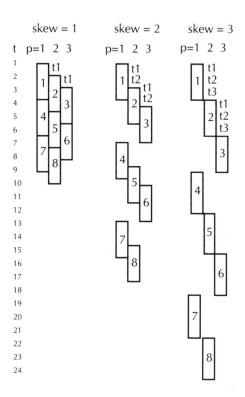

Figure 8.8   Execution scenarios for $N = 8$, $k = 3$, and skew = 1, 2, 3

Combining the two sources of delay, and noting the startup time for each of the k processes, plus the speed of each processor, we get the elapsed time for the entire **pipe** as a function of number of statements and skew:

$$r_0 k + r_1 \left\{ (N-1) \sum_{i=1}^{\text{skew}} t_i + \sum_{i=1}^{k} t_i \right\}$$

= process startup time + time for N iterations using k processes

Now, we must consider communication delays introduced by sending **mapin/ mapout** data to and from the k processes. Note that each time a statement is executed, it must receive an update from the main process. That is, before each of the k statements begins, we must copy the latest values of the variables into the local process. If we assume that the size of the data to be mapped is S, then the communication delay for each iteration is $k(w_0 + w_1 S)$, where w_0 is message initiation time, and w_1 is transmission time per character.

There are $(N-1)$ rounds that must receive updates, so this introduces an additional delay of $k(N-1)(w_0 + w_1 S)$ time units. Combining the processing time delay with the communication time delay yields the overall total:

$$T_k = r_0 k + r_1 \left\{ (N-1) \sum_{i=1}^{\text{skew}} t_i + \sum_{i=1}^{k} t_i \right\} + k(N-1)(w_0 + w_1 S)$$

Example 8.8

Suppose a **pipe** and the machine it runs on have the following characteristics:

S = 1,000 characters
w_0 = 10 ms
w_1 = 0.001 ms/character
r_0 = 100 ms
r_1 = 10 ms/operation

where ms is milliseconds, and an operation is roughly equivalent to a multiplication.
    Compare the execution times of sequential versus parallel implementations, assuming $k = 7$, skew = 1, $N = 1,000$, and $t_i = t$. Thus,

$$\sum_{i=1}^{\text{skew}} t_i = t$$

and

$$\sum_{i=1}^{k} t_i = kt$$

Sequential Solution

$$T_1 = r_0 + r_1 N \sum_{i=1}^{k} t_i = 100 + 10\,(1000) \sum_{i=1}^{k} t_i$$

$$= 100 + 10\,(1000)\,(kt) = 100 + 70000t$$

Pipe Solution

$$T_k = r_0 k + r_1 \left\{ (N-1) \sum_{i=1}^{\text{skew}} t_i + \sum_{i=1}^{k} t_i \right\} + k(N-1)(w_0 + w_1 S)$$

$$= 100\,(7) + 10\,\{999t + kt\} + 7\,(999)\,(10 + 1000\,(0.001))$$

$$= 700 + 9990t + 70t + 7\,(10989) = 77623 + 10060t$$

Assuming $t = 1$, the sequential version takes 70,100 ms, compared to 87,683 ms for the **pipe** version. The **pipe** runs slower. But, assuming $t = 10$, the comparison is 700,100 ms for the sequential version, compared to 178,223 ms for the **pipe**. In this case, the **pipe** speedup is $700100/178223 = 3.9$.

The best speedup we can hope for is k, assuming no overhead. A more realistic speedup includes overhead. In fact, if the overhead is too great, the advantages of a **pipe** are lost. Including overhead,

$$\text{Speedup} = \frac{r_0 + r_1 N \sum_{i=1}^{k} t_i}{r_0 k + r_1 \left\{ (N-1) \overset{\text{skew}}{\sum_{i=1}^{k} t_i} + \sum_{i=1}^{k} t_i \right\} + k(N-1)(w_0 + w_1 S)}$$

This expression reduces to a simplified version when overhead is ignored, i.e., $r_0 = w_0 = w_1 = 0$ and we assume $(N-1) = N$, for large N and small k:

$$\text{Speedup} = \frac{Nk}{(N)\,\text{skew} + k} = \frac{k}{\text{skew}} \qquad 1 \leq \text{skew} \leq k$$

So, we see the effects of skew on speedup. The best theoretical speedup occurs when skew = 1, and the worst occurs when skew = k.

With the parameters given in Example 8.8, we get the following speedup:

$$\text{Speedup} = \frac{100 + 10Nkt}{100k + 10\{(N-1)\,\text{skew}\,(t) + kt\} + k(N-1)(10 + 0.001S)}$$

Again, assuming $(N-1) \approx N$, and dropping the term $0.001S$, the even more simplified speedup becomes:

$$\text{Speedup} = \frac{100 + 10Nkt}{100k + 10t\,((N)\,\text{skew} + k) + 10kN}$$

If we once again assume that N is very large, this further reduces to,

$$\text{Speedup} = \frac{k}{\text{skew} + k/t}$$

Example 8.9

In the previous example, we assumed $t = 1$, and obtained a sequential time of $100 + 70,000t$. The **pipe** time was $77,623 + 10,060t$. For what value of t does the **pipe** yield a speedup of 2?

Assuming the target machine parameters of the previous example, we get the following speedup formula:

$$\text{Speedup} = \frac{100 + 70000t}{77623 + 10060t} = 2.0$$

Solving for t, we get $t = 155146/59940 = 2.6$. Compare this answer with the two approximations derived in Example 8.8:

$$\text{Speedup} = \frac{k}{\text{skew} + k/t} = 2.0 \Rightarrow t = 2.8$$

$$\text{Speedup} = \frac{k}{\text{skew}} = 2.0 \Rightarrow t \text{ independent}$$

8.6 APPLICATIONS OF PIPE

The following examples were selected to illustrate how parallelism applies to a variety of areas, when it does *not* pay off, and how to apply the analysis techniques presented in this chapter. We use a matrix calculation to illustrate the techniques and to show when a **pipe** cannot give worthwhile speedups; a merge algorithm to show that parallelism has applications in business data processing; and finally a hashing example, to illustrate how we might convert a sequential algorithm into a parallel algorithm.

8.6.1 Solution to Vandermonde Linear System

A Vandermonde linear system is a special case of a linear system of equations, where the coefficients are powers of $x[1..n]$. We want to solve for $w[1..n]$ in:

$$
\begin{bmatrix}
1 & 1 & \cdots & 1 \\
x_1 & x_2 & \cdots & x_n \\
x_1^2 & x_2^2 & \cdots & x_n^2 \\
\cdots & \cdots & \cdots & \cdots \\
x_1^{n-1} & x_{n-1}^{n-1} & \cdots & x_n^{n-1}
\end{bmatrix}
\cdot
\begin{bmatrix}
w_1 \\
w_2 \\
w_3 \\
\cdots \\
w_n
\end{bmatrix}
=
\begin{bmatrix}
q_1 \\
q_2 \\
q_3 \\
\cdots \\
q_n
\end{bmatrix}
$$

The sequential program for solving this special linear system is based on a Pascal program given by Press et al. (see References at chapter end):

```
procedure vander(var w, q: doublevector; var x : doublearray);
var
     k1, k, j, i: integer;
     xx, t, s, b: double;                    { Double precision real   }
     c: doublevector;                        { c[1..n] of double precision   }
begin
     if n = 1 then w[1] := q[1]
     else begin
          for i := 1 to n do c[i] := 0.0;
          c[n] := -x[1];
          for i := 2 to n do begin
               xx := -x[i];
               for j := n + 1 - i to n - 1 do c[j] := c[j] + xx * c[j + 1];
               c[n] := c[n] + xx
          end;
          for i := 1 to n do begin
               xx := x[i];
               t := 1.0;
               b := 1.0;
               s := q[n];
               k := n;
               for j := 2 to n do begin
                    k1 := k - 1;
                    b := c[k] + xx * b;
                    s := s + q[k1] * b;
                    t := xx * t + b;
                    k := k1
               end;
               w[i] := s / t;
          end
     end
end
```

This program contains many opportunities for parallelization. For example, the loop for initialization of c_i can be converted to a **fan**, because there are no dependencies:

```
for i := 1 to n do c[i] := 0.0;
```

becomes:

```
fan i := 1..n
{ /* Do nothing */ }
mapout 0.0 to c[i];
```

Similarly, the nested loops below can be converted to parallel form as follows.

```
for i := 2 to n do begin
    xx := -x[i];
    for j := n + 1 - i to n - 1 do c[j] := c[j] + xx * c[j + 1];
    c[n] := c[n] + xx
end;
```

First, the inner loop can be converted to a **fan**, because its dependencies obey the iteration diagram of a **fan** (see Figure 8.7). The jth iteration contains an antidependency on the $(j + 1)$th iteration, because of $c[j + 1]$. But, because there is only one statement in the body of the loop, this loop-carried dependency manifests itself as an iteration dependency.

The inner loop is converted to a **fan**:

```
for i := 2 to n do begin
    fan j := n + 1 - i..n - 1
    mapin c[j] to cj;
          c[j + 1] to cj1;
          -x[i] to xx;
    { double cj, cj1, xx;
      cj := cj + xx * cj1}
    mapout cj to c[j]
    endfan;
    c[n] := c[n] - x[i]
end;
```

Now the outer loop can be converted to a **pipe**, with two statements. This is left as an exercise for the reader. We continue on to the more interesting nested loop, below:

```
for j := 2 to n do begin
    k1 := k - 1;
    b := c[k] + xx * b;
    s := s + q[k1] * b;
    t := xx * t + b;
    k := k1
end;
```

This loop can be simplified by removing the extra variable, $k1$, and substituting forward in the statements that use $k1$. This leads to the following loop, which we want to convert into a **pipe**:

```
for j := 2 to n do begin
    b := c[k] + xx * b;
    s := s + q[k - 1] * b;
    t := xx * t + b;
    k := k - 1
end;
```

The iteration diagram for this loop is shown in Figure 8.9a. Note the loop-carried dependencies linking iteration i with iteration $i + 1$. Also note the antidependencies caused by variable b. This loop appears to resist parallelization due to the numerous dependencies. But we can apply the techniques introduced earlier, and gain a small amount of parallelism from this loop.

The forward loop-carried dependencies can be eliminated by eliminating k. That is, we can rewrite the loop in a form that does not use k at all. Replacing k by $(n - j + 2)$ and $(k - 1)$ by $(n - j + 1)$ does not alter the result, but removes the dependency on k, as shown in Figure 8.9b. The loop now becomes:

```
for j := 2 to n do begin
    b := c[n − j + 2] + xx * b;
    s := s + q[n − j + 1] * b;
    t := xx * t + b;
end;
```

We can do one more trick: substitute variables bb and bbb into the loop so that the dependencies are converted to those shown in Figure 8.9c, corresponding to the modifications shown below:

```
for j := 2 to n do begin
    b := c[n − j + 2] + xx * b; bb := b;
    s := s + q[n − j + 1] * bb; bbb :=  bb;
    t := xx * t + bbb;
end;
```

It is not necessary to implement this in the **pipe**, because **mapin** creates duplicates anyway. Therefore, the **pipe** for this loop is:

```
pipe j := 2..n
mapin c[n − j + 2] to cnj2;
      x[i] to xx;
      b to b;
      s to s;
      q[n − j + 1] to qnj1;
      t to t;
{ double cnj2, xx, b, s, qnj1, t;
      1: b := cnj2 + xx * b;
      2: s := s + qnj1 * b;
      3: t := xx * t + b }
mapout b to b; s to s; t to t
endpipe
```

8.6.2 Merging Two Lists

One of the most frequent operations in data processing, besides sorting, is that of merging. Given two lists, $L1$ and $L2$, each in ascending order, combine them into a single list $LOUT$ which is also in ascending order. This operation can be done in sequential Pascal as follows:

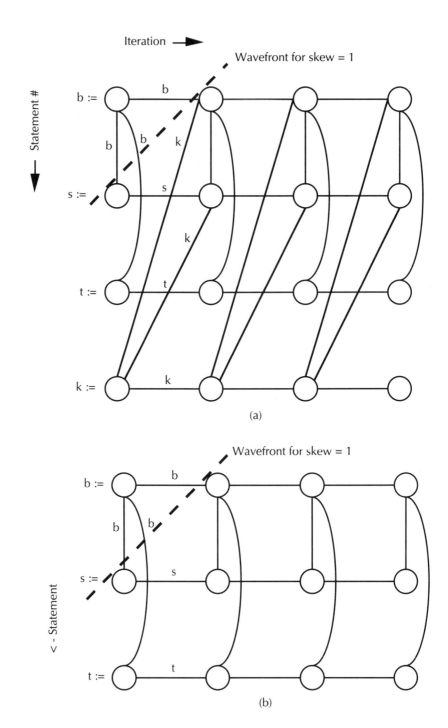

Figure 8.9   Conversion of sequential Vandermonde loop to a pipe: (a) original dependencies, (b) combine statements s := and k :=

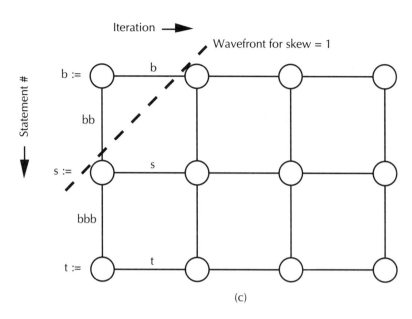

Figure 8.9 (Continued) Conversion of sequential Vandermonde loop to a pipe: (c) remove dependency between b := and t :=

```
procedure Merge( L1, L2 : list; var LOUT : listout);
var i, j : integer;
begin
    i := 1; j := 1;
    while (i <= N) and (j <= N) do begin
        LOUT[i + j – 1] := minimum(L1[i], L2[j]);
        if L1[i] < L2[j] then i := i + 1 else j := j + 1;
    end; {while}
    for i := i to N do LOUT[i + j – 1] := L1[i];
    for j := j to N do LOUT[i + j – 1] := L2[j];
end {Merge}
```

Only one of the two **for** loops at the end of the merge is performed, because only one list contains additional elements to merge when the other list is fully merged. In either case, these loops are easily converted into a **fan**, because there are no dependencies:

```
procedure Merge(L1, L2 : list; var LOUT : listout);
var i, j : integer;
begin
    i := 1; j := 1;
    while (i <= N) and (j <= N) do begin
        LOUT[i + j – 1] := minimum(L1[i], L2[j]);
        if L1[i] < L2[j] then i := i + 1 else j := j + 1;
    end;{while}
```

```
    fan i := i..N
    mapin L1[i] to L1
    {element L1}
    mapout L1 to LOUT[i + j − 1]
    endfan;
    fan j := j..N
    mapin L2[j] to L2
    {element L2}
    mapout L2 to LOUT[i + j − 1]
    endfan;
end {Merge}
```

But, what about the conditional loop, below ? Can it be parallelized? This is left as an exercise for the reader.

```
    i := 1; j := 1;
    while (i <= N) and (j <= N) do begin
        LOUT[i + j − 1] := minimum(L1[i], L2[j]);
        if L1[i] < L2[j] then i := i + 1 else j := j + 1;
    end; {while}
```

8.6.3 Finding Perfect Hashing Functions

As a final illustration of the power and limitations of pipes, we will implement a *perfect hashing function search algorithm*. The basic idea of such an algorithm is to find a function that maps integers into a table, one-to-one, without collisions which would result in more than one comparison. Such functions are very useful for high-speed lookups, because they achieve a lookup in one comparison.

We will illustrate the perfect hashing function, and then give a sequential algorithm for finding a function that yields perfect hashes in the minimum-sized table. That is, we will attempt to find the smallest hash table such that a function of the form,

$$H(w) = (w + s) \text{ div } M$$

yields a mapping from w onto $H(w)$ without conflict. This problem can be solved only when the set of integers to be mapped, w, are known in advance.

Example 8.10

Consider the hashing function $H(w) = (w + 1)$ **div** 5, which maps the squared integers $\{2, 4, 8, 16\}$ into a table of four locations without collision. This is a perfect hashing function because four numbers are mapped into the four locations of the table.

w	$H(w)$	Table location
1	$(1 + 1)$ **div** 5 = 0	0
4	$(4 + 1)$ **div** 5 = 1	1
9	$(9 + 1)$ **div** 5 = 2	2
16	$(16 + 1)$ **div** 5 = 3	3

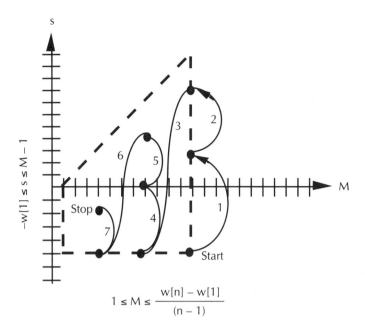

Figure 8.10 Search space, and search path for perfect function search

In this example, $s = 1$ and $M = 5$. Note that no table locations are left unused, and only four locations are needed to hold the four numbers.

The problem we must solve is stated as follows: Given a set of n numbers $w = \{w_1, w_2, ..., w_n\}$ in ascending order, what are the best values of s and M such that $H(w)$ yields the smallest table? This is an optimization problem that searches the space of all allowable solutions, until the best one is found. This search is shown in Figure 8.10, and is given in a sequential form, below.

The search starts at the lowest possible value of s, and the highest possible value of M, because these values lead to the smallest table. We increment s first, because the table size is held down while we look for a fit. Finally, the value of M is decreased, and the search along the s-axis resumed. This is shown in Figure 8.10 as a vertical search along s followed by a horizontal search along M. The sequential code is

```
procedure Perfect(w : keys; var s, M : integer);
var
      i, del, min, nexth, nextm, h : integer;
begin
      s := −w[1]; M := (w[n] − w[1]) div (n − 1);        { Initial trial values }
      repeat  {Horizontal search}
            i := 1; nexth := Hash(w[1], s, M);            { Hash is a proc }
            del := (nexth + 1) * M −w[1] − s;             { Restart values }
            min := del;
```

```
        repeat {Vertical search}
            i := i + 1; H := nexth; nexth := Hash(w[i], s, M);
            del := (nexth + 1) * M – w[i] – s;
            min := minimum(min, del);
        until (h = nexth) or (i = n);
        if h = nexth then begin
            s := s + min;
            nextm := (w[i] + s) div (nexth + 1);
            i := 1;
            if s >= M then begin
                s := –w[1]; m := nextm – ord(m = nextm)
            end;
        end;
    until (i = n ) or (M = 1);
end
```

This is a brute force algorithm that can consume large amounts of sequential computer time, especially if the magnitude of key $w[n]$ is high, and $w[1]$ is small. In fact, the computational complexity is proportional to the search space shown in Figure 8.10. This space is computed by adding the area of the lower rectangle to the upper triangle:

Complexity = area of rectangle + area of triangle

$$= w[1]\left\{\frac{w\lfloor n\rfloor - w\lfloor 1\rfloor}{n-1} - 1\right\} + 0.5\left\{\frac{w[n] - w[1]}{n-1} - 1\right\}\left\{\frac{w[n] - w[1]}{n-1} - 1\right\}$$

$$= O\left(\left\{\frac{w[n] - w[1]}{n-1} - 1\right\}^2\right)$$

Assuming $w[n]$ is much larger than $w[1]$, we can ignore $w[1]$, and $(n-1)$ is approximately n:

$$\text{Complexity} = O\left(\left\{\frac{w[n]}{n}\right\}^2\right)$$

Naturally, we want to improve the time to make this calculation. So, what can be parallelized in this code? What happens if we convert the two (nested) **repeat-until** loops into **pipes**?

```
pipe
    mapin w[1..n] to key[1..n];
            s to sopt; M to mopt;
    { keys key[1..n];
```

integer H, sopt, mopt, nexth, nextm, i, del, min;
    1: i := 1;
    2: nexth := Hash(key[1], sopt, mopt);
    3: del := (nexth + 1) * mopt − key[1] − sopt;
    4: min := del;
    5: **pipe**
      mapin i **to** i;
             nexth **to** nexth;
             key[1..n] **to** key[1..n];
             sopt **to** sopt;
             mopt **to** mopt;
             min **to** min;
      { **integer** H, sopt, mopt, nexth, nextm, i, del, min;
        1: i := i + 1;
        2: H := nexth;
        3: nexth := Hash(key[i], sopt, mopt);
        4: del := (nexth + 1) * mopt − key[i] − sopt;
        5: min := minimum(min, del)}
      mapout min **to** min; nexth **to** nexth;
      until (h = nexth) **or** (i = n);
    6: **if** h = nexth **then begin**
      sopt := sopt + min;
      nextm := (key[i] + sopt) **div** (nexth + 1);
      i := 1;
      if sopt >= mopt **then begin**
          sopt := −key[1]; m := nextm − ord(m = nextm)
      end;
    end}
mapout sopt **to** s; mopt **to** m;
until (i = n) **or** (mopt = 1);

The check for flow-correctness of this parallel version is left as an exercise for the reader. If successful, the algorithm is sixfold faster than its sequential version, because the outer loop contains six stages. The inner loop is potentially fivefold faster because it has five stages. However, these estimates ignore overhead.

8.7 KEYWORDS AND CONCEPTS

A **pipe** achieves loop parallelism at the statement level, much like the **fan** and **par** constructs. But, **pipes** are not synchronized after each iteration. Instead, the statements in the body of a **pipe** are executed asynchronously, staggered in time, so that statements from earlier iterations overlap with the same statements from later iterations. Statements from different iterations execute at the same time.

We have defined the conditions under which highly dependent sequential loops can be rewritten as parallel **pipe** loops. They are used when it is not possible to use a **fan** or a **par**, due to dependencies. But in general, **pipes** return limited speedup, so they should be used only after **fan** and **par** have been considered.

A **pipe** implements a form of *systolic parallelism* with the following features:

- Statements are numbered and executed in order.

- Iterations are not tightly synchronized, but statement $j < k$ is always executed before statement k, in each iteration. Statements from different iterations execute at the same time.

- Backward loop-carried dependencies are safe, but *forward loop-carried* dependencies can lead to flow errors. A **pipe** must be carefully designed to remove forward dependencies.

- Parallel execution is achieved by overlapping iterations of the loop body, achieving at most a k-fold increase in performance for a loop of $N \geq k$ iterations.

The concepts of *grain packing* and *skew* were introduced to handle forward loop-carried dependency. These reduce parallelism, but allow limited parallelism to be mined from highly dependent loops.

The following keywords and concepts summarize the ideas of the chapter:

Conditional pipe   The **pipe** construct replaces conditional and counting loops; hence, one can have either conditional or counting **pipes**. For example, if the sequential loop is a **while-loop**, then we replace it with a conditional **pipe**, and if the sequential loop is a **for-loop**, we replace it with a counting **pipe**.

Degree of parallelism   The degree of parallelism is equal to the maximum number of parallel processes that are active at the same time. Thus, the degree of parallelism of a pipe is $(k - 1)$, where k is the number of stages in the pipe. If we skew the stages, then the degree of parallelism is $(k - \text{skew})$. But, this is not the same as the speedup of a pipe, because of overhead.

Forward loop-carried dependencies   One of the most subtle sources of a flow error in **pipes** is the dependency of a subsequent loop iteration on a former iteration. This kind of loop-carried dependency may be removed by skewing the stages of the **pipe**.

Wavefront   We use wavefront analysis (iteration statement diagrams) to check the flow-correctness of **pipes**.

PROBLEMS

1   In a **pipe** with k statements, with skew = 1, forward dependencies that extend beyond $(k - 1)$ pose no risk. Why?

2   What is the relationship between the statement number and the amount of skewing needed to guarantee flow-correctness?

3 Compute the expected speedup on a machine and for a **pipe** with the following parameters: $S = 1,000$ characters, $w_0 = 10$ ms, $w_1 = 0.001$ ms/character, $r_0 = 100$ ms, $r_1 = 10$ ms/operation. Assume $N = 20$, $k = 10$, $t_i = i$, and skew = 2.

4 What is the best possible speedup expected for a pipe with skew = 3 and $k = 27$?

5 Derive a formula for the value of skew that yields $T_k = T_1$. In other words, when the speedup is 1, what is the value of skew?

6 Compute the speedup of the following pipe. List your assumptions.

```
pipe i := 1,2..N;          /* Fork k = 3 parallel processes, but stagger them */
mapin a[i – 1] to am1;
      b[i] to bi;
{ float am1, bi, ci, a;
      1: a := am1 + bi
      2: bi := 2 * bi
      3: ci := a – 1 }
mapout a to a[i];
       bi to b[i];
       ci to c[i]
endpipe
```

7 Can the following loop be parallelized? If so, give a pipe that solves this parallelization problem. Also, show the iteration diagram.

```
for i := 2 to n do begin
    fan j := n + 1 – i..n – 1
    mapin c[j] to cj;
          c[j + 1] to cj1;
          –x[i] to xx;
    { double cj, cj1, xx;
          cj := cj + xx * cj1}
    mapout cj to c[j]
    endfan;
    c[n] := c[n] – x[i]
end;
```

8 Rewrite the Vandermonde linear system program in parallel form. Analyze your parallel version, and estimate the speedup over its sequential version assuming the parameters given in this chapter.

9 Under what conditions of processor speed and communication delay is it practical to implement the **pipe** in the parallelized version of merge?

10 Show that the inner and outer **pipes** of the parallel perfect hashing function search algorithm are flow-correct. Under what conditions?

11 Compute the speedup of the parallel version of the perfect hashing function search algorithm. Use the processor parameters given earlier.

12   Can the following be parallelized? Why or why not?

```
i := 1; j := 1;
while (i <= N) and (j <= N) do begin
      LOUT[i + j − 1] := minimum(L1[i], L2[j]);
      if L1[i] < L2[j] then i := i + 1 else j := j + 1;
end; {while}
```

REFERENCES

W. H. Press, B. P. Flannery, S. A. Teukolsky, W. T. Vetterling, *Numerical Recipes*, Cambridge University Press, Cambridge England, 1989.

CHAPTER 9

The Client–Server Model

The **fan**, **pipe**, **tree**, and **par** constructs described thus far solve the problem of expressing fine-grained parallelism. They also provide efficient mechanisms for *static control* of parallelism, which makes them suited to applications where a program's process structure does not vary during program execution. But for large-grained applications, or programming situations where the processes are dynamically created during program execution, we need another construct.

In this chapter we will define the *method call mechanism* which provides for *large-grained data flow* parallelism, *modularity*, and dynamic creation and destruction of parallel processes. This mechanism is also called *remote procedure call (RPC)*, but as you will see, our method call mechanism improves on the RPC mechanism by incorporating the advantages of object orientation. RPC, combined with object orientation, yields the safety advantages of *encapsulation*, the flexibility of asynchronous and dynamic process activation provided by *message-passing*, and the use of *path expressions* to simplify synchronization. When paths, objects, and dynamic processes are merged into one, the result is a powerful mechanism for *client–server computing*.

We will introduce the concept of a large-grained process as *encapsulated* procedures or methods defined on some *object*. That is, a *large-grained process* is the activation of a method. Recall that an object encapsulates both data and function. Hence, a large-grained process is an *active method* which manipulates the data encapsulated in a corresponding object.

Finally, we will introduce the idea of a *server* as a way to structure large-grained computations. A server is an object plus processes to perform the actions of the object's methods. A server supports one process per activation of a method. But because a server can encapsulate many methods, and each method may be invoked by more than one process, a server may support many processes. This allows us to define *client–server parallelism* as two processes which collaborate in parallel; the client process calls one or more methods of the server; and the server provides subordinate processes to carry out the work of the client.

The client–server model will be shown by example to be a very flexible and powerful programming mechanism for encapsulating shared data and methods, implementing dynamic creation and destruction of processes, and managing synchronization of tasks. We will give two illustrations: the producer–consumer synchronization problem, whose solution is needed to implement the supervisor/worker paradigm of parallel programming; and matrix algebra (specifically, back substitution).

9.1 CLIENTS AND SERVERS

A *large grained computation* is one that takes a relatively long time compared to the communication delay in message-passing. Babb (see References at chapter end) popularized the notion of large-grained data flow computation in 1984, but the idea of increasing the size of each computation to balance the cost of communication has been known for some time. The *grain packing problem* associated with the *min-max problem* states that the size of each parallel process in a parallel program should be equal to the time it takes to send data to or receive data from the process. The best size of a process is the computation time it takes to offset communication time. Thus, a *grain* is a piece of code that is executed by a process, and a large grain is a piece of code that consumes a relatively large amount of time.

Large-grained data flow is implemented by large-grained servers, which are actually control-flow mechanisms for achieving parallelism while at the same time guaranteeing flow-correctness. Due to the relatively large size of the grains, this model is appropriate under the following conditions:

1 The cost of communication is so high that it does not permit fine-grained parallelism.

2 Processes are created and destroyed dynamically; i.e., the degree of parallelism is not known until the program executes.

The second feature is a by-product of the dynamic nature of process activations. Each time a method is called, a process is activated to execute the code in the method. But due to branches and delayed input, the number and kind of method calls may not be known beforehand. Thus, it is necessary to dynamically create processes *on the fly*, as the program executes.

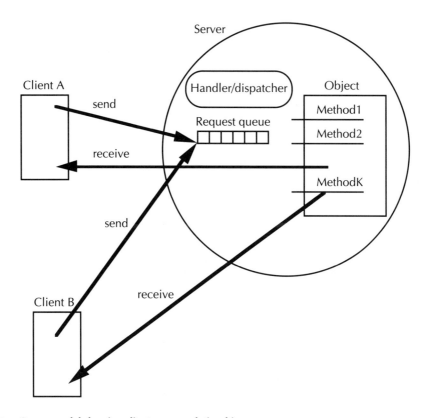

Figure 9.1   Server model showing client–server relationship

Most grains are decided by the application rather than by the desire to optimize computation. That is, we typically equate modularity with grains. In fact, we define the syntax of a grain as a method, and equate grain activation with a request for service from a server. A *server* is any object plus a process to enqueue or dequeue requests, and other processes to handle method activations.

A server is comprised of messages, processes, an object, and a request queue as follows (see Figure 9.1):

1   A request queue containing the names of the desired methods, and their parameters.

2   A handler/dispatcher process for dispatching method requests.

3   An object containing encapsulated data and methods.

4   A send/receive message pair for activating methods and communicating results.

5   Zero or more active processes, one for each method activated by a client.

Figure 9.1 shows one or more client processes being served by a server. A *client* is any process that receives services from one or more server methods.

When a client sends a request to a server, the request is immediately placed on the request queue by the server's handler/dispatcher processor. The dispatcher creates a new process for each activation of a method. Note that there can be many parallel processes running simultaneously within one server. When a method process has completed its work, the results are communicated back to the client through a return message. The client receives the message, and continues on.

The send/receive mechanism is *asynchronous*. That is, the client does not wait for the reply after sending a request to a server. Instead, the client continues in parallel with the method it called, and only waits if it reaches its receive point before the method process sends its reply. A client–server pair establishes a fork/join process pair, much like the **par** construct. However, unlike the **par**, a method request sent to a server is executed as a single, dynamic, self-synchronizing process.

Because each server may service more than one client at a time, it is necessary to synchronize access to encapsulated data. Thus, the handler/dispatcher must also enforce a *synchronization policy* which specifies the order of method activation. We will propose *path expressions* as directives to the handler/dispatcher process, which will implement a synchronization policy established by a path expression defined for every object.

In summary, the concept of a server is a combination of ideas:

1   A server is an object plus one process for each method activation.

2   Method calls are handled by a special handler/dispatcher process which controls the enqueing and dequeing of calls.

3   Method calls are asynchronous; i.e., the client does not block and wait after a call.

4   The data encapsulated inside a server are self-synchronized by the path expression defined on the object.

5   More than one client–server pair can be established concurrently.

In the following sections we will formalize the syntax and semantics of servers and show how to apply them to typical large-grained calculations. The key features of the semantics of a server are:

1   Servers are dynamic: the number of parallel processes and their type are not known until after the program begins executing.

2   Servers are modules that encapsulate data and methods; each method may incorporate fine-grained or large-grained parallelism.

3   Servers achieve parallelism by establishing an asynchronous client–server relationship between pairs of processes.

4   Activation of parallel (method) processes are synchronized by a path expression and the handler/dispatcher.

9.2 CLASSES, OBJECTS, AND SERVERS

An *object-oriented system* Ψ consists of a set of modules called *classes C*, a set of *inheritance relations H*, and a mapping function Φ that associates pairs of classes such that one is a superclass and the other is a subclass:

1    $\Psi = \{C, H, \Phi\}$. An object-oriented system.

2    $C = \{c_0, c_1, c_2, ..., c_{k-1}\}$. k classes, with a unique root class c_0.

3    $H = \{h_{1,1}, h_{1,2}, ..., h_{2,1}, h_{2,2}, ..., h_{m,n}\}$. nm inheritance relations.

4    $\Phi : C \times C \Rightarrow H$. An inheritance relation function that associates a superclass c_i with subclass c_j. One class, c_0, is the unique *root class*, which is the superclass of all other classes. All classes are associated with c_0 through transitive closure in Φ. In this case, Φ defines a tree, because there is no multiple inheritance.

In addition, let each class define a set of states, S_j, and a set of functions, F_j:

$$c_j = \{S_j, F_j\}$$

C_i is a superclass of c_j if there exists an inheritance relation $c_i \rightarrow c_j$ and c_i is a parent of c_j. Likewise, c_j is a subclass of c_i if $c_i \rightarrow c_j$ exists. Finally, let $p = p_1, p_2, ..., p_L$ be an *inheritance chain* in Ψ extending from the root class c_0 to c_j. The inheritance chain p is defined by a sequence in H. Then, each state and function in c_j is defined by *inheritance, extension,* or *override* as follows:

$$S_j = \bigcup_{i=1}^{L} \{S_{p_i}\} + e_j$$

which means that the state S_j is the concatenated sum of superclass states, plus extensions obtained by adding state variables. In other words, class c_j inherits the states of all L of its superclasses. In addition, it extends these states by simple concatenation. Extension is defined by the concatenation set e_j. Overrides are defined by the set ϑ_j, and the remaining functions derive their definitions from superclasses:

$$F_j = e_j + \vartheta_j(F_{p_i}) + \bigcup_{i=1}^{L} \{F_{p_i} - \vartheta_j(F_{p_i})\}$$

which describes new functions, override, and inheritance of functions. Similarly, the functions defined on c_j are obtained by extension e_j, overrides, $\vartheta_j(F_{pi})$, and inheritances from the L superclasses of c_j.

Now we are in a position to define an *object-oriented parallel program* as a collection of dynamic instances of classes called *objects*, messages which allow objects to communicate in a point-to-point manner, and a correspondence which associates pairs of objects with messages:

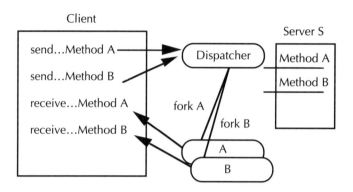

Figure 9.2   Messages result in forked processes when sent to a server

1    $P = \{\mathbf{O}, M, \psi\}$. An object-oriented parallel program consists of objects, messages, and a rule for associating messages with pairs of objects.

2    $\mathbf{O} = \{obj_1, obj_2, ..., obj_k\}$. Set of instances of classes, i.e., objects.

3    $M = \{\mu_{1,1}, \mu_{1,2}, ..., \mu_{2,1}, \mu_{2,2}, ..., \mu_{m,n}\}$. nm messages among objects.

4    $\lambda : \mathbf{O} \times \mathbf{O} \Rightarrow M$. A mapping function that associates messages with objects.

Each of the objects in $\mathbf{O}$ may be used in a server; i. e., S is defined as follows:

$$S = (Obj, Proc, D, Q)$$

A server comprises an object, a set of processes, Proc, a handler/dispatcher process, and a request queue. Obj $\in \mathbf{O}$, Proc $= (p_1, ..., p_k)$, and D, Q are defined in Figure 9.1.

Figure 9.2 illustrates a server with two active methods. The client process sends requests for the services of methods A and B of server S. The dispatcher process spawns two processes, one for method A and another for method B. The two processes carry out the methods, and send a reply back to the client. The client does not wait unless the reply is not yet ready when the receive point is reached.

9.3 SYNTACTIC STRUCTURE OF OBJECTS

The concepts described above can be converted into a practical syntax for parallel programming by applying information hiding, encapsulation of data and synchronization rules, inheritance, and dynamic instantiation. *Information hiding* means we separate the interface from the implementation. *Encapsulation* means we prevent access to the state of an object except by methods defined on the object. *Inheritance* means we can reuse an inherited method rather than rewrite it. *Dynamic instantiation* means we create objects as needed.

First, we separate the interface from the implementation. The interface construct contains the names of all superclasses that provide inherited properties; the path expression specifies a synchronization path; and the method headers specify a *message protocol* for client processes to obey:

interface <classname> {
superclass <classname>;
path <path-expression>;
method <function-header-list> }

The implementation part of a server-object is its executable code, illustrated below. If the code is inherited from a superclass method, the **inherit** keyword is used in place of <Function-Body>. If the code is intended to override a superclass method, the **override** keyword is used. If the code is to extend the subclass, <Function-Body> provides that code. In the last two cases, constants, types, variables, and methods are encapsulated by the server as specified in <Function-Body>.

code <classname> {
<const-list>;
<type-List>;
<var-List>;
method <Function-Header> [**inherit**]
    [**override**]
    [<Function-Body>] }   /* Optional... */

The interface and code segments are compiled separately so that changes to one will have a limited impact on the other. Placing the path expression in the interface block instead of in the implementation block cleanly separates synchronization from implementation. More importantly, state, function, and synchronization are fully encapsulated, so that message-passing is the only coupling mechanism among client–server modules.

Abstract classes are interface modules, only. That is, they consist of an **interface** block and no **code** block. All methods defined in an abstract class must be overridden by methods defined in subclasses. An abstract class is useful for establishing an interface called a *protocol*. A protocol establishes an interface for an entire class of objects.

Example 9.1

An abstract data type with simple operations INSERT, GET, PUT, and PRINT is given below. The TABLE class stores strings of information which are indexed by an integer key. Note how the inputs to each function are indicated by the keyword **in**, and outputs are indicated by the keyword **out**, such as in Ada™.

interface TABLE {
  superclass LIST;
  method
    INSERT(**in integer** key, info);   /* Add a new record to TABLE */
    GET(**in integer** key; **out string** info); /* Look up and get string */
    PUT(**in integer** key; **in string** info); /* Change existing entry */
    PRINT( );}   /* Print entire TABLE */

The TABLE class inherits its state and function from the LIST superclass. Some functions are inherited from the LIST superclass, and some are obtained by extensions or overrides. The keywords **override** and **inherit** are used to specify which methods override others of the same name in LIST, and which methods are inherited. When neither keyword is used, the method is added as an extension to the subclass.

```
code TABLE {
  method
    INSERT override;              /* Replace INSERT */
    {  /* override code goes here */  }
    GET inherit;                  /* Reuse GET   */
    PUT inherit;                  /* Reuse PUT   */
    PRINT                         /* Extend by concatenation of PRINT */
    {  /*...Code for printing the table, here...*/  }
}
```

Objects are dynamic instances of classes. Thus one or more objects of type TABLE are created with the **new** function, and destroyed with the **dispose** function:

```
TABLE P, Q ;                    /* Reference pointers to objects P and Q */
.
.

send(TABLE) to new;             /* Asynchronous call to create new TABLE */
send(TABLE) to new;             /* Create a second table   */
receive(P) from new;            /* Reference to TABLE stored in P   */
receive(Q) from  new;           /* Reference to TABLE stored in Q   */
.
.

send(key, info) to P->INSERT;   /* Add a new record to P */
.
.

send(key) to Q->GET;            /* Ask for string   */
.
.

receive(info) from Q->GET;      /* Info string is returned */
```

The first two send/receive pairs establish the servers and assign P and Q to point to them. The send to P->INSERT tells server P to insert a string into the table. The send to Q->GET requests that server Q look up a string. Later, the string is returned at the receive point. The only parallelism in this example occurs between the last two statements, i.e., send/receive.

The **new** and **dispose** functions are actually system methods, i.e., **system->new** and **system->dispose**. However, all system methods are abbreviated as shown above. Therefore, it is not necessary to write *system->*.

Parameterized *constructor* and *destructor* functions are optionally provided by the programmer as in C++. Constructor and destructor methods have the same name as their class. A constructor method is executed only once when the object is created. A destructor is executed only once for each object, when the object is destroyed.

Constructor and *destructor* functions are defined by the programmer, using ~ to signify the destructor. The next example revises the previous example to include explicit constructor and destructor methods.

Example 9.2

Modify the previous example to show how to define constructor and destructor methods. These methods are automatically called whenever an object is created or disposed.

```
interface TABLE {
  superclass LIST;
  method
    TABLE (in integer init, out integer err);   /* Creator function  */
    ~TABLE (out integer err);                    /* Destructor function  */
    INSERT(in integer key, info);                /* Add a new record to TABLE  */
    GET(in integer key; out string info);        /* Look up and get string   */
    PUT(in integer key; in string info);         /* Change existing entry  */
    PRINT( );}                                    /* Print entire TABLE */
```

In this version, the constructor and destructor methods can be specified by the user as any processes that are executed when objects of this class are created or disposed. The parameters in the constructor specify the size of the table (amount of space to be allocated), and the err parameter returns any error condition that may have arisen when the allocation was done. A similar error condition is returned by the destructor.

The following sketches how these may be used to create, use, and then destroy one or more instances of TABLE. The implementation block might look like the following:

```
code TABLE {
  method
    TABLE{                            /* Creator function  */
      /* Code goes here */
      };
    ~TABLE{                           /* Destructor function  */
      /* Code goes here */
      };
    INSERT override;                  /* Replace INSERT  */
    {   /* Override code  */  }
    GET inherit;                      /* Reuse GET   */
    PUT inherit;                      /* Reuse PUT   */
    PRINT                             /* Extend by concatenation of PRINT  */
    {  /*...Code for printing the table, here...*/   }
    }
```

Now, suppose we use two instances of TABLE. The parameters of the constructor and destructor are provided by the client when the object is created and destroyed. The values of the parameters are used by the server process to configure the object. For example, suppose table *P* is of size 200, and table *Q* is of size 100:

```
send (TABLE, 200) to new;           /* Create space, and call constructor */
send (TABLE, 100) to new;
receive (P, error) from new;        /* Error in constructor? */
```

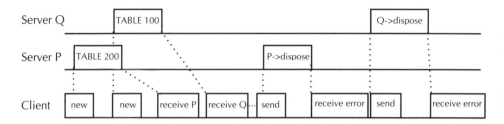

Figure 9.3   **Timing diagram of client–server interaction for TABLE objects *P* and *Q* showing the constructor and destructor phases**

```
if error then ...
receive (Q, error) from new;
if error then ...
    .
    .
    .
send() to P->dispose;              /* Execute destructor for P */
receive(error) from P->dispose;
send() to Q->dispose;              /* Execute destructor for Q */
receive(error) from Q->dispose;
if error then ...
```

This code would be executed from the client process, which sends messages to the two servers for *P* and *Q* (see Figure 9.3). The *P* and *Q* objects might reside on the same or different processor. In either case, the constructor, destructor, INSERT, GET, PUT, and PRINT methods are carried out by each server, in the order specified by the path expression in TABLE (no path expression is shown in this example—see the next section).

These constructs do not support *multiple inheritance*. Thus, all class hierarchies are trees rather than lattices. But *polymorphism* is supported, because a method in class *A* may have the same name as a method in class *B*, even when the two methods are not in the same chain of the inheritance tree. Thus, two different objects, say LIST1 and LIST2 may be instantiated from different classes, but still implement their own versions of INSERT, GET, PUT, and PRINT.

9.4 SYNCHRONIZATION OF OBJECTS

Functions defined on an object may be invoked by *asynchronous* **send/ receive** messages. That is, the input parameters of the destination method are passed to the method by a **send** message. The sender *does not* wait for a returned value. At a later time, the result computed by the destination method is returned as a **receive** message. The sender *does* wait at the **receive** statement until the receive phase is completed. Timing for asynchronous send/receive messages and method activation is easily visualized using a timing diagram as shown in Figure 9.3.

The TABLE server example can be used once again to illustrate how parallel accesses to table entries can be overlapped in time.

Example 9.3

Using the previous example of a TABLE, illustrate how to insert new elements into table *P*, and then how to modify these elements:

```
send (5, "Five") to P->INSERT;      /* Add record to TABLE P  */
send (1, "New") to P->INSERT;       /* Asynchronously add a record */
send (1, "Replaced") to P->PUT;     /* Change record 1     */
send (5) to P->GET;                 /* Look up key = 5     */
  .
  .
  .
receive (info) from P->GET;         /* Returned value is "Five" in info */
```

The messages sent to P->INSERT and P->PUT require no return value; hence these functions may be executed in parallel. The P->GET function, however, returns a value in variable info; hence the receiver must wait for the returned result before continuing execution. Thus, **sends** run in parallel with the sender, but **receives** set up a *barrier* until the return value is obtained.

The scheme illustrated in the previous example is insufficient to protect access to the state of an object. Note that P->INSERT and P->PUT can interfere with one another. A race condition between P->INSERT and P->PUT can lead to indeterminate access to the same item.

Example 9.4

Consider what happens when the following two accesses happen at about the same time.

```
send (1, "New") to P->INSERT;       /* Create record 1 */
send (1, "Replaced") to P->PUT;     /* Simultaneous update to record 1    */
```

If INSERT is done slightly before PUT, then the result is probably as intended. But, if PUT is done slightly before INSERT, the attempted PUT would probably fail because no entry with key = 1 exists.

We can solve the problem of race conditions in servers by specifying a synchronization policy for all objects of a class. We do this using the simplicity of a *path expression* which specifies the order of activation of methods. Each identifier in the regular expression is a method name, and the operators are as described in the previous chapter.

The path expression constraint can be tested by drawing a timing diagram to visualize a scenario whereby concurrent access is attempted. The scenario will reveal a flow error in the program, if we look at the worst case.

Example 9.5

A path expression for the TABLE object is shown below. The path expression specifies a limited number of concurrent activations of methods: INSERT, PUT, or PRINT in parallel with GET. Parallel INSERT and PRINT are forbidden as are PUT and PRINT and PUT and GET.

```
interface TABLE {
  superclass LIST;
  path INSERT + PUT + GET + PRINT + PRINT GET;
  method
    TABLE (in integer init, out integer err);   /* Creator function */
    ~TABLE (out integer err);                    /* Destructor function */
    INSERT(in integer key, info);                /* Add a new record to TABLE */
    GET(in integer key; out string info);        /* Look up and get string */
    PUT(in integer key; in string info);         /* Change existing entry */
    PRINT( );}                                    /* Print entire TABLE */
```

What happens if one or more client processes invoke P>INSERT twice, P>PUT once, and P>GET once, followed by a P>PRINT? Assuming these messages arrive at object *P* in the order listed above, the request queue of the *P* server will contain the following requests:

P>INSERT;	Head of queue
P>INSERT;	
P>PUT;	
P>GET;	
P>PRINT;	Tail of queue

The patterns in the path expression are matched against the request queue, and we instantly recognize a match with one INSERT. Thus, INSERT is processed, and once again we match the patterns. INSERT is matched a second time. Then, PUT is matched, and when it finishes, GET and PRINT are matched, simultaneously. Thus, all of the requests are executed according to the path expression. In this case, GET and PRINT are the only processes that are allowed to run at the same time. This scenario is shown as a timing diagram in Figure 9.4a.

But, suppose the following requests are made and appear in the request queue:

P>INSERT;	Head of queue
P>PRINT;	
P>GET;	
P>PUT;	Tail of queue

In this case, INSERT is executed by itself, then PRINT and GET are executed in parallel because they match the pattern PRINT GET. Finally, PUT is executed by itself (see Figure 9.4b). The order of the terms in the regular expression does not matter: PRINT GET and GET PRINT are both recognized as parallel activations of methods PRINT and GET.

9.5 BOUNDED BUFFER PROBLEM REVISITED

Chapter 2 gave a solution to the *bounded buffer problem*, which can be used to formulate a general client–server class that can be reused whenever two processes wish to buffer their communications. For example, when two processes run at different speeds but communicate through a buffer (to accommodate the different speeds), they do so through a server called BBUFFER, which supports both producer and consumer methods.

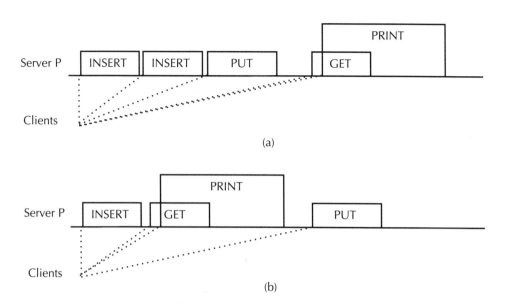

Figure 9.4 **(a) Timing diagram scenario for parallel GET and PRINT, (b) timing diagram scenario for parallel requests to INSERT, PUT, GET, and PRINT**

The key to improvement of the earlier bounded buffer solution is to note that producer and consumer indexes must be protected from indeterminism. Therefore, we need to define a class of counters that guarantee mutually exclusive access:

```
interface Counter {
path Inc + Dec;                          /* One or the other, but not both */
method
  Inc(in integer in; out integer in);    /* Increment in */
  Dec(in integer in; out integer in);    /* Decrement in */
}
```

Now, we can define a bounded buffer class using the improvements devised earlier:

```
interface BBUFFER {
  path [(n − in)(Produce)] + (in)(Consume);
  method
    BBUFFER (in integer n);              /* Creator function  */
    ~BBUFFER ();                         /* Destructor function  */
    Produce(in integer info);
    Consume(out integer info);
  }
code BBUFFER{
integer q, p, in;                        /* Instance variables = state of object  */
const n;                                 /* Set by constructor when object is instantiated  */
```

```
integer buffer[n];              /* Create this when object is instantiated */
process count Counter;          /* For Inc and Dec mutual exclusion */
method
Consume(out integer info)  {
  q := q mod n + 1;             /* Access 1..n, 1..n, 1..n, etc */
  info := buffer[q];            /* Get   */
  send(in) to count->Dec;       /* Decrement in by 1 */
  receive(in) from count->Dec;
  return };

Produce(in integer info) {
  p := p mod n + 1;             /* Access circular buffer   */
  buffer[p] := info;            /* Put   */
  send(in) to count->Inc;       /* Increment in by 1 */
  receive(in) from count->Inc;
  return };

BBUFFER (in integer n){         /* Creator function  */
  send(count) to new;           /* Create Inc/Dec server */
  receive(count) from new;
  return};

~BBUFFER (){                    /* Destructor function */
  return}
}
```

For every instance of BBUFFER, one or more Consume and Produce processes are created on the fly to carry out the requests made by one or more servers. The following example illustrates this.

Example 9.6

Consider two client processes that collaborate to do work; ClientA produces outputs that ClientB consumes. We want to run *A* and *B* at maximum speed, but because they have different patterns of access to messages between them, we set up a bounded buffer of size 100 to cushion communication. Let this server be called Mail, and the two clients ClientA and ClientB. The two clients run in parallel, and only communicate through Mail.

These processes must be set up and run. We do so in parallel as follows:

```
code MAIN
{ process  Mail BBUFFER;          /* Process pointers */
          ClientA Producer;
          ClientB Consumer ;
  /* Creations... */
  send(Mail, 100) to new;         /* Mail server   */
  send(ClientA) to new;           /* ClientA   */
  send(ClientB) to new;           /* ClientB   */
  receive(Mail) from new;         /* Server is up...*/
  receive(ClientA) from new;      /* ClientA = Producer   */
```

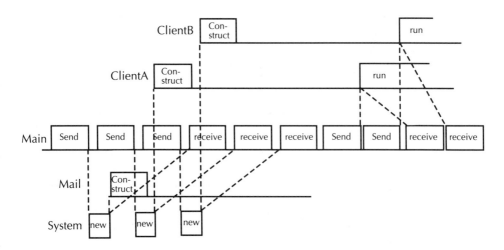

Figure 9.5   **Timing diagram scenario for Producer ClientA, Consumer ClientB, and bounded buffer server**

```
receive(ClientB) from new;          /* ClientB = Consumer   */
send() to ClientA->run;             /* Start running Clients */
send() to ClientB->run;
receive() from ClientA->run;        /* Wait here until done   */
receive() from ClientB->run;        /* These are barriers    */
send() to Mail->dispose;            /* Kill server, too   */
receive() from Mail->dispose;       /* Be tidy   */
}
```

The timing diagram for creating the two Clients and single server is shown in Figure 9.5. Note that the three processes are brought into existence by the MAIN process. This scenario starts life for ClientA, ClientB, and Mail, but it does not show what happens between ClientA, ClientB, and Mail. This interaction is governed by the code for ClientA->run and ClientB->run, shown below.

```
interface CONSUMER {               /* This will be ClientB   */
method
run();
}

interface PRODUCER {               /* This will be ClientA   */
method
run();
}

code CONSUMER {
integer msg[100];
method
run(){
```

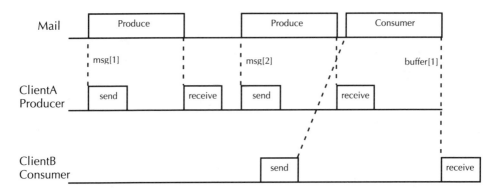

Figure 9.6   **Timing diagram scenario for ClientA, ClientB, and Mail server when two messages are produced for Mail, and one is consumed**

```
for(i := 1; not done; i++){
    send() to Mail->Consume;
    receive(msg[i]) from Mail->Consume;
};
return};
```

The code for the Producer is left as an exercise for the reader. A timing diagram scenario is shown in Figure 9.6. In this scenario, Client A produces msg[1] and msg[2] for the Mail server to store in its buffer. Client B consumes the first message from buffer[1]. Assuming both clients initially request Mail service at the same time, the path expression is used to select the appropriate method to activate. But, in Figure 9.6, ClientB requests access slightly after the second request by ClientA. This places ClientB behind ClientA on the request queue of Mail.

A general Producer-Consumer configuration for multiple client access to a bounded buffer is shown in Figure 9.7. This model is frequently used in supervisor/worker paradigms where one process supervises the work of all others. Each worker process communicates with the supervisor process through the Mail server, which is simply a bounded buffer server.

Applications of the supervisor/worker paradigm abound. We list only a few here:

1   Clearly, a distributed e-mail message system can be implemented with the supervisor/worker paradigm. The supervisor is a process that runs forever, and simply dispatches messages for its workers. Each worker sends and receives its mail, without synchronization among peers. Due to the differences in the frequency and size of messages, the workers run at different speeds. The Mail bounded buffer smooths out the accesses, but guarantees that all messages are received in the order they are sent.

2   Ray tracing in computer graphics is a candidate for the supervisor/worker paradigm. Each ray of light from a source to the viewer's eye is traced through a series of reflections and absorptions. Suppose 1,000 rays are followed through an image by 50 workstations running in parallel. We set up

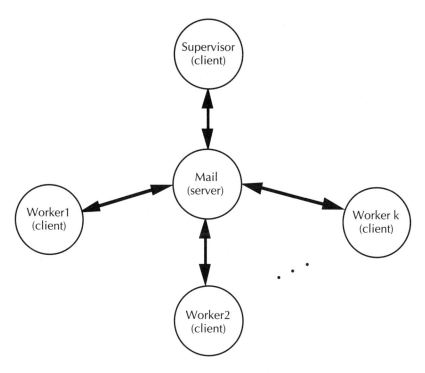

Figure 9.7 The supervisor/worker paradigm is a special case of the client–server paradigm that uses the bounded buffer server as a central mail message storage object.

one supervisor process to monitor the progress of 50 worker processes, one per workstation. This means that $1,000/50 = 20$ rays are traced by each workstation process. The supervisor sends a series of messages to each worker, and then each worker returns answers through the mail server, as they are found. Because some rays are absorbed before others, the time to trace all 20 rays may vary from workstation to workstation. The bounded buffer server smooths these time differences without holding up peer workers.

3 We want to compute some physical property by a finite element method. For example, we might compute the heat flow through a machine part by partitioning the part into regions. Due to the shape of the part, some regions will consist of more grid points than others. So, some workers will take longer to compute the heat flow within their sections than others. In addition, the workers must communicate with one another at the boundaries of their regions. The Mail server is used to buffer these communications. As in the e-mail example, the supervisor process dispatches the exchanged information in the order it is received.

9.6 MATRIX ALGEBRA REVISITED

In earlier chapters we presented a variety of matrix algebra algorithms written in fine-grained form. These algorithms can be used to implement the methods of a server which provides matrix algebra for client processes. That is, we can encapsulate the matrix values, along with the algorithms that manipulate them, in the form of a server and then simply instantiate the server for each matrix we want to process.

The following example also illustrates how to combine large-grained client–server objects with fine-grained parallelism. The fine-grained parallel algorithms are implemented as methods on a server, and then these methods are run in parallel with other methods. Therefore, parallelism is found at two levels: at the large-grained method activation level, and at the fine-grained statement level. This provides an enormous opportunity to exploit *massively parallel* hardware. But, we must be careful that such programs are flow-correct.

This technique is general. It can be applied to all sorts of algorithms, not just matrix algorithms. Most data structure operations such as INSERT, DELETE, LOOKUP, SUM, and PRINT can be encapsulated in a class that does all of the work for any client. When applied to a database system, the operations of JOIN, SELECT, and PROJECT are candidates for the server model.

Example 9.7

The problem is to encapsulate a linear system containing $Ax = b$ inside a server. To do this, we first define a class LinSys, with the appropriate operations to carry out the I/O, inner product, and summation steps. Then, we instantiate objects with A, x, and b as the state. The methods are activated as large-grained parallel processes, but within each parallel process, we implement fine-grained parallelism.

We use the fine-grained algorithms developed in earlier chapters, plus an algorithm to do *back substitution*. Recall that back substitution works only on a system of linear equations that have been diagonalized. That is, solve $Ax = b$, for a lower-diagonal matrix A, and vector b. This means solving the folowing equations:

$$x_1 = b_1 / a_{11}$$
$$x_2 = [b_2 - a_{21}x_1] / a_{22}$$
$$x_3 = [b_3 - (a_{31}x_1 + a_{32}x_2)] / a_{33}$$
$$\vdots$$

$$x_k = \left[b_k - \sum_{i=1}^{k-1} a_{ki}x_k \right] / a_{kk}$$

A class for matrix algebra, showing only the code needed for back substitution is shown below. Back substitution is implemented as method BACKSUB. The other methods perform various other operations on $Ax = b$. For example, the PUT and GET methods implement I/O routines for loading/retrieving the state of the server with matrix A, and vectors b and x. Implementation of other operations (LU decomposition, for example) is left as an exercise for the reader.

```
interface LinSys {
  path INNER + ROWSUM + BACKSUB + PUTX + PUTB + PUTA + GETX GETB GETA;
  method
    LinSys(in integer N);                   /* Creator */
    INNER(in integer k);                    /* Inner product of row – column k */
    ROWSUM(in integer k);                   /* Sum of row k */
    DIAG();                                  /* Diagonalize Ax = b   */
    BACKSUB();                               /* Back substitution calc */
    PUTX(in integer i; in float elem);      /* Store in x */
    PUTB(in integer i; in float elem);      /* Store in b */
    PUTA(in integer i,j; in float elem);    /* Store in A */
    GETX(in integer i; out float elem);     /* Retrieve element of x */
    GETB(in integer i; out float elem);     /* Retrieve element from b */
    GETA(in integer i,j; out float elem);   /* Retrieve element from A */
  }

code LinSys {
  const N;
  float  A[1..N][1..N], b[1..N], x[1..N];
  method
    BACKSUB(){
    X[1] := B[1] / A[1,1];
    pipe j := 2..N;                          /* Could be for j := 1, N   */
    mapin A[j, 1..(j – 1)] to v[1..(j – 1)];  /* Row j to vector   */
           x[1..(j – 1)] to u[1..(j – 1)]     /* Vector-to-vector   */
           b[j] to bj; A[j, j] to ajj;
    { float u[1..(j – 1)], v[1..j – 1];
    1: /* Summation to get v[1]...    */
       /* Left as an exercise for the reader */
       /* What goes here? */
    2: u[j] := (bj – v[1]) / ajj;            /* v[1] contains sum   */
    mapout u[j] to x[j]                       /* Result is in X   */
    endpipe;
```

The determination of the flow-correctness and performance of this code is left as an exercise for the reader. For example, is this an appropriate use of a **pipe**? Does the destructive summation performed by the **tree** cause a problem?

To use this, create a server as follows, and call the appropriate methods:

```
process Lin LinSys;
  .
  .
  .
send(Lin, 100) to new;                       /* Startup a 100 × 100 system   */
  .
  .
  .
send() to Lin->DIAG;                         /* Solve Ax = b for diagonal   */
  .
  .
  .
send() to Lin->BACKSUB;                      /* Do the back substitution   */
```

9.7 KEYWORDS AND CONCEPTS

In this chapter we have defined the *method call mechanism* which provides for *large-grained data flow* parallelism, *modularity*, and dynamic creation and destruction of parallel processes. This mechanism yields the safety advantages of *encapsulation*, the flexibility of asynchronous and dynamic process activation provided by *message-passing*, and the use of *path expressions* to simplify synchronization. The result is a powerful mechanism for *client–server computing*.

This model is appropriate under the following conditions:

1   The cost of communication is so high that it does not permit fine-grained parallelism.

2   Parallelism is dynamic; i.e., the potential for parallelism is not known until the program executes.

We have introduced the idea of a *server* as a way to structure large-grained computations. A server is an object plus processes to perform the actions of the object's methods. A server supports one process per activation of a method. But, because a server can encapsulate many methods, and each method may be invoked by more than one process, a server may support many processes. This allows us to define *client–server parallelism* as two processes which collaborate in parallel; the client process calls one or more methods of the server; and the server provides subordinate processes to carry out the work of the client.

The following keywords and concepts summarize the ideas of this chapter:

Active method   In the client–server model presented here, methods are dormant until a process is created to execute the method. Thus, an active method is a process.

Asynchronous   Methods are activated by a message which arrives at the server. The server checks the path expression to guarantee proper synchronization, and then a process is created to run the method. This is all done in parallel with the client which made the request. When we dissociate the client from the server in this manner, we say the method is activated asynchronously.

Client–server computing   A client is a process that sends messages to servers. A server is a collection of processes which provide services to client processes. This leads to client–server parallelism, and is the crux of client–server computing.

Constructor and destructor   Servers are created on the run, in a process known as dynamic instantiation. When created, a constructor procedure is activated, and when destroyed, a destructor procedure is activated. Therefore, a server is self-configuring and self-destructing.

Encapsulation   Encapsulation in the client–server model means more than information hiding. It also means that the path expression which governs synchronization is put into the interface block of the server, so that we can separate it from implementation. Thus, the state is invisible, but the server's path expression is made visible.

Inheritance   The server is also an object, and therefore, servers inherit methods from their parent classes.

Large grained computation   A large-grained computation is a computation that takes significantly more time than the communication delay required to provide data to the grain. That is, large-grained data flow means large-grained processes.

Path expression   Methods are self-synchronizing in the client–server model. This is done through path expressions, which define the order of activation of methods. Path expressions implement a sychronization policy.

PROBLEMS

1   Give the code of PRODUCER that works with the CONSUMER code of ClientB, shown in section 9.4.

2   Draw a timing diagram scenario for the PRODUCER/CONSUMER solution of problem 1.

3   Can the CONSUMER process be implemented as follows? Explain how this differs from the implementation given above.
```
code CONSUMER {
integer msg[100];
method
run(){
for(i := 1; not done; i++){
    send() to Mail->Consume};
for(i := 1; not done; i++){
    receive(msg[i]) from Mail->Consume}
};
return};
```

4   Give the interface and implementation parts of a LinSys class that can solve $Ax = b$ using LUD decomposition and back substitution. Is your system flow-correct? Be careful to preserve the state of the system (*Hint*: **tree** aggregation is destructive).

5   Is the back substitution code given in this chapter flow-correct? Why or why not?

6   Design and implement a fully functional LinSys server, complete with I/O, LU decomposition, and back substitution.

7   Is the **pipe** in LinSys really useful? How much parallelism is in this **pipe**? Suggest an improvement to the LinSys server that will yield better performance.

8   Complete the LinSys code by filling in the missing parts indicated by :

1: /* Summation to get v[1]...   */
    /* Left as an exercise for the reader */
    /* What goes here? */

REFERENCES

R. G. Babb, Parallel Processing with Large Grain Data Flow Techniques, *IEEE Computer*, **17(7)**:55–61, July 1984.

CHAPTER 10

Software Implemented Fault-Tolerance

Fault-tolerance is the ability of a system to continue to operate in the presence of errors. A *fault-tolerant computing system* is one in which correct answers are obtained from each processing step in the presence of errors. Software Implemented Fault-tolerance (SIFT) uses redundant software routines to implement fault-tolerance.

In a redundant system, each processing step is augmented by one or more steps, which are implemented by hardware or software units, such that each independent unit computes a *trial result*. The trial results are compared in some manner, and one of them is selected as the correct result. The idea of a trial result, as opposed to a solitary result, is central to the concept of SIFT.

In this chapter we will show how to use parallel and distributed software to implement SIFT. We will propose two fundamental methods: voting, and backup/recovery. Voting is a method whereby k parallel trial results of a processing step are compared and the result obtained by the majority of the processes is used. The remaining $(k - n)$ trial results are discarded. Backup/recovery is a method whereby k sequential trials are used to obtain the correct result, and each trial is tested to see if it is correct. If this is not the case, the system recovers and tries again.

The voting technique uses parallel processes to obtain trials which are used to determine the correct answer. The backup/recovery technique uses sequential trials to obtain the correct answer. In the latter case, performance degrades when errors are corrected. In addition, a side effect of backup/recovery called the *domino effect* may occur, which can cause the entire system to halt when even a simple fault is corrected.

Finally, we will illustrate the domino effect and propose a theoretical solution called *MRS-structured* design. Unfortunately, MRS-structure is difficult to implement, so we will weaken it to a simpler form, and show how to use this form to solve the bounded buffer server problem once again. This time, however, the solution is fault-tolerant.

10.1 SOFTWARE IMPLEMENTED FAULT-TOLERANCE

Software implemented fault-tolerance (SIFT) implements fault-tolerance through software redundancy. That is, more than one software routine is used to compute the same result, and then the correct result is selected from among the alternatives. The alternative values are called *trials*, and the goal of SIFT is to efficiently compute trials and correctly select one trial as the result.

There are two fundamental approaches to redundancy, and hence SIFT. The first method uses parallel processes (each computing a different algorithm) to compute k trial values, compares those values, and selects the majority value as the correct result. This is called *majority voting*.

The second approach uses alternative algorithms to sequentially compute up to n trial values. If the first trial value is incorrect, the system recovers from the error by backing up, restoring the previous state of the program, and then attempting to find a second trial value using a different algorithm. The trial calculation followed by backup and restore is repeated until alternatives are exhausted, or the correct result is obtained. This is called the *backup / recovery* method.

Voting and backup/recovery methods are useful for a number of SIFT applications. These applications can be classified as follows:

1   Voting
- Redundant I/O, e.g., mirrored disk drives
- Alternative algorithms for the same calculation, e.g., correcting round-off errors
- Stochastic algorithms, e.g., speeding up *Monte Carlo simulations*

2   Backup/recovery
- Robustness, e.g., recovery from detectable errors
- Graceful degradation, e.g., trading performance for recoverability
- Backtracking algorithms, e.g., state-space searches

In the remainder of this chapter, we will illustrate each of these applications after we first propose language constructs for expressing voting and backup/recovery algorithms.

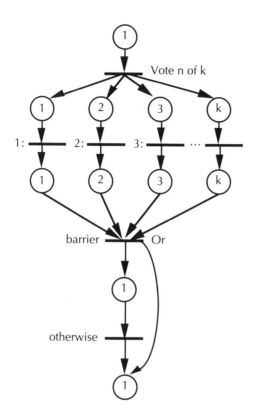

Figure 10.1 Graph of vote construct for SIFT. Note the OR transition, which represents a branch after the barrier.

10.2 VOTING

In any fault-tolerant system, *redundancy* is used to tolerate errors. Thus, redundant disk drives containing identical data are used to tolerate failure in one or more disks. Redundant algorithms might be used in a similar fashion to tolerate algorithmic errors. For example, a list of numbers might be sorted by two different algorithms, and if one fails to produce an ascending list of numbers, the other result will be used.

Regardless of the method of producing a redundant result, some form of redundancy is needed. The redundant results are called *trials*, and it is assumed that we can always select the correct result from among the trials. These trial results are produced by redundant routines called *trial processes*.

Clearly, multiple processing elements can be used to produce trials, see Figure 10.1. The simplest form of this is voting. A voting system is one in which k trials are computed, and then the majority value is taken as the correct result. Suppose k parallel processes are used to compute k trials at the same time. The k

trials are compared and one selected. In a voting system, the majority trial value is selected as the correct value. Thus, k parallel processes are used to compute a single *reliable* result.

For example, three different square-root algorithms might be used to simultaneously calculate one correct square-root. We assume that if at least two of the trials agree, the correct result is equal to the majority result. Thus, three trials are calculated at once, compared, and the majority value taken as the correct result. But, what happens if they all disagree?

In Figure 10.1, k processes are used to compute trial values, which are compared by voting. If n trials agree, their value is taken as the correct result. But, if n identical trial results cannot be obtained, the **otherwise** clause is executed. In general, n out of k trials form a majority when $n > k$ **div** 2. For example, if $k = 3$, then $n = 2$ agreements are needed to obtain a majority.

The general vote construct is given below:

```
vote n of k, error-bound          /* Error bound may be dropped   */
mapin <mapin-values>
1: <trial #1>;
2: <trial #2>;
    .
    .
k: <trial #k>;
otherwise <failure-exception>
mapout <mapout-trial-values>
endvote
```

The execution semantics of this construct are shown in Figure 10.1. To obtain a majority, n must be greater than k **div** 2. The k parallel processes are computed simultaneously, and then the k trials compared. If n of the k trials agree, their value is mapped out as the result. If, however, voting fails, the <failure-exception> routine is executed and no trial value is selected as a correct one.

In this construct, it is not necessary for $n > k$ **div** 2. The voting succeeds whenever n trials agree. Thus, if only $n = 2$ of $k = 5$ trials agree, the vote succeeds, and an agreed upon result is returned by the vote. Hence, it is possible to compute *minority votes* as well as majority votes in the same manner.

The **vote** construct behaves much like the **par** construct. That is, both execute possibly different routines at the same time, and produce outputs at their barriers. In fact, the **par** construct can be used to simulate the vote construct as shown below:

```
par i := 1..k
mapin <mapin-values>
1: <trial #1>;
2: <trial #2>;
    .
    .
k: <trial #k>;
mapout <mapout-values>
endpar
```

send(n, <mapout-values>) **to** votefor;
receive(<result-value>, n_matching_trials) **from** votefor;
if n_matching_trials < n **then** <failure-exception>

Note how the alternatives simultaneously produce *k* trials. The *votefor* method returns the number of matches found in *n* matching trials. If at least *n* trials match, the returned value is equal to the match in <result-value>.

Example 10.1

We wish to write a parallel majority voting algorithm for testing the accuracy of floating point roundoff. The following algorithm produces a correct result when floating point multiplication and division are totally accurate. If inaccurate, the result produced is 0.0.

vote 2 **of** 3
mapin A **to** Left
1: {**float** Left;
    Left := Left }
2: {**float** Left;
    Left := 2.0 * (Left / 2.0)}
3: {**float** Left;
    Left := (Left * 2.0) / 2.0}
otherwise {**float** Left;
    Left := 0.0}
mapout Left **to** A;
endvote

For example, the three processes might produce the following trials in parallel:

A	$p = 1$	$p = 2$	$p = 3$	Majority result
0.0	2.0	0.0	0.0	0.0
1.0	2.0	~1.0	~1.0	?
2.0	2.0	~2.0	~2.0	?

Depending on the accuracy of the floating point multiplication and division, either the calculated result or the failure result is returned. The tilde (~) indicates floating point approximations of 1.0 and 2.0.

This example illustrates the purpose of the error-bound parameter in **vote**. Voting can be made *fuzzy* by permitting the trials to agree within some error bound. The **vote** above can be revised to permit a fuzzy majority.

Suppose we are willing to accept floating point round off up to an error bound of 0.001. Then, the vote is written as follows:

vote 2 **of** 3, 0.001
mapin A **to** Left
1: {**float** Left;
    Left := Left }
2: {**float** Left;
    Left := 2.0 * (Left / 2.0)}
3: {**float** Left;
    Left := (Left * 2.0) / 2.0}

Program I/O

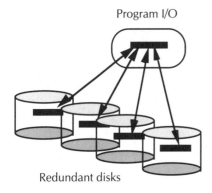

Redundant disks

Figure 10.2   Mirroring with redundant disks

otherwise {**float** Left;
    Left := 0.0}
mapout Left **to** A;
endvote

Now, a majority consists of 2 trials that are equal to within ±0.001. Thus, the following possibilities exist:

A	$p = 1$	$p = 2$	$p = 3$	Majority result
0.0	2.0	0.0	0.0	0.0
1.0	2.0	~1.0	~1.0	~1.0
2.0	2.0	~2.0	~2.0	~2.0

The result is an approximation. Thus, a fuzzy vote produces a majority result in the presence of the round off error typically found in most numerical calculations. This modification of strict voting is extremely useful for scientific programming.

10.2.1 Redundant I/O

One common technique for increasing the reliability of a computer system is to improve the reliability of its storage. In the case of disk drives we can do this with *mirroring*, as shown in Figure 10.2. Each record of the file is written to k disks, duplicating the entire file k times. Each time a system writes to or reads from a record, it writes to or reads from all disks.

Example 10.2

Suppose, $k = 3$ disks are used to store three copies of a single file. Files f1, f2, and f3 contain identical information. The system methods readf and writef perform the file I/O when instantiated by system send/receive methods that are asynchronously called from the application code. To protect against an error, we select the majority (out of 2 of 3 trials) as follows:

vote 2 **of** 3
mapin rec_no **to** r
1. { **integer** r; **string** rec; **send**(r) **to** f1->readf; **receive**(rec) **from** f1->readf};
2. { **integer** r; **string** rec; **send**(r) **to** f2->readf; **receive**(rec) **from** f2->readf};
3. { **integer** r; **string** rec; **send**(r) **to** f3->readf; **receive**(rec) **from** f3->readf};

otherwise { **send**('Disk Error') **to** sys->output};
mapout rec **to** result
endvote

The three alternatives are simultaneously computed, and the trial results compared. If two or more trials agree, the result is the majority value. If there is no majority, the "Disk Error" message is sent to output.

10.2.2 Alternative Algorithms

One of the most often used techniques of scientific programming is that of alternative algorithms. This technique attempts to produce correct approximations by computing trials using several different algorithms. Then the trials are compared by fuzzy voting, and the ones which most nearly agree are taken as the correct answer. We will illustrate this concept using a simple numerical application, but the technique is best used when the outcome is not known ahead of time.

Example 10.3

As a demonstration of fuzzy voting and the utility of alternative algorithms, consider the problem of estimating the universal constant π. At least three methods are known for estimating π on a finite precision computer:

1   Arctan: $\tan(1) = \dfrac{\pi}{4}$,   so $\pi = 4 \times \arctan(1)$.

2   Integration: $4 \times \displaystyle\int_0^1 \frac{dx}{1+x} = 4 \times \arctan(1) = \pi$.

3   Series: $\arctan(x) = x - \dfrac{x^3}{3} + \dfrac{x^5}{5} - \cdots$,

so $\pi = 4 \times \arctan(1) = 4 \times \left(1 - \dfrac{x^3}{3} + \dfrac{x^5}{5} - \cdots\right)$.

Let these algorithms be implemented as the servers: arctan4, integrate4, and series4, respectively. Each returns a number which is an approximation to π. Which one of these approximations is best? If we trust the majority, then the following produces the accepted approximation:

vote 2 **of** 3, 0.000001
/* No mapin values */
1:{ **float** pi; **send**(1) **to** math->arctan4; **receive**(pi) **from** math->arctan4};
2:{ **float** pi; **send**(0,1) **to** num->integrate4; **receive**(pi) **from** num->integrate4};
1:{ **float** pi; **send**(1) **to** calc->series4; **receive**(pi) **from** calc->series4};
mapout pi **to** approx
otherwise { **send**('Inaccurate pi') **to** output}
endvote

If at least two approximations agree within the error bound (0.000001), then that value is returned. If none of the approximations agree within the error bound, then the error message is produced.

10.2.3 Stochastic Algorithms

A third class of voting algorithms are called stochastic, because they derive their answers by means of statistical averages. We will illustrate this class through a simple coin tossing simulation.

Example 10.4

Suppose three coins are tossed (simultaneously, or one at a time) to produce a run of heads (H) and tails (T). For example, a run might be HHH, TTT, HTH, TTH, or so forth. Clearly, there are eight possible outcomes of this game. If the coins are fair, then each outcome is as likely as all others. But if the coin is not fair, what is the probability of getting all Hs or all Ts? How often do we get HHH or TTT?

The following is a trivial stochastic algorithm for determining the frequency of HHH or TTT outcomes of the coin-tossing game. It is a brute–force algorithm which simply counts the number of times all coins agree, and uses this count to estimate the observed frequency in 1,000 tosses. A server called *toss* returns a new random number each time it is requested.

```
count := 0;
for( i := 1; i ≤ 1000; ++){
    count := count + 1;
    vote 3 of 3
    1: { integer r; char coin;            /* First coin   */
        send() to toss->random; receive(r) from toss->random;
        if r ≤ 0.5 then coin = 'H' else coin := 'T'};
    2: { integer r; char coin;            /* Second coin   */
        send() to toss->random; receive(r) from toss->random;
        if r ≤ 0.5 then coin = 'H' else coin := 'T'};
    3: { integer r; char coin;            /* Third coin   */
        send() to toss->random; receive(r) from toss->random;
        if r ≤ 0.5 then coin = 'H' else coin := 'T'};
    otherwise { count := count – 1 }      /* Backoff   */
    mapout coin to coin;                  /* vote here   */
    endvote;
};
freq := count / 1000;
send(freq) to output;
```

This algorithm uses voting to decide whether all trials match, instead of correcting an error. Similar stochastic algorithms might be expressed in this manner, but in many cases, it is better to use a **fan** or a **par**.

10.3 BACKUP/RESTORE

An alternative to voting is the backup/restore method of SIFT. In this approach, alternative algorithms are used sequentially to recover from an error. This approach is also based on a criterion called an *acceptance test*. Thus, backup/recovery SIFT differs from voting as follows:

1   Backup/recovery is sequential, not parallel like voting.

2   Backup/recovery is based on an acceptance test, not on trials.

3   Error recovery greatly degrades performance, voting marginally affects performance.

Performance is degraded only when errors occur, because backup and recovery are done sequentially, and require that the acceptance test be applied to an alternative routine. This approach seems to be less useful than voting, but backup/recovery SIFT is more general, because any acceptance test may be used.

Backup/recovery should be used to achieve:

1   Robustness, e.g., recovery from detectable errors.

2   Graceful degradation, e.g., trading performance for recoverability.

3   Backtracking algorithms, e.g., state-space searches.

Backup/recovery SIFT is powerful but dangerous, because it can lead to total failure unless the proper backup/recovery structure is designed into the application. This topic will be fully explored in the final section of this chapter.

10.4 THE BACKUP CONSTRUCT

The general form of the backup/recovery construct is shown below:

backup <acceptance-test>
mapin <mapin-values>
1: <first-alternative-routine>;
2: <second-alternative-routine>;
.
.
.
k: <last-alternative-routine>
otherwise <failure-exception>
mapout <mapout-values>
endbackup

This construct defines alternative routines which are called into action only when predecessors fail to satisfy the acceptance test. That is, a copy of <mapin-values> is made, and the routine <first-acceptance-test> is executed. If <acceptance-test> is TRUE, the variables <mapout-values> are returned to the program. If <acceptance-test> is FALSE, the variables <mapin-values> are restored from the copy, and <second-alternative-routine> is executed. This process of trial-backup/recovery-trial is repeated until <acceptance-test> is TRUE, or until all alternatives have been tried. If all alternative routines fail to satisfy the acceptance test, the **otherwise** routine <failure-exception> is executed.

The following sequential code is roughly equivalent to **backup**:

```
i := 1; fail := FALSE; copy( <mapin-values>);
repeat
      case i of
            1: <first-alternative-routine>;
            2: <second-alternative-routine>;
            .
            .
            .
            k: <last-alternative-routine>;
            otherwise fail := TRUE
      end;
      if (not <acceptance-test>) and (not fail)
            then begin i := i + 1; restore (<mapin-values>) end;
until (<acceptance-test>) or fail;
if fail then <failure-exception>;
```

The *copy* routine makes a backup copy of the variables <mapin-values> so that they can be restored by the *restore* routine. Each time the loop is traversed, *i* is incremented so that the next alternative in the sequence is tried. Either the acceptance test will be satisfied, or else the routine <failure-exception> will be executed.

Example 10.5

Consider the following reliable code for sorting elements of array $x[1..n]$. Suppose two sorting servers are used as alternatives; one which is fast and another which is slower but simpler. The acceptance test is obtained by scanning the sorted list and returning TRUE if its elements are in ascending order. The **backup** construct holds two alternatives:

```
backup ascending                       /* Ascending is a Boolean variable   */
mapin x[1..n] to list[1..n];           /* Sort x   */
1: { string list[1..n];
      send(list, n) to p->bitonic;     /* The fast sort   */
      receive(list) from p->bitonic;
      send(list) to q->up;             /* Scan for ascending order   */
      receive(ascending) from q->up};
2: { string list[1..n];
      send(list, n) to s->quicksort;   /* The simpler sort   */
      receive(list) from s->quicksort;
      send(list) to q->up;             /* Scan for ascending order   */
      receive(ascending) from q->up};
otherwise { send('Sort Failed') to output
endbackup
```

The backup/restore approach can be used to implement reliability with graceful degradation. But, it may also be used to implement back tracking algorithms such as in tree searches and graph traversals.

10.5 THE DOMINO EFFECT

It may come as a surprise to learn that systems of backup/restore constructs can quickly become complex. In fact, they can become dangerous, unless carefully designed. In the following, we will illustrate the *domino effect*, and then propose a solution called *MRS SIFT* or *MRS conversations*.

The name domino effect is very descriptive. A failure in a process forces rollback to a previous state of the process. The messages sent or received beyond this state are put into question, because they may have been a source of the error, or they may need to be sent a second time. What happens to the interprocess communications? Must they be canceled and then correct ones sent once again? This is called *rollback propagation*, or simply, *R-propagation*.

10.5.1 Rollback Propagation

In previous examples, we were careful to send messages to different servers in the event of a backup/recovery phase. This simplifies the problem that we are about to discuss. When error recovery leads to repeatedly sending messages to the same processes, we risk a complete failure of the system. This is illustrated in Figure 10.3a for an arbitrary 3-process system.

In the timing diagram of Figure 10.3a, we indicate recovery points by a vertical bar, and the backup action by a backward pointing arc. Recovery points are also called *marks*, and are indicated by an *M*. Backups are sometimes called *rollbacks*. Rollbacks occur when an error is detected, and the process returns to a previous mark, and attempts to repeat the messages sent out and received.

Message-passing is shown as a dotted line between the sender and the receiver. Not knowing which actions are **sends** and which are **receives**, the best we can do is to show the existence of communications between two processes. As an example, Figure 10.3a shows backup/recovery points placed after every third communication.

When a recovery point is reached, the copied **mapin** values are restored and used to repeat an alternative trial. This trial sends and receives message to or from the *same* distant server process as in earlier trials. This is the source of the problem in message-passing systems, because from the perspective of the server process, two or more messages arrive for the same purpose. How is the server to know which message is correct, and which is incorrect? In Figure 10.3b, we see that the need to repeat the same messages among pairs of processes leads to complete collapse of the entire system. This is called the *domino effect*, and is of major concern in SIFT.

In Figure 10.3b a failure occurs in P1, causing P1 to rollback to its most recent mark. This is shown as the arc numbered 1. Then, because the communications between P1 and P2 are no longer valid, P2 is forced to rollback to a mark which will permit it to accept new input messages from P1. This is shown as arc 2. But, P2 invalidates messages sent by it to P3; thus, P3 must rollback to its earliest mark. This is shown as arc 3. Continuing in this fashion, P3 invalidates earlier messages from P2, which rolls back to its starting point (arc 4), and finally P1 is forced back to its starting point (arc 5).

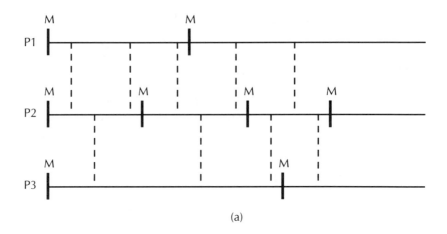

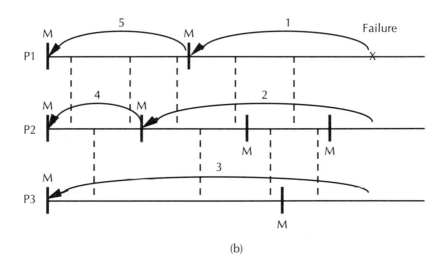

Figure 10.3   Domino effect in a system of 3 processes which communicate by message passing: (a) interprocess communication through send/receive messages, showing backup/recovery points (M) after every third message, (b) domino of 3-process system caused by failure in one process (P1)

The domino effect can destroy an entire software system when only a small error occurs in one process. It is a major challenge to the design of message-passing systems. We will present a partial solution to this problem called mark-receive-send (MRS) design, but the complete solution remains unknown, and is a research question.

Suppose we attempt to prevent the domino effect from occurring in an arbitrary message-passing SIFT program. This problem was studied by Russell, Kim, and others (see References). In 1980, Russell proposed a structuring law called MRS.

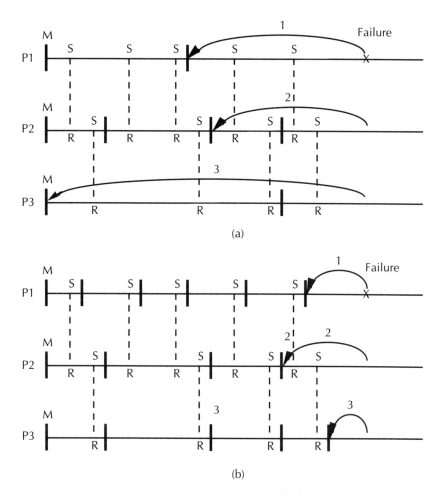

Figure 10.4 Limitations in the domino effect made possible by MRS structure: (a) domino of producer–consumer server system when server follows an MRS law, but consumer–producer clients mark after every third communication, (b) domino of producer–consumer server system when server follows an MRS law, but consumer–producer clients mark after every communication.

In an *MRS-structured* SIFT program, a mark is placed after every series of **sends** but before a new series of **receives**. That is, the sequence M, R, R, ..., R, S, S, ..., S, M, ..., is established by placement of a mark after a series of **sends** but before a new series of **receives**.

Figure 10.4 illustrates the effect of the MRS structure on the producer–consumer client–server system described in the previous chapter. **Sends** are indicated with an S, and **receives** are indicated with an R. In addition, the MRS theory assumes messages need not be sent a second time unless they are invalidated by a rollback.

In Figure 10.4a we illustrate the effects of the same failure of Figure 10.3 on an MRS-structured server, but with two different rules governing the clients. In Figure 10.4a, we place a mark after every third producer **send**, and every third consumer **receive**. Even so, the MRS pattern of the server limits the rollback as shown. The rollback at arc 1 invalidates the final two **sends** prior to the failure. These **sends** must be received again by the server, which means rollback arc 2 occurs. But the chain reaction continues, because the rollback of the server invalidates the final two **receives** of the consumer. Rollback arc 3 causes the consumer to restart.

10.5.2 Implementing Recovery

In Figure 10.4b the limitation of rollback is even greater, because a mark is placed after every communication by both producer and consumer clients. Thus, only very limited rollback occurs. The problem with this solution, however, is that marks are very expensive, because they make copies of backup/recovery values.

The second problem with the theory of MRS structure is one of implementation. How can we implement the rollback of one process by another? Notice how some rollbacks are limited to the immediate predecessor mark, while others extend arbitrarily beyond the nearest mark. In general, a fault-tolerant process must maintain a list of all rollback points established since process creation, in case a rollback of arbitrary length occurs.

Efficient, domino-free, MRS-structured SIFT systems are hard to implement. This remains an area in need of additional research, and is a topic beyond the scope of this book. However, a simple version of the MRS theory can be implemented as follows. Each process pair involved in a communication is synchronized such that there is never a rollback beyond one communication. To do this, we must place a mark after every communication.

Example 10.6

Consider the consumer–producer problem illustrated in Figure 10.4. In light of the simplified MRS structure proposed above, there is no need to draw a timing diagram, because a mark is placed after every **send/receive**. Hence, a failure in a send causes an immediate backup and resend.

Now, consider the producer–consumer client–server application. Simple transmission errors can be detected and corrected using a *checksum* routine to compute checksums of the messages as they are sent, and again after they are received. If the two checksums are unequal, we rollback the previous **send**, and **send** again. The code below uses only two trials to illustrate this idea. More trials may be used without loss of generality.

First, we add the checksum parameter to the interface of our earlier solution. The variable *chksum* is a sum computed before sending a message, and then again after receiving each message. The *error* parameter is used to communicate between client and server, indicating whether an error has occurred.

```
interface BBUFFER {
  path [(n − in)(Produce)] + (in)(Consume);
    method
      BBUFFER (in integer n);          /* Creator function */
      ˷BBUFFER ();                      /* Destructor function */
```

```
        Produce(in integer info; in integer chksum; out boolean error);
        Consume(out integer info; out integer chksum);
        }
code BBUFFER{
integer q, p, in;                        /* Instance variables = state of object    */
const n;                                 /* Set by constructor when object is instantiated    */
buf_rec buffer[n];                       /* buffer[n].data and buffer[n].check */
integer newsum;                          /* Create this when object is instantiated    */
process count Counter;                   /* For Inc and Dec mutual exclusion */
method
Consume   {
        q := q mod n + 1;                /* Access 1..n, 1..n, 1..n, etc */
        info := buffer[q].data;          /* Get    */
        chksum := buffer[q].check;       /* Pass-on the checksum    */
        send(in) to count->Dec;          /* Decrement in by 1 */
        receive(in) from count->Dec;
        return };

Produce {
        send(info) to sys->checksum;
        receive(newsum) from sys->checksum;
        if newsum = chksum
            then {
                    p := p mod n + 1;            /* Access circular buffer    */
                    buffer[p].data := info;      /* Put info    */
                    buffer[p].check := chksum;   /* Put check sum    */
                    send(in) to count->Inc;      /* Increment in by 1 */
                    receive(in) from count->Inc;
                    error := FALSE }
            else error := TRUE;
        return };
}
```

The client processes use this server in the following way. This code is incomplete, but illustrates the central idea:

```
code PRODUCER {
integer newsum, msg[100];                /* Checksum, messages to produce    */
boolean done, no_error;                  /* Working variable, acceptance test    */
method
run(){
for(i := 1; not done; i++){
    backup no_error                      /* Identical trials    */
    mapin msg[1] to message;
    1: {  send(message) to sys->checksum;        /* Same as 2    */
          receive(newsum) from sys->checksum;
          send(message,newsum) to Mail->Produce;
          receive(no_error) from Mail->Produce};
        2: {  send(message) to sys->checksum;        /* Same as 1    */
          receive(newsum) from sys->checksum;
          send(message,newsum) to Mail->Produce;
          receive(no_error) from Mail->Produce};
```

```
        mapout                          /* Nothing */
        endbackup;
   };
   return};

   code CONSUMER {
   integer newsum, chksum, msg[100];      /* Check sums, messages to get */
   boolean done, no_error;                /* Flags   */
   run(){
   for(i := 1; not done; i++){
        backup no_error
        mapin                           /* Nothing */
        1: {  send() to Mail->Consume;
              receive(message,chksum) from Mail->Consume;
              send(message) to sys->checksum;
              receive(newsum) from sys->checksum;
              no_error := (newsum = chksum)};
        2: {  send() to Mail->Consume;        /* Same as 1   */
              receive(message,chksum) from Mail->Consume;
              send(message) to sys->checksum;
              receive(newsum) from sys->checksum;
              no_error := (newsum = chksum)};
        mapout message to msg[i]
        endbackup
   };
   return};
```

Clearly, this is not a very efficient solution, because it tightly synchronizes the two clients. This was necessary to enforce the immediate rollback, in case of a failure. In addition, checksum error detection is not very general. But, this simplification is easy to implement, as shown.

10.6 KEYWORDS AND CONCEPTS

In this chapter we have shown how to use parallel and distributed software to implement SIFT. We have proposed two fundamental methods: voting, and backup/recovery. Voting is a method whereby k parallel trial results of a processing step are compared and the k majority result is used. The remaining trial results are discarded. Backup/recovery is a method whereby k sequential trials are used to obtain the correct result, each trial is tested to see if it is correct, and if not, the system backs up and tries again.

A side-effect of backup/recovery, the *domino effect*, may occur which can cause the entire system to halt when even a simple fault is corrected. We have illustrated the domino effect and proposed a theoretical solution called *MRS-structured* design. Unfortunately, MRS structure is difficult to implement, so we have weakened it to a simpler form, and have shown how to use this form to solve the bounded buffer server problem.

The following keywords and concepts summarize the ideas of this chapter:

Acceptance test Faults are detected by making tests, called acceptance tests, which are predicates that return TRUE or FALSE. A checksum test is an example of an acceptance test.

Backup/recovery When an error is detected, the parallel program can either substitute an alternative value for the value in question, or it can backup to a previous state, and attempt to recover by taking an alternative path through the program.

Domino effect When backup is used to recover from an error, the system is in danger of subsequent backups, which can lead to system-wide failure. This scenario is called the domino effect.

Fault-tolerant computing system A fault-tolerant system is one that can continue to operate even though errors occur.

Majority voting Faulty values can be corrected by computing alternative values. But how does the program know which value is true and which is an error? The majority value is assumed to be correct in majority voting systems.

Marks If backups are to be used to correct a fault, the backup state must have been saved before the fault occured. The saved states of a program are called marks.

MRS-structured MRS (mark-receive-send) systems are more resilient than non-MRS systems, because they resist the domino effect. In an MRS system, a mark is placed before every sequence of **receives** and **sends**. Thus, when a fault is detected, the length of the rollback is limited.

R-propagation The cause of the domino effect is rollback propagation, or R-propagation. One rollback initiates another, etc., until the entire system collapses.

Redundant software Like redundant hardware, redundant software resists faults by using alternative procedures to compute the same algorithm. If one version of the algorithm fails, then an alternative one is tried.

Rollback A process is rolled back to a previous mark whenever a fault is detected. Faults are assumed to have occurred when an acceptance test fails.

PROBLEMS

1   Define software fault-tolerance, SIFT, rollback, recovery, trial result, and R-propagation.

2   Propose flow, anti-, and output dependency axioms for majority voting and backup constructs. How might they be used to prove the flow-correctness of these two constructs?

3   Propose flow-correctness axioms for MRS-structured fault-tolerant programs. Explain your proposals.

4   What purpose might there be for minority voting? For example, what does it mean for 2 of 5 processes to agree?

5   In what way is a **vote** different than a **par**?

6   Give an example that uses fuzzy voting. Use the **vote** construct to illustrate the solution to your example.

7   Give algorithmic examples of redundant, alternative, and stochastic voting.

8   Draw a timing diagram for the following communications performed by a single process: R, R, S, S, R, S, R, S, S, S, S, R. Draw the marks needed to make this an MRS-structured process.

9   Redraw Figure 10.4 to show what happens if a mark is placed immediately after all sends, but no marks are placed after receives. Does this prevent the domino effect?

10 Prove than an MRS-structured SIFT program is domino-free when all processes alternate between **send** and **receive**.

REFERENCES

K. H. Kim, Programmer transparent coordination of recovering parallel processes, Report to HQ Space and Missile Systems Organization, Los Angeles, August 1978.

B. Randall, System structure for software fault tolerance, *ACM SIGPLAN Notices*, **10(6)**, June 1975.

D. L. Russell, State restoration in systems of communicating processes, *IEEE Trans. on Software Engineering*, **SE-6(2)**, 183–194, 1980.

K. H. Kim, and L. Welch, Distributed Recovery Blocks, *IEEE Trans. Computers*, May 1989.

CHAPTER 11

Programming in the Large

Programming in the small (PITS) is the process of writing small routines to perform some algorithm. On the other hand, *programming in the large* (PITL) is the process of combining building blocks into larger building blocks to arrive at an overall program structure. PITL deals with the design of an application, while PITS is restricted to the implementation of an algorithm. For the most part, this book has shown how to program in the small.

In this chapter we will describe a graphical notation for the design of parallel and distributed software systems that emphasizes PITL. That is, we will show how to design a parallel program, rather than how to implement an algorithm. We will do this by assigning a graphical object to each construct previously discussed. Then, we will show how to use these graphical objects as building blocks to design an application. However, our examples will still be restricted to small ones, because large ones would take too much space.

One of the problems of large system design is that of clutter. A large system has many parts, and if we attempt to understand a system by looking at all of its parts in one sweeping view, we can be overcome by detail. To combat this complexity, most PITL notations involve *abstraction* in the form of hierarchy and *information hiding*. Thus, the graphical notation we propose must incorporate hierarchical decomposition of actions and data, as well as hiding of implementation details.

The PITL system proposed here uses a multiple-windowing scheme to implement hierarchical views, and graphical icons to hide implementation level text. A simple box is used to represent some action. This box is connected by incoming

245

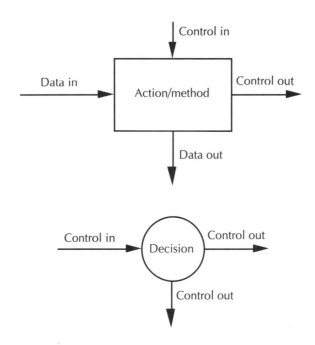

Figure 11.1   Basic building blocks of parallel program design

control paths from its top and outgoing paths from its right side. Data flows into the box from its left side, and leaves from its bottom. Thus, a simple box diagram shows both control flow and data flow.

Boxes can be decomposed into other boxes or textual code. A box that contains text is called a primitive box, because it cannot be decomposed further. A composite box is one that contains more boxes.

Circles are used to denote the fundamental parallel programming constructs of **fan**, **pipe**, **par**, **tree**, **backup**, and **vote**, as well as sequential constructs such as **if**, **loop**, and **case**.

11.1 THE BASIC BUILDING BLOCKS

Figure 11.1 shows the basic building blocks for constructing a PITL parallel program design. The rectangular box contains either implementation of an action in the form of source program text, e.g., a PITS algorithm, or another (decomposed) collection of icons representing a deeper level of design. Typically, a top level box is decomposed into many levels of intermediate boxes, ending with a *leaf box* containing PITS text. Boxes containing text of sequential code are also called *primitive boxes*.

In Figure 11.1, we note a *control circle* which contains either a decision predicate such as **if**, **loop**, or **case**, or a parallel programming control construct such as **fan**, **pipe**, **par**, or **tree**. Circles combine flows of control to define how the parts of the program are to be executed, both in sequence, and in parallel. An analysis of the *control flow* of a PITL design is sufficient to understand the parallelism within the design. The circle hides the details of the decision predicate or control construct.

Arcs connect boxes and circles. *Data arcs* define access to data and **mapin/ mapout** distributions. *Control arcs* define the behavior of the entire program, as a hierarchical network of flows. The overall diagram is annotated as needed to document the design.

Example 11.1

Consider the example of Figure 11.2. The top level box, Figure 11.2a, shows only the overall inputs and outputs to the entire application. The START control arc indicates a starting point, while the STOP arc (at the right) indicates a stopping point. Think of these arcs as signals that activate and deactivate the entire program. The two variables x and y are shown as input variables, and the two variables u and v are shown as output variables.

The next level is a decomposition of the top level box (see Figure 11.2b). Note where the variables from the top level are visible in this level. Also, note how the inputs are connected to the boxes that use and define them. For example, variable u is defined by Box 1.1, and used by Boxes 1.2 and 1.4. Variables x and y are defined in the top level box, and used in the lower layer boxes. Variable z is local to the lower layer, and so it is visible only within that layer. Output variables u and v are visible to the top layer. All data access is shown in the lower diagonal of each diagram. All control flow is shown in the upper diagonal of the diagram.

Control flow arcs START and STOP are visible at the lower layer, where START defines the first action to be done in the lower layer, and STOP defines the end of the sequence.

The control circles are marked with their semantics: *seq* for *sequential*, and *if* for *choice*. In the case of a choice, two output control arcs emanate from the circle. Each one is labelled with the decision predicate which activates the arc. Thus, the diagram of Figure 11.2b illustrates an **if-then-else** construction.

A textual representation of the design is:

top-Level(**in** x, **in** y, **out** u, **out** v):
    Box 1.1(**in** x, **out** u);
    Box 1.2(**in** u, **out** z);
    if x > 0 **then** Box 1.3(**in** y, **in** z, **out** v) **else** Box 1.4(**out** u, **in out** v);
end.

The implementation of the box code is given in a lower level decomposition. This is not shown in Figure 11.2.

What makes this kind of graphical programming interesting is that we can easily distinguish the control flow and data flow portions of the design. We can further make this visual inspection useful for deciding which portions of the program can be executed in parallel rather than sequential execution. Finally, we can also use this diagram to visually inspect the program for flow dependencies.

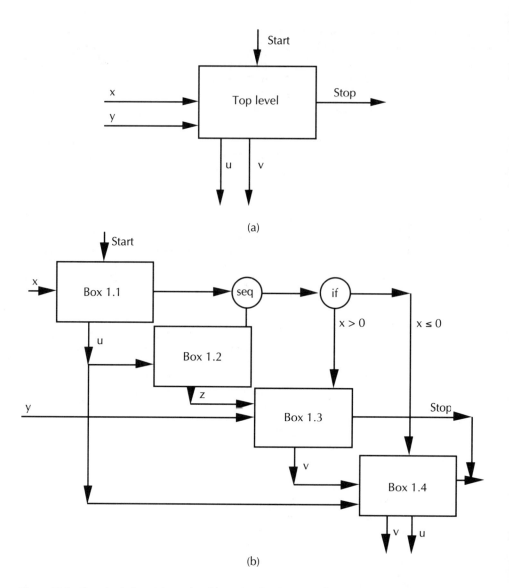

Figure 11.2 Sample design: (a) top level box showing inputs and outputs to the entire design, and (b) decomposition showing data access and control flow

11.1.1 Fan, Par, Pipe, Tree

The basic building block idea is easily specialized into icons for each of the sequential and parallel programming constructs, as shown in Figure 11.3. The specialization is done by simply labeling each circle according to its structure, and associating a box with each routine.

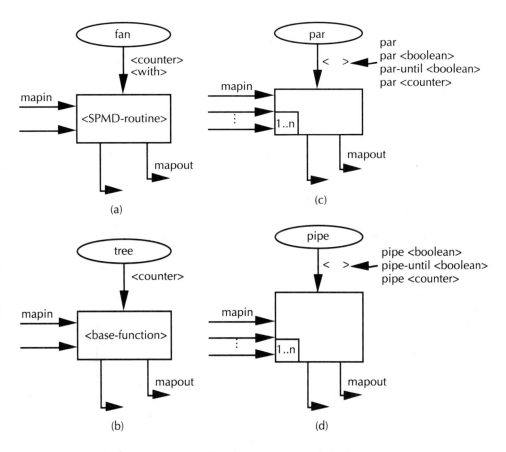

Figure 11.3 **Parallel construct icons: (a) fan, (b) tree, (c) par, and (d) pipe**

For example, Figure 11.3a shows how to represent a **fan** as a control circle labelled fan and a control arc labelled with the **fan** arguments. The **mapin** distributions are data flow arcs coming in from the left, and the **mapout** distributions are data flow arcs coming out of the bottom of the box. The box itself contains the code for the SPMD calculations.

Figure 11.3a shows a similar representation of a **tree**. Clearly, **fan** and **tree** are data-parallel constructs because they contain a single SPMD routine as shown by a box. They contain similar input and output data arcs as well. The major difference between a **fan** and a **tree**, as far as the graphical design is concerned, is the fact that a **fan** performs a "pure" SPMD operation, while a **tree** performs a "pure" reduction operation.

The **par** and **pipe** icons share a common form as shown in Figures 11.3c and 11.3d. Like the **fan** and **tree**, they consist of control circles which control a box; **mapin** and **mapout** are shown along the lower diagonal of the diagram, and the control arcs are shown along the upper diagonal.

Because **par** and **pipe** clauses may contain different routines, the boxes of these two parallel constructs are divided into *pages*—one page for each clause. The user must select which page to view, when decomposing the **par** or **pipe** box. Figures 11.3c and 11.3d show the clauses as numbered pages, 1..*N*. In most cases the boxes will contain PITS text, but they may be decomposed into additional layers of design.

Example 11.2

Consider the enumerated decompositions of the outer **pipe** in the hashing function given in Chapter 8. This program contains both sequential and parallel control, but we illustrate only the nested pipes in the core of the program, in Figure 11.4. The decomposition is given only for page 5, corresponding to the fifth stage of the outer pipe.

Notice how the **mapin** and **mapout** accesses are represented. These are taken directly from the textual routine. The same is true for the decision predicates. Thus, it is almost possible to understand the control portion of the program even though the details of the individual stages are hidden.

Now, consider a second example, also taken from Chapter 8. The Fibonacci algorithm shown in Figure 11.5 illustrates a small amount of control and shows how to define a box as a sequential routine. Although only page 1 is shown in Figure 11.5, there is also code associated with page 2. This code is hidden until the page is turned, revealing the second stage of the pipe (not shown in the figure).

11.1.2 Client–Server Notation

The client–server graphical design involves two parts: the definition of the class structure of server objects, and the definition of the message-passing channels whenever servers are used. The first definition can be done in a rather traditional manner, with a *inheritance diagram* as shown in Figure 11.6.

In Figure 11.6, the name of the server and class appears inside the circle. The names of methods are listed below, and the relationship among the methods defined in subclasses is made explicit by drawing a line between superclasses and subclasses. For example, an *inherit* line means the definition of a method is inherited from its superclass. The *override* line means that the method is redefined within the subclass.

When the server is used, we must specify message-passing as a control circle, see Figure 11.7. In most cases, the server method accesses the data passed to it by a message, and then computes some return values, which it passes back to the client. The client and server run asynchronously, and without any coordination other than the *path expression* given in the server's interface.

Example 11.3

The design of the mail server described in several earlier earlier chapters can now be given. Figure 11.8 shows the various levels of a simple producer–consumer version of the mail server. The definition of the server is also shown in the form of a hierarchical class diagram.

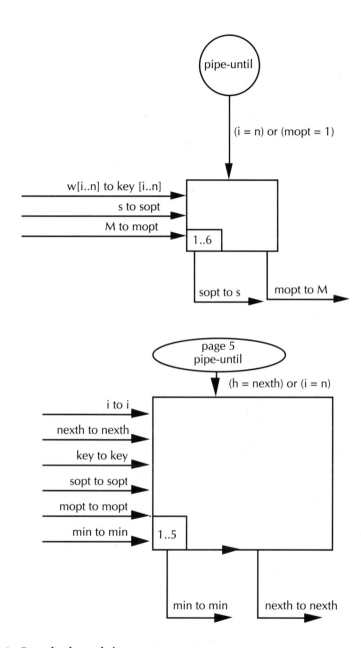

Figure 11.4   Example of nested pipes

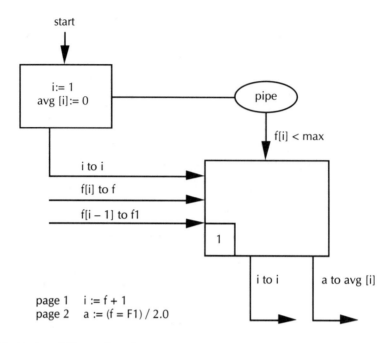

Figure 11.5   **Design of Fibonacci number generator program**

11.1.3 Fault-Tolerance

The graphical representation of fault-tolerance constructs are simple extensions of the basic box and circle notation. We can think of **vote** and **backup** as forms of control flow. These each have n decompositions, depending on the amount of redundancy in the control construct. Figure 11.9 shows how similar these control structures are to all the others.

Example 11.4

As a simple example of a fault-tolerant design, consider the fault-tolerant mail server of the previous chapter. This design is rather plain, as seen in Figure 11.10. Both decompositions for the producer method are shown.

11.2 COMPLETE PROGRAMS

The previous illustrative fragments survey the fundamental ideas of parallel program design and PITL. But, they do not give much insight into how one might use them to design a complete application. Suppose we use this approach to design an application that sorts a list, and an application that uses a client–server for solving a linear system by *back substitution*.

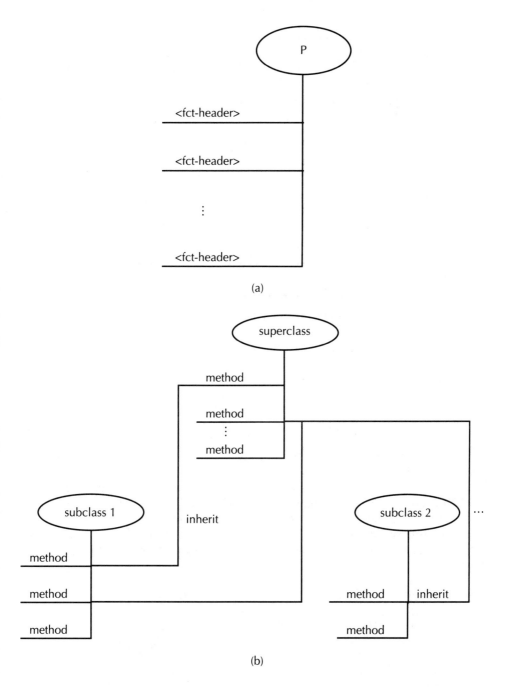

(a)

(b)

Figure 11.6   Definition of a server and the class hierarchy showing (a) override relations and (b) inheritance

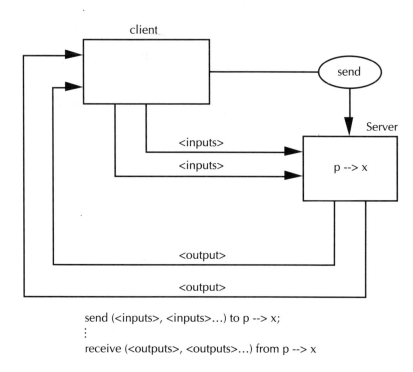

send (<inputs>, <inputs>...) to p --> x;
⋮
receive (<outputs>, <outputs>...) from p --> x

Figure 11.7   **Message-passing is a control flow operation.**

11.2.1 Bitonic Sort

The *bitonic sort* program of Chapter 5 involves several sequential and parallel constructs. It is shown as a multilevel design in Figure 11.11. The top level shows all inputs to the for-loop that does each pass of the bitonic sort algorithm. The BITONIC level shows what happens inside of the for-loop. Notice that the for-loop is composed of an outer **fan** and then a number of nested **fans** and for-loops. The two inner **fans** are decomposed and shown in Figure 11.11. The textual code is repeated here for convenience, and annotated according to the concepts introduced in this chapter:

```
for i := 1..logn                    /* Top level for-loop */
{
    k := power2(i − 1);             /* Start BITONIC Level */
    fan t := 1..k                   /* Fan circle of Figure 11.11 */
    {}
    mapout False to b[t]            /* Output of fan circle */
    endfan;
```

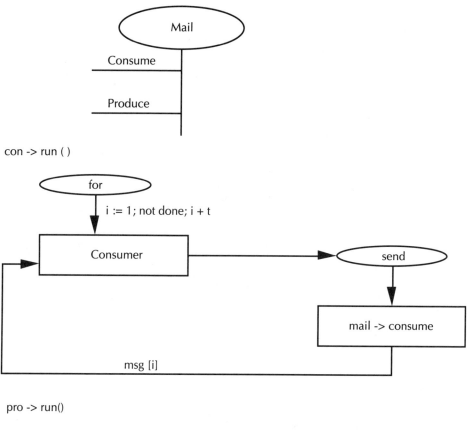

con -> run ( )

pro -> run()

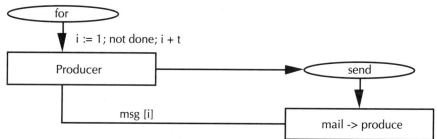

Figure 11.8   Mail server definition and design of producer–consumer pair

```
for t := (i – 1)..logn4          /* For circle in BITONIC level */
{   fan j := 1..power2(t)         /* Fan j in BITONIC level */
    mapin b[j] to RHS;
    { int RHS;                    /* RHS in Figure 11.11 */
    RHS := comp( RHS )}
    mapout RHS to b[j + power2(t)]
    endfan;
};
```

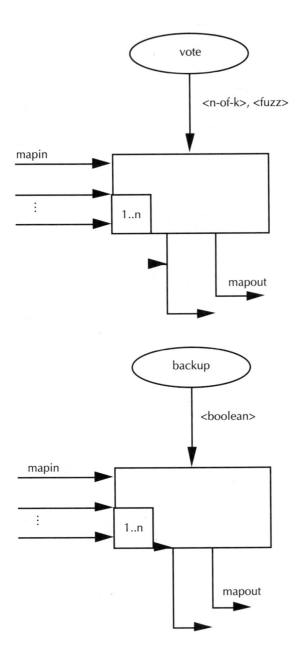

Figure 11.9   Fault-tolerance control constructs

Producer

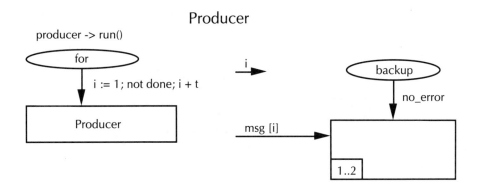

Producer 1 & 2

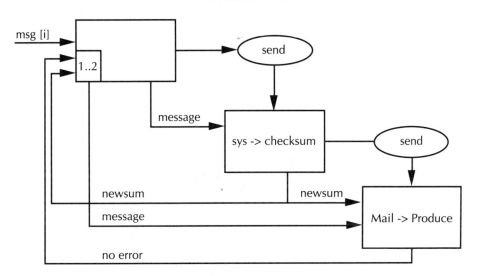

Figure 11.10 Fault-tolerant version of mail server

```
for j := i..1                       /* For circle */
{
    m := power2(j − 1);             /* Do this first, in Figure 11.11 */
    fan  p := 1, 2 * m..N;          /* Fan p in BITONIC Level */
        q := 1..m
    mapin d[p + q − 1] to Left;
        d[p + q − 1 + m] to Right;
        b[this] to bit
    { int Left, Right, bit;          /* Swapping in Figure 11.11 */
        if bit = False
        then if Left < Right then swap(Left, Right)
        else if Right > Left then swap(Left, Right)
    }
```

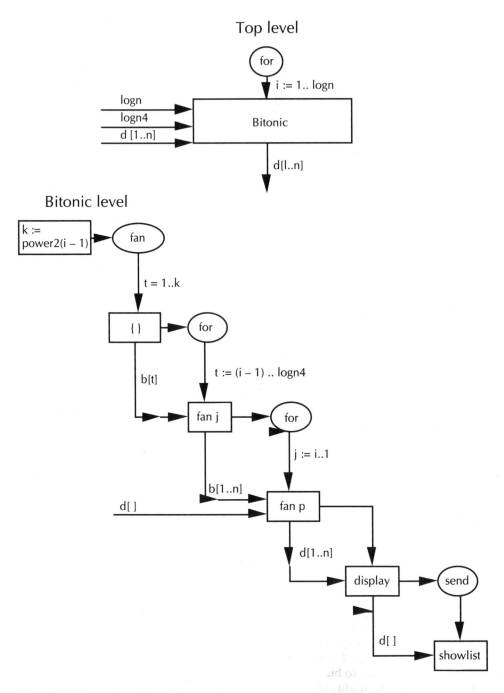

Figure 11.11 Complete design of bitonic sort program

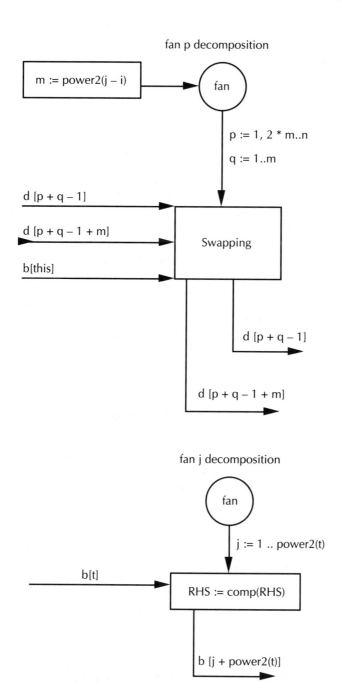

Figure 11.11 (Continued) Complete design of bitonic sort program

```
        mapout Left to d[p + q − 1];
              Right to d[p + q − 1 + m]
              endfan;
    }
    showlist(d);
}
```

We have used a short cut in one of the control arcs of Figure 11.11. Whenever the flow of control is sequential, we can leave off the **seq** circle, since it is implied. The control arc between boxes **fan** p and display is an implied sequential control arc. Thus, these two boxes are always executed sequentially.

The only parallelism in this example is contained within the **fans**. This can be clearly seen by visual inspection of the upper diagonal of the graphical design. All control lines are sequential, hence all of the flows are sequential. Thus, if any parallelism exists, it must be contained within decompositions, i.e., within the boxes. Further inspection of the boxes reveals that the three **fans** contain parallelism.

Visual inspection can also tell us something about the flow-correctness of the design. We look for multiple occurrences of variable names as labels on data arcs. For example, $b[j]$ and $b[j + power2(t)]$ appear together in the bitonic level. They are outputs from boxes which might be done in parallel. If so, is there an output dependency? As it turns out, these are performed sequentially, so there is no flow dependency error. Similarly, $d[1..n]$ and $d[]$ appear together, but again, the sequential control structures assure flow-correctness.

11.2.2 Client–Server Back Substitution

The back substitution algorithm was given in several earlier chapters. The design shown in Figure 11.12 uses a server whose methods are shown in the adjacent object diagram. Only the BACKSUB method is shown as a graphical decomposition. Furthermore, only one page of the pipe is shown as **tree** 1.

As it turns out, this design is incorrect! Why? The error is in the **tree** construct. The **tree** construct cannot be used to sum the vector elements resulting in $v[i]$. The reason is left as an exercise for the reader.

In general, each method of a class must be specified as a graph containing decomposable boxes and data/control arcs. These designs are reusable in the sense that once created, they can be saved and reused by others.

In addition, designs can be analyzed to guarantee flow-correctness properties. What is the flow-correctness error in Figure 11.12?

11.3 PERFORMANCE VISUALIZATION

The same technique of visualizing the design applies to visualizing the performance of the parallel program while it is executing. Perhaps the simplest example of this is the dynamic display of a Gantt chart as it unfolds in time.

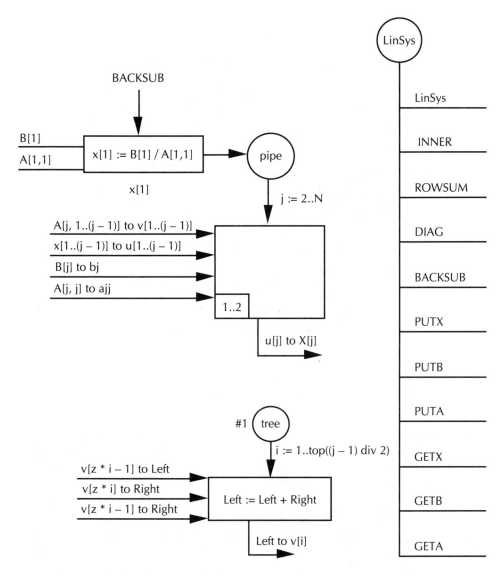

Figure 11.12 Design of backsubstitution method

Figure 11.13 illustrates a Gantt Chart at some instant in time, for a **fan** that is running $N = 100$ processes on $k = 8$ processors. The value of $k < N$ was chosen to optimize this particular **fan**. Processes are numbered in the Gantt chart.

Note how the processes are staggered in time. This occurs because of the overhead associated with starting up processes and distributing messages.

Similar displays are shown for other parallel program constructs.

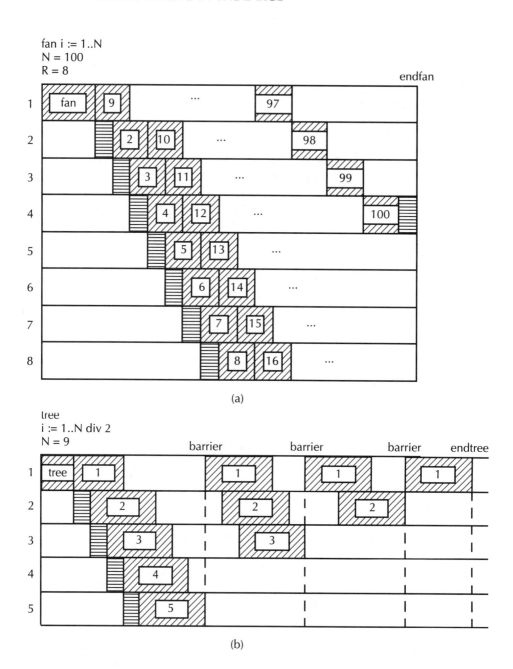

Figure 11.13 Performance visualization of executing parallel program—dynamic Gantt charts: (a) fan, (b) tree, (c) par, and (d) pipe

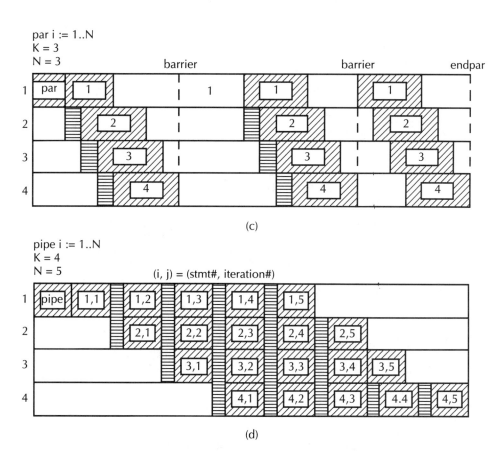

Figure 11.13 (Continued) Performance visualization of executing parallel program—dynamic Gantt charts: (a) fan, (b) tree, (c) par, and (d) pipe

11.4 KEYWORDS AND CONCEPTS

In this chapter we have described a graphical notation for the design of parallel and distributed software systems. We have proposed a parallel program design notation for parallel programming in the large. This notation assigns a graphical object to each construct previously discussed.

The PITL system proposed here uses a multiple-windowing scheme to implement hierarchical views, and graphical icons to hide implementation level text. A simple box is used to represent an action. A box is connected by incoming control paths from its top, and outgoing paths from its right side. Data flows into the box from the left, and leaves through the bottom. This simple diagram shows both control flow and data flow.

The following keywords and concepts summarize the ideas of this chapter:

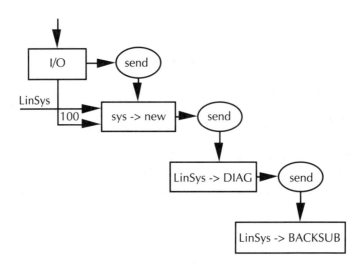

Figure 11.14 Design of program that uses LinSys

Control arcs   The graphical design notation uses control arcs to express control flow parallelism, and data flow arcs to express data flow. Thus, both paradigms are supported.

Control circle   A control circle is used to show both sequential and parallel control flow. The control circle can be a **branch, loop, fan, par**, etc.

Inheritance diagram   A visual representation of the class hierarchy and inheritances is used to express the inheritance options in an object-oriented design.

Programming in the large (PITL)   Programming in the *small* is basically algorithm design and implementation. To build complete applications, we need programming in the *large*. This is the purpose of PITL design notations such as the one proposed here.

PROBLEMS

1   Can the design of the solution to a linear system of equations shown in Figure 11.14 be improved by making some of the routines run in parallel with the others? Why or why not?

2   Verify that the design shown in Figure 11.15 is correct for solving a system of equations using Gaussian elimination. What is missing? Can you provide a complete design?

3   What is wrong with the tree in the LinSys BACKSUB design of Figure 11.12?

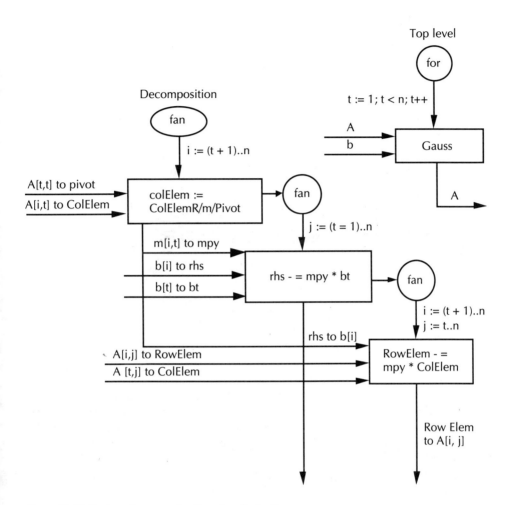

Figure 11.15 Design of program for Gaussian elimination

APPENDIX

Summary of Flow-
Correctness Axioms

We require a flow-correct parallel program to obey three synchronization predicates: *flowdependency, antidependency,* and *output dependency,* defined as follows. If a data dependency exists, and if the intention of the
programmer is to eliminate indeterminism, then the appropriate dataflow predicate must be TRUE:

1   FLOW. Programmer intent is to define x, then use x:

FLOW(x, t) :-
       ($\exists \Delta t > 0$ | DEF(x, t − Δt)),   e.g., x := 1; at $t = 0$
       USE(x, t).   y := x; at $t = 1$

2   ANTI. Programmer intent is to use x, then redefine it:

ANTI(x, t) :-
       ($\exists \Delta t > 0$ | USE(x, t − Δt)),   e.g., y := x; at $t = 0$
       DEF(x, t).   x := 1; at $t = 1$

3   OUT. Programmer intent is to define or output x, twice:

OUT(x, t) :-
       ($\exists \Delta t > 0$ | DEF(x, t − Δt)),   e.g., x := 0; at $t = 0$
       DEF(x, t)   x := 1; at $t = 1$

This notation is read, "FLOW(x, t) is true if the following clauses are all true." Clauses are separated by commas, and the predicate is terminated by a period. The notation "∃ $\Delta t > 0$ |," is read, "there exists a Δt greater than zero such that."

We are particularly interested in these predicates when $\Delta t > 0$ fails, leading to potential race conditions. That is, we are interested in cases where $\Delta t = 0$, and a dependency exists such that a variable is simultaneously used, defined, or doubly defined.

In general, a *flow anomaly* leads to an incorrect parallel program when $\Delta t = 0$. This indicates a *race condition*. Race conditions lead to indeterminism in the resulting value of a variable.

SUMMARY OF PERFORMANCE MODEL PARAMETERS

We use linear approximations in the following definitions, even though the phenomenon we are modelling is rarely linear. The following symbols will be used throughout.

p The parallel processing hardware contains p identical processors and their memory.

N The parallel program can be partitioned into N tasks.

t_i Task i takes t_i time units to execute. Times t_j and t_i may differ for $j \neq i$.

r_1 *Processor time* (the inverse of processor speed) measured in units of time to perform some operation. The definition of an operation will change occasionally, but in general it is some basic arithmetic operation such as addition, multiplication, move, copy, etc.

r_0 *Processor setup time*, measured in time units. This is the time it takes to initiate a process on some processor. This estimate includes overhead due to the operating system.

In addition, we assume the execution time of a task is a function of the length of its input data, S. Therefore, the estimated *execution time* of a task is $F(S)$. The *execution time delay* of a task includes its setup time and depends on processor speed,

R Execution time delay of a process. $R = r_0 + r_1 * F(S)$, where S is the length of input to the process.

We use the following quantities to estimate communication times:

w_1 *Communication time* (the inverse of bandwidth) of the interconnection network, measured in time units. This time delay is caused by transmission speed, routing delays, and other overhead.

w_0 *Communication setup time*, measured in time units. This is the time it takes to initiate a message, including buffer creation, packaging the characters, and so on.

w_{ij} *Communication time* between tasks t_j and t_i depends on locality and processors: if t_j and t_i are placed on the same processor, $w_{ij} = 0$. Otherwise, w_{ij} = startup time + message size * transmission time per character, e.g., $w_{ij} = w_0 + w_1 * S_{ij}$.

I Processors are connected by some interconnection network, which we ignore. We also ignore network contention. Both of these factors can alter our estimates in dramatic ways, but we do not address them here.

SUMMARY OF PARALLEL PROGRAMMING CONSTRUCTS

The fundamental building blocks of parallel programming are:

fan   do n identical processes in parallel, once.

tree   do n identical processes in $\log_2(n)$ phases as a binary tree.

par   iteratively do n different processes in parallel, until predicate fails.

pipe   iteratively do n different processes overlapped in time, until predicate fails.

method   do one task potentially containing many parallel processes.

vote   fault-tolerant parallel n-of-k voting: k results computed in parallel.

backup   fault-tolerant sequential rollback and recovery.

Data Parallel Fan

fan \<counter\>
with \<boolean-constraint\>
mapin \<distribution-list\>
{ \<SPMD-routine\>}
mapout \<aggregate-list\>
endfan

The elapsed time of a **fan** is:

$$T_k = (r_0 + r_1 + w_0 + w_1) + r_1F(S) + (k - 1)(w_0 + w_1S)$$

$$S = d / k$$

where d is the size of the original data. Hence, the speedup of a **fan** is given by:

$$\text{Speedup} = \frac{r_0 + r_1F(d)}{(r_0 + r_1 + w_0 + w_1) + r_1F(d/k) + (k - 1)(w_0 + w_1S)}$$

Given $F(S) = S^n$, what is the best value for k? The optimal value of k is selected so that computation and communication times are balanced. We look at the two most common assumptions; $n = 1$, and $n = 2$.

Optimal k: Linear Algorithm

$$k = \sqrt{\frac{d\,(r_1 - w_1)}{w_0}}$$

$$r_1 > w_1$$

$$F(S) = S$$

Optimal k: Quadratic Algorithm

$$A = \sqrt{\frac{d^4 r_1^2}{w_0^2} + \frac{d^3 w_1^3}{27 w_0^3}}$$

$$B = \frac{d^2 r_1}{w_0}$$

Then the optimal solution is given by the cube root expression:

$$k \doteq \sqrt[3]{B + A} + \sqrt[3]{B - A}$$

Note that $(k - 1)$ is approximately equal to k for $k \gg 1$. This assumption greatly simplifies the mathematics so the equation can be more easily solved:

$$k \approx \sqrt[3]{\frac{2d^2 r_1}{w_0}}$$

$$F(S) = S^2$$

Parallel Reduction Tree

tree <counter>
mapin <mapping>
{ <base-function> }
mapout <mapping>
endtree

A **tree** converts an $O(N)$ time complex sequential process into $N/2$ processes that execute in $O(\log_2 N)$ time. A binary tree of processes is formed, each of the $\log_2 N$ levels of the tree contains parallel siblings which are performed in parallel as a phase. The first phase processes $N/2$ tasks; the second phase processes $N/4$ tasks; the ith phase processes $N/2^i$ tasks; and so on until $N/N = 1$ task remains. The $\log_2 N$ phases are done in sequence, hence the **tree** takes at least $O(\log_2 N)$ time to complete.

The **tree** construct is used to perform *reductions* on regular data. For example, given a list of numbers stored as an array, summation reduction can be performed in $\log_2 N$ phases to obtain a sum; maximum/minimum reduction can be done to obtain the largest/smallest element of the array; and other similar operations which can be distributed across the regular array can be performed in $O(\log_2 N)$ time instead of $O(N)$ time.

The elapsed time of a **tree** is:

$$T_{tree} = \sum_{k=N/2}^{1} T_k = \sum_{k=N/2}^{1} (r_0 + r_1 + w_0 + w_1) + r_1 F(S) + (k-1)(w_0 + w_1 S)$$

$$= (r_0 + r_1 + w_0 + w_1) \log_2 N + \sum_{k=N/2}^{1} \{ r_1 F(S) + (k-1)(w_0 + w_1 S) \}$$

Under all of the assumptions made in this book, speedup is $O(N/\log_2 N)$.

Independent Loop Par

par
<body>
endpar

par <boolean-test>
<body>
endpar

par
<body>
until <boolean-test>

par<counter>
<body>
endpar

where <body> is defined as a list of labelled clauses:

```
<id1> : <mapin>{<routine1>}<mapout>;
<id2> : <mapin>{<routine2>}<mapout>;
.
.
.
<idk> : <mapin>{<routinek>}<mapout>;
```

The **par** statement is used to implement MIMD parallelism, independent loops, or a limited form of general loop parallelism. In general, the **par** construct mimics three forms of looping, and one form of MIMD parallelism. This requires four forms of the **par**.

The variable <id$n$> is unique and merely numbers the statements. Each <id> clause is assigned to a process; thus, k processes are executed in parallel. Each variable <routine$n$> is a procedure containing declarations of local variables and one or more statements. The optional <mapin> and <mapout> directives work as they do in **fan** and **tree**, causing messages to be passed into and out of the parallel processes of the **par** statement.

Let the S characters of input data to a **par** be distributed in sizes given by S_i. This will be determined by the problem. The amount of computation at each process is $F(S_i)$. For each iteration, the elapsed time of a serial **par** (single processor) is:

$$T_1 = r_0 + r_1 \left(\sum_{i=1}^{n} F(S_i) \right)$$

and the elapsed time for a parallel **par** (n processes) is :

$$T_n = \mathbf{M}_{i=2}^{n} \{ [r_0 + r_1 F(S_1)] ; [(i-1)(w_0 + w_1 S_i) + r_0 + r_1 F(S_i) + w_0 + w_1] \}$$

The maximum function selects the *critical path*, which is $[r_0 + r_1 F(S_1)]$, or one of the other n paths of length $[(i-1)(w_0 + w_1 S_i) + r_0 + r_1 F(S_i) + w_0 + w_1]$. The critical path may *not* be through the nth clause if $F(S_n) << F(S_i)$ for some $i \neq n$.

In many cases, it is reasonable to assume that all processes are approximately the same in terms of data length and execution time. That is, $S_i = S_0$ and $F(S_i) = F_0$, where S_0 and F_0 are relatively small constants. Under these conditions, the critical path is through clause $i = n$, so the speedup for a single iteration is:

$$\text{Speedup} = \frac{r_0 + n r_1 F_0}{(n-1)(w_0 + w_1 S_0) + r_0 + r_1 F_0 + w_0 + w_1} = O(1)$$

This is counterintuitive. But, if we ignore communication delays, the intuitive result is obtained, i.e., $w_0 = w_1 = r_0 = 0$:

$$\text{Speedup} = \frac{nr_1F_0}{r_1F_0} = \frac{n}{1} = O(n)$$

Dependent Loop Pipe

pipe <boolean-test>
mapin <mapin-list>
{<body>}
mapout <mapout-list>
endpipe

pipe
mapin <mapin-list>
{<body>}
mapout <mapout-list>
until <boolean-test>

pipe<counter>
mapin <mapin-list>
{<body>}
mapout <mapout-list>
endpipe

The **pipe** construct implements a loop containing flow-dependent statements. Specifically, any sequential loop containing flow dependencies caused by serial OUT, ANTI, and FLOW patterns as well as loop-carried dependencies can be converted into an iterative **pipe**. Specifically, the **pipe** mimics three forms of looping.

The execution time of a sequential loop with N iterations and k statements, where statement i takes t_i time units to execute is:

$$T_1 = r_0 + r_1 N \sum_{i=1}^{k} t_i$$

In a **pipe** equivalent of this loop, each skew delay equals the time of a corresponding statement, so a skew of 1 adds a delay of t_1; a skew of 2 adds a delay of $t_1 + t_2$, and so forth. Thus, the total amount of skewing for the entire **pipe** is:

$$(N-1) \sum_{i=1}^{skew} t_i$$

Combining the two sources of delay, and noting the process startup time for each of k processes, plus the speed of each processor, we get the elapsed time for the entire **pipe** as a function of the number of statements and the skew:

$$r_0 k + r_1 \left\{ (N-1) \sum_{i=1}^{\text{skew}} t_i + \sum_{i=1}^{k} t_i \right\}$$

= process startup time + time for N iterations using k processes

There are $(N-1)$ rounds that must receive updates, so this introduces an additional delay of $k(N-1)(w_0 + w_1 S)$ time units. Combining the processing time delay with the communication time delay yields the overall total:

$$T_k = r_0 k + r_1 \left\{ (N-1) \sum_{i=1}^{\text{skew}} t_i + \sum_{i=1}^{k} t_i \right\} + k(N-1)(w_0 + w_1 S)$$

The best speedup we can hope for is k, assuming no overhead. A more realistic speedup includes overhead. In fact, if the overhead is too great, the advantages of a **pipe** are lost.

$$\text{Speedup} = \frac{r_0 + r_1 N \sum_{i=1}^{k} t_i}{r_0 k + r_1 \left\{ (N-1) \sum_{i=1}^{\text{skew}} t_i + \sum_{i=1}^{k} t_i \right\} + k(N-1)(w_0 + w_1 S)}$$

This expression simplifies when overhead is ignored; i.e., let $r_0 = w_0 = w_1 = 0$ and assume $(N-1) = N$ (large N) and small k:

$$\text{Speedup} = \frac{Nk}{(N)\,\text{skew} + k} = \frac{k}{\text{skew}} \qquad 1 \le \text{skew} \le k$$

The best theoretical speedup occurs when skew = 1, and the worst occurs when skew = k.

CLIENT–SERVER MODEL AND METHOD CALL

The *large-grained model* is appropriate under the following conditions:

1   The cost of communication is so high that it does not permit fine-grained parallelism.

2   Parallelism is dynamic; i.e., the degree of parallelism is not known until the program executes.

A *server* is comprised of messages, processes, object, and request queue as follows:

1   A request queue containing the name of the desired method, and the method's parameters.

2   A handler/dispatcher process for dispatching method requests.

3   An object containing encapsulated data and methods.

4   A send/receive message pair for activating methods and communicating results.

The syntactic expression of these ideas is as follows:

interface <classname> {
  superclass <classname>;
  path <path-expression>;
  method <function-header-list> }

The implementation part of a server-object is its executable code. If the code is inherited from a superclass method, the **inherit** keyword is used in place of the <function-body> routine. If the code is intended to override a superclass method, the **override** keyword is used. If the code is to extend the subclass, <Function-Body> provides that code. In the latter two cases, constants, types, variables and methods are encapsulated by the server as specified in <Function-Body>.

code <classname> {
  <const-list>;
  <type-List>;
  <var-List>;
  method <Function-Header>   **[inherit]**
                                  [override]
  [<Function-Body>] }   /* Optional */

Methods defined on the server's object are activated when they receive a message. Messages are sent, and received by way of the **send** and **receive** primitives:

send(<input parameters>) **to** <object>->method-name>;
receive(<output parameters>) **from** <object>-><method-name>;

Thus, methods are activated in parallel with the client process, forcing the client to wait only when a return value is accepted by a **receive**.

FAULT-TOLERANCE

Parallel Vote

vote n **of** k, error-bound   /* Error-bound may be dropped   */
mapin <mapin-values>
1: <trial #1>;
2: <trial #2>;
.
.
.
k: <trial #k>;
otherwise <failure-exception>
mapout <mapout-trial-values>
endvote

To obtain a majority, n must be greater than k **div** 2. The k parallel processes are computed simultaneously, and then the k trials compared. If n of the k trials agree, their value is mapped out as the result. If voting fails, however, the routine <failure-exception> is executed and no trial value is selected as the correct one.

Backup and Recovery

An alternative to voting is the backup/restore method of SIFT. In this approach, alternative algorithms are used sequentially to recover from an error. This approach is also based on an acceptance criteria called an *acceptance test*.

Backup/recovery SIFT differs from voting as follows:

1   Backup/recovery is sequential, not parallel like voting.

2   Backup/recovery is based on an acceptance test, not on trials.

3   Error recovery greatly degrades performance, while voting marginally affects performance.

Performance in backup/recovery SIFT is degraded only when errors occur, because the backup and recovery are done sequentially, and require that the acceptance test be applied to an alternative routine. This approach seems to be less useful than voting, but backup/recovery SIFT is more general, because any acceptance test may be used.

Backup/recovery should be used to achieve:

1   Robustness, e.g., recovery from detectable errors.

2   Graceful degradation, e.g., trading performance for recoverability.

3   Backtracking algorithms, e.g., state-space searches.

The general form of the backup/recovery construct is shown below:

backup <acceptance-test>
mapin <mapin-values>
1: <first-alternative-routine>;
2: <second-alternative-routine>;
.
.
.
k: <last-alternate-routine>
otherwise <failure-exception>
mapout <mapout-values>
endbackup

This construct defines alternative routines which are called into action only when predecessors fail to satisfy the acceptance test. That is, a copy of the **mapin** values is made, and the routine <first-acceptance-test> is executed. If the acceptance test is TRUE, the **mapout** values are returned to the program. If the acceptance test is FALSE, the **mapin** values are restored from the copy, and <second-alternate-routine> is executed. The pattern of trial–backup/recovery–trial is repeated until the acceptance test is TRUE or all alternatives have been tried. If all alternative routines fail to satisfy the acceptance test, the **otherwise** routine <failure-exception> is executed.

Index

About the Author

Ted Lewis is currently Professor and Chairman of Computer Science at the Naval Postgraduate School, Monterey, California. He is the author of 18 computer books, including his most recent co-authored book *Introduction to Parallel Computing*, (with Hesham El-Rewini) Prentice Hall 1992, and many scientific papers on high-performance computing. He is also the current editor-in-chief of *Computer* magazine, the flagship publication of the IEEE Computer Society. He has previously served as editor-in-chief of the Computer Society.

Lewis has made technical contributions to cryptography, distributed computing, parallel programming, and object-oriented framework design. He has also been a consultant to the governments of Taiwan, Egypt, and Mexico, as well as numerous companies throughout the world. He received his PhD in 1971 from Washington State University, and has been a member of the faculty of Computer Science of Oregon State University, University of Missouri-Rolla, and the University of Southwestern Louisiana.